A ginormous "
unending love & role modeling &
gracious hospatality ♡

Paul & Chris

10-22-13

THE
EMPERORS
WHO HAD NO
CLOTHES

EXPOSING THE HIDDEN ROOTS OF THE EVOLUTIONARY AGENDA

The Emperors Who Had No Clothes: Exposing the Hidden Roots of
the Evolutionary Agenda
Copyright ©2013 by Milt Marcy
Printed in the USA
ISBN-13: 978-1477478509
ISBN-10: 1477478507
LCCN: 2012908924

DEDICATION

FOR many years my son, Matt Marcy (1976 – 2011), told me, "Dad, you need to write a book." Some of the best suggestions I ever got in life were given to me by him, so I always took his comments seriously, but I told him that I didn't think there was anything I could write about that hadn't already been written about very well by someone else. I wanted to write about something that no one had written about before and I wanted it to be a subject that was very important for people to hear about.

In 2009 it became crystal clear that I was being directed by God himself to write about the subject that you will read about in this book. It has been a labor of love in the sense that I have been producing something that people need to hear.

This book is dedicated to Matt, my biggest fan, as I was his.

ACKNOWLEDGMENTS

MANY people have been a big help in the writing of this book. I am sure I will leave some out that I should have mentioned. If you are one of those I sincerely apologize. I first need to recognize my son, Matt who was a major inspiration for my writing it. Others who inspired me were Dave Pattillo, J. D. Mitchell, Don Chittick, Henry Morris III, John Morris, James Johnson, Rob Mullin, Phillip O'Donnell, Howard Mudder, Pete Beach, Derald Dieterich, Phil Yount, John Winquist, Rick Harrison, Don Wadkins, Dan Lumley, Heath Lourwood and many others.

Technical assistance was provided by J. D. Mitchell, Rick and Sylvia Thompson, Doris Marcy and others. I would like to thank J. D. Mitchell, Rob Mullin, Sylvia Thompson and Professor James Johnson for their suggestions involving some changes, additions and subtractions to the original manuscript.

Lastly, I want to thank our Lord and Savior, Jesus Christ, without whom none of the rest would have made any difference.

TABLE OF CONTENTS

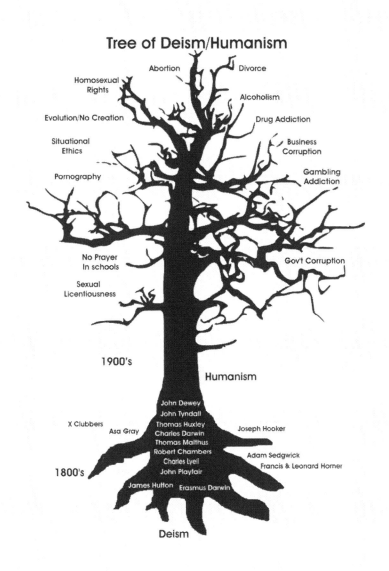

Tree of Deism/Humanism

Abortion

Divorce

Homosexual
Rights

Alcoholism

Evolution/No Creation

Drug Addiction

Situational
Ethics

Business
Corruption

Pornography

Gambling
Addiction

No Prayer
In schools

Gov't Corruption

Sexual
Licentiousness

1900's

Humanism

John Dewey
John Tyndall
X Clubbers   Thomas Huxley
Asa Gray   Charles Darwin   Joseph Hooker
Thomas Malthus
Robert Chambers
Charles Lyell   Adam Sedgwick
John Playfair   Francis & Leonard Horner

1800's

James Hutton   Erasmus Darwin

Deism

PREFACE

N O less of a philosophical sort than Mark Twain once made the statement, "Before I sit down for breakfast each day I've believed six lies." Notice that he said he believed the lies, not just that he was told six lies. I'm sure he was over-stating the case somewhat, but many times it is very difficult to discern the truth, and even the best of us get fooled more often than we would like to admit. In this day of specialized knowledge it is even harder to get at the truth. Does your car really need all that work your mechanic says it does? Does your computer really need to be discarded, causing you to have to buy a new expensive replacement? In the past, people such as Benjamin Franklin, Isaac Newton, and others had knowledge across a wide spectrum of disciplines, and it was considered normal. Now, you have no choice but to trust the "experts" because there is just too much for one person to know, even if we are just talking about the daily activities of our lives.

Of course, the benefit to this modern way of life is that we are able to have wonderful things like cars, airplanes, computers, televisions, etc. We are also able to buy the products of an industrial age that uses sophisticated machines and processes to produce products not available before. A tremendous amount of information is at our fingertips.

While people from ancient times did not have the division of labor we have now, they still must have been afflicted with the same scourge of cheating and outright dishonesty that we have today.

1

Anyone who has read the book of Proverbs or even the prophets in the Bible has run across numerous references to the dishonest scales that were used by merchants of that time. There are other references to worldly savvy businessmen taking advantage of the simple minded or the poor and downtrodden. Consider Ezekiel 22:27: "Her princes in the midst thereof [are] like wolves, ravening the prey, to shed blood, [and] to destroy souls, to get dishonest gain.

If we go all the way back to the beginning of the human race we find the same problem. Adam and Eve didn't even have to contend with other human beings initially, but they had the biggest deceiver of all confronting them directly with his lies. Even though that event was in the distant past, there is much we can learn from it, because the basic principles involved do not change. Satan was a deceiver then, and he is just as much of a deceiver today; some of the details are changed, but he uses the same methods he used then. He was able to deceive the original couple by appealing to their pride. He convinced them that by disobeying God and eating of the forbidden fruit they could rise to a level equal with God Himself.

Artwork by Matt Marcy

Pride can be on a personal level or it can be corporate. When our favorite sports team wins, it is corporate. We have pride in our country, pride in our company, etc. I believe we also have pride in the age in which we live. We look back at those who went before us and like to speculate on how much better we have it than they. They were so ignorant, uneducated and unaware in the minds of many of us. Pride can be used to accomplish much good, but Satan often uses it to accomplish his purposes to turn us away from God.

Our sin is much like the one in the Garden of Eden. We imagine that we don't need God. In fact, many have even been convinced that there is no god. After all, we don't have any scientific evidence that there is, do we? And in this age, scientific evidence trumps all other kinds of evidence. I think we could even say that, for many, science has replaced religion. In court nowadays, the psychiatrist has often replaced the church pastor as the expert witness as to the character of the defendant or a witness. We place all of our trust in science and assume it is our faithful watchdog that will always protect us and lead us to truth. It has our well-being as its number one goal. It is devoid of petty jealousies and special interests. It is completely objective. The scientist allows the evidence to lead him to the truth. No one would ever use science to seek their own personal goals over the welfare of the public at large.

In this book I will show you that all of the above statements are false and that it is greatly to your benefit to take measures to seek out the truth in these matters. I want to show you that the people that brought you our current reigning worldview paradigm never had your interests at heart to begin with, and they still don't today. They had an agenda that was and still is well hidden. Many church leaders have noted the moral breakdown rampant in today's world, citing (correctly, I think) the fact that fewer people now believe in the God of the Bible. I believe the authority of the Bible has been undermined by the compromise that has been made on the literal meaning of the text. Hoping to retain people by compromising on these issues, the opposite has happened. People have seen right through the smokescreen that the church has been intimidated by secularists to the point that it is no longer willing to stand for anything that really matters. In short, the average person is much more intelligent and worldly-wise than the clergy has given him credit for, and because of that, the kingdom of God is losing more and more people to secularism.

Today's western world demands that we look at things through secular eyes. Even Christians are expected by the secularists to leave God out of all discussions unless we are in church. This idea is one of the manifestations of humanism. Humanist philosophy says that man is the ultimate measure of all things and that man controls his own destiny. There is no god above us that has any power over human affairs. Humanists may be atheists, agnostics or religious people, but if you are religious, your religion must be left out of the public sphere. Keep it to yourself. One has to wonder how strong the religious people's religion is if they are willing to play by those rules.

These are the first two tenets of the humanist manifesto, drawn up in 1933 by the American Humanist Association:

> **FIRST:** Religious humanists regard the universe as self-existing and not created. [cosmological evolution]
>
> **SECOND:** Humanism believes that man is a part of nature and that he has emerged as a result of a continuous process [biological evolution].

As shown above, evolution is the foundation of humanism. Is it any wonder that Julian Huxley, a staunch atheist and grandson of the great evolutionist, Thomas Huxley (a.k.a. Darwin's Bulldog), was a past president of the American Humanist Association? Humanism must defend evolution against all attacks, because if evolution is destroyed, the basis for humanism will be destroyed. Aldous Huxley, humanist and evolutionist, the brother of Julian Huxley and also grandson of Thomas Huxley, said:

> I had motive for not wanting the world to have a meaning; consequently assumed that it had none, and was able without any difficulty to find satisfying reasons for this assumption. The philosopher who finds no meaning in the world is not concerned exclusively with a problem in pure metaphysics, he is also concerned to prove that there is no valid reason why he personally should not do as he wants to do, or why his friends should not seize political power and govern in the way that they find most advantageous to themselves.... For myself, the philosophy of meaninglessness was essentially an instrument of liberation, sexual and political.

This makes it easier to understand why the media reaction is so extreme when, for example, a presidential candidate states that he or she doesn't believe in evolution or that they believe evolution should be allowed to be questioned in the classroom. In a practical sense, this subject should not have anywhere near the prominence it does. The president does not make decisions about these matters. Why would he even be asked what he believes about this? In reality, isn't this a rather obscure subject to bring up to a person being considered for leadership of the free world? What other aspect of classroom instruction comes up every four years in the presidential race and invariably makes the editorial page? Even though many Christians may be asleep at the wheel on this controversy, the humanists know full well the implications of allowing a toehold in public instruction or political leadership to those who don't accept evolution. The questioner in this situation is not concerned about the future president making a decision affecting classroom instruction; he really wants to know what that person's world-view is. Do they closely adhere to Biblical principles or do they compromise like most other people? The secular members of the press feel threatened if the president abides closely to Biblical principles, and will often cast aspersions on the intelligence of that candidate. However, they will never get into an intellectual debate.

Professor Richard Lewontin, the famous geneticist at Harvard University, made the following statement that could sum up the motivation for many evolutionists and humanists:

> We take the side of [evolutionary] science *in spite* of the patent absurdity of some of its constructs, *in spite* of its failure to fulfill many of its extravagant promises of health and life, *in spite* of the tolerance of the scientific community [and popularization by the media] for unsubstantiated just-so stories, because we have a prior commitment, a commitment to materialism. It is not that the methods and institutions of science somehow compel us to accept a material explanation of the phenomenal world, but, on the contrary, that we are forced by our *a priori* adherence to material causes to create an apparatus of investigation and a set of concepts that produce material explanations, no matter how counter-intuitive, no matter how mystifying to the uninitiated. Moreover, that materialism is an absolute, for *we cannot allow a divine foot in the door.* (Italics and brackets mine) [1]

Lewontin also said,

> Evolution is unproven and unprovable. We believe it because the only alternative is special creation, and that is unthinkable. [2]

If people would take these famous evolutionists at their word, this book would be unnecessary.

[1] Ibid
[2] Ibid

Why is there so much affinity between evolutionism, humanism, agnosticism and atheism? What other field of study has so many vociferous adherents in a seemingly unrelated field? Do we find history professors off pushing scientology or math professors publishing books on the occult? I think the answer is fairly obvious: No, we don't. There is a strong connection between evolution and religion and it is my belief that we would not even have a discipline today called evolution if it was not for its importance in eradicating Christianity from the world stage.

Throughout the book when I refer to religion I am referring to Christianity unless otherwise stated, since in times past Islam and the eastern religions were not very well known in Western Europe and America. It has been said that evolution is a religion, but I will not take that approach in this book. I prefer to look at it as more of an anti-religion or a philosophy that doesn't include God, since religions are expected to give some answers about ultimate realities, while evolution simply creates more questions and gives no definite answers. And as I will posit, the purpose for which it was designed was to oppose Christianity and nothing else.

Mankind has always sought to evade any responsibility toward God. It started right in the Garden of Eden when Adam and Eve attempted to hide from God after the first sin, and it's been going on ever since. God always requires something of those who follow him, and that is frightening for a lot of people. What they fail to understand is that He rewards His followers with far more than they can ever give Him. There is an element of faith required in order to put this principle into action, so those who aren't willing to trust God do the opposite and run from Him. Part of that running is a mental game of constructing an intellectual edifice that seemingly blocks God out of one's world. The thinking is if we can convince ourselves, and then others, that there is no such thing as God, maybe we can evade any responsibility to Him.

The well-known philosopher of science, Michael Ruse, a strong proponent of evolution, made the following statement:

> Evolution is promoted by its practitioners as more than mere science. Evolution is promulgated as an ideology, a secular religion—a full-fledged alternative to Christianity, with meaning and morality. I am an ardent evolutionist and an ex-Christian, but I must admit that in this one complaint—and Mr. Gish is but one of many to make it— the literalists are absolutely right. Evolution is a religion.

This was true of evolution in the beginning, and it is true of evolution still today. Evolution therefore came into being as a kind of secular ideology, *an explicit substitute for Christianity* [Italics mine]. [3]

Three hundred years ago most everyone in the western world believed in the biblical timeline in regard to the creation of the world; that God created the world and the universe by divine fiat about 5,700 years earlier, and he did it in six literal days. For anyone to suggest otherwise was considered scandalous. Then, in the 18th century the western world experienced the Enlightenment, an ironic name for a period when the exploits of man were placed above the awe and wonder of God. Another name for that period is "the age of reason." That term reminds me of Judges 21:25 in the Bible, which says, "In those days there was no king in Israel; every man did that which was right in his own eyes." That verse is the final commentary on a tragic period in the history of Israel when chaos reigned supreme and man's reason was the ultimate judge in all things. There was no universal standard for conduct, just as we are today losing our universal standard, the Bible.

Creating a realistic picture of life in the middle ages and how it led into the enlightenment is important to understanding how we got to where we are today. The church became a very oppressive institution from about the fifth century onward. Prior to that, it was the governments, mainly Rome, which oppressed individual Christians. As the centuries wore on, the church became more and more controlling, eventually joining forces with governments to control every aspect of the lives of the people. The abuses of the Church of Rome later became the abuses of the Church of England as well. A strange paradox presents itself in the fact that the invention of the printing press made it possible for Bibles to be produced *en masse* so that more people had access to the Word of God. That alone was the main stimulus for people to learn to read. Then, as more people learned to read and as the market demanded it, the number of secular books began to grow in number. This all led to more technological progress. As technology moved forward it created a larger class of wealthy people, as it always does. Something about material blessing seems to make people feel they no longer need God. The idea of God for many, though certainly not all, wealthy people is an inconvenience. Jesus said, "It is easier for a camel to go

---

[3] www.answersingenesis.org, famous quotes of evolutionists

through the eye of a needle than for a rich man to enter the kingdom of God" (Matthew 19:24). Nevertheless, we note that there have been many who were both rich and true followers of Christ, among them, Joseph of Arimathea, who took responsibility for the body of Christ when He was removed from the cross. The general result, however, of God's material blessings upon people down through the ages has been a turning away from God. The ironic indirect result, then, is that the printing of Bibles eventually led to people turning away from God.

Out of the 18th century came James Hutton, a man who inherited a degree of wealth and lived the last half of his life in relative leisure. He was involved in the Scottish Enlightenment. He was the first notable person in Britain to contradict the biblical account of our origins, proposing long ages and gradual changes as the method by which our present earth came to be. This concept came to be known as *uniformitarianism*. He never directly confronted the Genesis account of origins and the flood; he simply ignored them. Given that most people accepted Genesis as being true, that was probably the wisest course of action he could have taken to avoid their wrath. He also waited until late in life to publish his ideas, probably not wanting to live the best years of his life being branded a heretic, or even worse, an agent of the Devil.

In 1797, the year Hutton died, Charles Lyell was born. Lyell became fond of Hutton's ideas regarding the long age of the earth and the gradual change over time through processes only observable at the present. Lyell had a strong desire to see the accepted cosmology of Genesis 1-11 join the dust bin of history. His major work, *Principles of Geology*, was published in three volumes between 1830 and 1833. The key to all of Lyell's works was the phrase, "the present is the key to the past." The only catastrophic events allowed were volcanoes, earthquakes and floods of the size that were observed in his time.

Charles Darwin read Lyell's book and saw the theories presented as an opportunity to extend uniformitarianism into the field of biology. Darwin was independently wealthy and never worked after he was 27 years old. He spent his time tinkering with his evolutionary ideas, but he was very timid and didn't seem to have the will to go public with them. He was well aware that his ideas would be offensive to many, and his wife and her family were, for the most part, very conservative Unitarians. He never could get past the idea that God allows bad things to happen, and when his favorite daughter got sick and died, it seemed to accelerate his feelings of antipathy toward God. Still, he probably would have kept those ideas to himself if not for the urging of his friends, one of whom by that time was Charles Lyell, to publish the book which came to be known as *The Origin*. Some of his other friends were Thomas Huxley, later known as Darwin's bulldog, Joseph Hooker, who followed his father as director of the famous Kew Gardens in London, and Herbert Spencer, a well known atheist writer. His friends and several others met rather frequently and called themselves the X Club. Darwin himself was not a part of the group. There were nine altogether, sharing a common worldview. They had no use for Christianity or its organ in England at that time, the Church of England.

Thomas Huxley especially, more than any of the others, took Darwin's ideas and ran with them. He was an eloquent speaker, and was able to back theologians into a corner when they tried to defend Genesis from attack. He had more than a cursory knowledge of the scriptures. In fact, at times one might think he knew them better than some of the clergymen he debated, which in some cases wasn't saying much. Huxley was consumed with wanting to elevate science above the scriptures in the minds of all he came into contact with. For instance, Huxley was invited to speak at an event. Dinner was provided before Mr. Huxley was scheduled to speak and a local cleric was asked to say grace before the meal. A reporter, in giving his account of the event, noted that it was really odd that they had invited both Huxley and God to the same event! So, in the minds of the public, there was no doubt that Huxley and God were at opposite ends of the spectrum.

After the seed was planted by Hutton, Lyell and others, the X Clubbers were very successful in force-feeding evolution to a backslidden British public and facing down the clergy. As Britain was the dominant political and cultural society in the world at that time, it wasn't long before evolution was entrenched as a force to be reckoned with, not only in science, but also in religion, around the world. As we get into the book we will get intimately involved in the lives of these history makers.

Theologians, recognizing the threat to the authority of the Bible, instead of confronting the threat, capitulated and granted that science was on the side of their opponents and went into damage control mode. That started in the 18th century with the gap theory, the idea that there is a gap of millions of years between Genesis 1:1 and 1:2. There were already many long age views bandied about a hundred years before Darwin codified the long age view. Compromising theologians such as Thomas Chalmers (1780 to 1847), who was the founder of the Free Church of Scotland, surmised that it would be advantageous to grant the people with long age views their point that the earth was millions of years old, if all the so-called supporting geology could be lumped into that time before the beginning of Genesis 1:2. This thinking reveals his naivity regarding the objectives of those who were proposing the long ages. They had no intention of allowing any compromises. Genesis 1:1 reads:

> In the beginning God created the heavens and the earth.

To any reasonable person verse two seems to modify verse one by giving additional details about how the earth was shaped and developed to make it suitable to support life, which was to come in only a few days. It reads:

> The earth was without form, and void; and darkness was on the face of the deep. And the Spirit of God was hovering over the face of the waters.

There is no indication from the text that billions of years of earth history lie between these two verses. The compromise was made because the gap theorists thought the long age of the earth was an established fact, so they needed to come up with a way to have a very old earth and also keep a high view of scripture. In the process, they actually tortured scripture by requiring the death of creatures, including "pre-Adamites" before Adam's sin brought death into the world.

One of Chalmers' lectures in 1814 was the first to seriously propose the gap theory as an alternative to the traditional view of Scripture. It should not be forgotten that Chalmers' home was in Edinburgh and the time period was right when John Playfair's and Sir James Hall's Friday Club was building some steam in Edinburgh advocating for Hutton's long age views. Certainly the long agers were getting the word out in Edinburgh that the Bible was not the only way that people should look at the history of the earth. Might I say they even intimidated a few theologians, Chalmers being one of them? The day-age theory was also popular, proposing that the days of creation were actually periods of eons of time. Again, while this idea had been around since the time of Augustine, it wasn't seriously considered until the mid-19th century when Arnold Guyot, an

American geologist and John William Dawson, a Canadian geologist sought to harmonize the biblical account with the long age views of Charles Lyell and others. By that time the long agers were in the majority and could not be ignored. The day-age theory appealed to 2 Peter 3:8 for support. That verse states: "One day is with the Lord as a thousand years and a thousand years as one day."

There are obvious problems, however. The Hebrew word for day, "yom", whenever used in scripture with a number, as it is in Genesis, always refers to a literal 24 hour day. Adding to that, the terms, "evening" and "morning" removes any remaining doubt about what is meant. Also, the rest of the creation account is presented as straight forward prose. There is no hint of any Hebrew poetry, so why would that one small section be the only part in the whole account that is poetic?

The argument could be made that the writer of the Genesis account could not have used a better way to indicate to his readers that they were literal days than the way he did. After all, "evening and morning, the first day" and "evening and morning, the second day", etc., is about as plain as the text could be expected to be if literal 24 hour days were intended. It should be noted that the Hebrews began their day in the evening and ended it at sundown the following evening.

Day-age has the same problem with sin before the fall that the gap theory has so it is no closer to being in line with the rest of the scriptures than its failed cousin, the gap theory. The motivation for the gap theory and the day-age theory was crass accommodation to the long agers for the purpose of appeasement.

A popular modern twist on the day-age theory is the framework hypothesis. This view was popularized by Reformed scholar, Meredith G. Kline in a 1958 article entitled, "Because It Had Not Rained." This non-literal view of the creation account attempts to turn that account into a rhetorical structure whereby the six days of creation comprise two couplets of three days. Day one is coupled with day four. God created the light on day one. He created the sun, which now gives us our light on day four. Day two is coupled with day five. On day two the firmament and the seas were created. On day five the creatures who inhabit the sky and seas were created. Day three is coupled with day six. On day three the dry land and the vegetation were created. On day six the creatures which inhabited the dry land appeared.

It is left to the reader to determine how long these "days" were, but the intention is to allow for vast periods of time. Day seven,

God's day of rest, correlates with all of the time since the creation, since the record does not give us an ending for day seven. As with the two aforementioned theories, the framework hypothesis needs to turn Genesis into a non-literal account.

There is plenty of reason to believe that Genesis one through eleven was *intended* to be a literal account, even if you believe it is wrong in what it tells us. The keepers of the Old Testament scriptures, the Jewish rabbis, have always believed that Genesis was a literal account of creation. Not all of them believed it was correct, but one would be hard pressed to find a Jewish text in all of the rabbinical literature that would deny that Genesis was to be taken literally. There was never any attempt to turn it into poetry. For example, one of the most revered rabbis of the last two thousand years, Maimonides, in the twelfth century, referred to the work of Ibn Ezra (1089-1164) when addressing the creation days' length. Ibn Ezra says, "One day refers to the movement of the sphere." This shows that at that time they were well aware that the earth was a ball and it leaves no doubt about how long the creation days were. [4]

Dr. Steven Boyd of The Master's College conducted a statistical study on the historicity of Genesis 1:1 –2:3 as a part of the RATE project, a multi-pronged research project that was aimed at demonstrating the correct (young) age of the earth. The other aspects of the study were scientific. Boyd's objective was to do a statistical analysis of the Hebrew language used in Genesis to determine if it could possibly properly be termed poetic and not prose, even though it had never been classified as poetry prior to modern times. Dr. Larry Vardiman reported on the results of that study:

> Dr. Boyd's statistical study concluded that Genesis 1:1–2:3 is indeed a narrative passage, not poetic, based on the relative frequency of the preterite verb form in the two types of passages. There is less than 1 chance in 10,000 that Genesis 1:1–2:3 is poetry. If Genesis is narrative, then it is not allegorical but historical, with the plain sense of the words corresponding to reality and the sequence of events corresponding to real time. [5]

---

[4] Creation, 26(2):53-55, March, 2004, Paul James-Griffiths
[5] Internet, Institute for Creation Research, Reading Genesis as History, Larry Vardiman, Ph. D.

Hebrew poetry, unlike English poetry, is not dependent upon rhyme and meter. James Johnson of the Institute for Creation Research describes the difference in his article about Hebrew poetry:

> Unlike the rhyme and rhythm of English poetry, Hebrew poetry is defined by informational parallelism — parallelism of meaning.[3] The paralleled thoughts may emphasize good and bad, wise and unwise, reverent and blasphemous. They may or may not recount historical events, although time and place, if mentioned at all, are less emphasized than in narrative prose. This informational parallelism—using comparative lines and phrases—portrays similarities and/or contrasts, or comparisons of whole and part, or some other kind of logical associations of meaning. [6]

We find lots of Hebrew poetry in the Psalms and Proverbs. Sometimes a line will reinforce the meaning in the previous line and sometimes it will be an opposite meaning. That kind of parallelism is not found in Genesis.

In modern times the most common compromise to the true meaning of Genesis is to just attribute the existence of the world and the universe to the work of evolution, but give God credit for putting the process in motion. For those people there are only two choices as to how Genesis is to be taken. It must be termed poetry or it is just plain wrong. If one subscribes to the poetry idea they may use one of the theories already discussed. However, it is becoming ever more popular, even among so-called evangelicals to place Genesis alongside the myths of pagan cultures. It is not surprising that these are some of the same people who are now compromising on bedrock doctrines like the virgin birth, the divinity of Christ and the resurrection. They have placed their hope in man, not God, and they will reap the fruits of their foolishness. There were many modifications of these ideas and other ones that have been thought up as well. But, let me make one thing perfectly clear: *They were all devised as a means of dealing with the challenges of evolution.* If they had been legitimate doctrines, they would have existed before the idea of evolution came into being.

---

[6] Internet, Institute for Creation Research, Genesis Is History, Not Poetry: Exposing Hidden Assumptions about What Hebrew Poetry Is and Is Not, James Johnson, p. 2

It is analogous to two people, let's call them Fred and John, walking down the street, when suddenly they round a corner and there stands Joe, Fred's mortal enemy. However, Joe seems pleasant enough as he pulls a small bottle out of his back pocket and says, "Here, Fred, take this bottle and drink it all. It tastes good and is good for you."

Fred is ready to drink it when John whispers to him, "I wouldn't drink that, Fred; it might be poisoned. Remember, that guy has it in for you."

Fred says, "I never thought of that, but I'm sure he would never do such a thing." John persists in reasoning with Fred until Fred finally says, "Well, lets see if we can put some other ingredients into it that will moderate the poison, then I'll drink it."

If it was designed to kill you why mess with it at all? Get rid of it! Sadly the modern church wants to incorporate evolution into their doctrine when its main purpose was, and still is, to kill the church, and it is pretty well along the way to doing just that.

Some modern evolutionists, realizing that there is no known way for evolution to have happened without the work of some outside agency, have proposed that aliens from other worlds came to earth and planted the seeds of evolution.

It may be simplistic, but there is a modern parallel in one of the most successful movie series of all time, *Star Wars*. Each film begins with the phrase, "A long, long time ago in a galaxy far, far away." It is easier to imagine that what you are seeing on the screen is real if it happened a long, long time ago in a place far, far away. Evolution has always had the, "long, long time ago," and now in the modern era they are adding the, "far, far away" part as it is increasingly obvious that it never happened here on earth.

Sometimes it is hard to enjoy the beauty of a forest when you are walking through it because the trees obstruct the view. Similarly, I believe that in our modern world, we are sometimes so busy living in it that we don't stop to notice how or why it changed. We need to look at what the very real consequences that we are experiencing today are, and how we got into this condition. What caused us to go from a God-fearing society a hundred years ago to a God-sneering one today?

Let's take a look.[7]

---

[7] Appendix A discusses the many ways our world has changed for the worse in the last few decades, with some pretty alarming statistical support.

CHAPTER 1
HOW DID WE GET HERE?

SOME principles can be applied with great consistency to civilizations all over the world, as far back in time as we have records. They were probably best expressed by Pastor Chuck Swindoll in the following quote:

> From bondage to spiritual faith,
> From spiritual faith to great courage,
> From great courage to liberty,
> From liberty to abundance,
> From abundance to leisure,
> From leisure to selfishness,
> From selfishness to complacency,
> From complacency to apathy,
> From apathy to dependency,
> From dependency to weakness,
> From weakness back to bondage. [8]

What is amazing about these phases in the life of a culture is the speed of transition from one phase to the next. One generation is all that is usually required to pass from one phase into another. In the three generations from David's rule, to Solomon and then to that of

---

[8] God's Masterwork, A Concerto in Sixty-Six Movements, vol. One by Charles R. Swindoll Copyright 1996 and page 61

Rehoboam and Jeroboam of the divided kingdoms, we see the nation of Israel go through several of those steps mentioned above. That was 3000 years ago, so this is not a new phenomenon.

Between 1517 and 1560, most of the countries of Western Europe received the full force of the Reformation. Some, like France, Spain and Italy, resisted and remained largely affiliated with the Roman church, but others were dramatically changed forever in many ways. One of those, and the country we are most interested in, in our study here, is Scotland.

The man who is credited more than any other in the conversion of Scotland is John Knox. Knox witnessed the burning at the stake of his mentor, George Wishart, in 1546. Knox then fled persecution himself and spent considerable time at Geneva studying under John Calvin. He visited Scotland at various times, but returned for the final time to live out his life there in 1560, and until his death in 1572 preached a fiery brand of Christianity that set Scotland on an irreversible course that would lead to undreamed of possibilities.

For the next 130 years, Scotland was a Christian nation, and an almost totally Protestant (Presbyterian) one. Because they were good Christian stewards, a law was passed in 1696 by Scotland's parliament, called the "Act for Setting Schools." It called for establishing a school in every parish in Scotland not already equipped with one. Each parish was now to supply a "commodious house for a school" and a salary for a teacher of not less than a hundred marks (or about sixty Scottish pounds or five pounds in English money) and no more than two hundred. [9] The cost was to be born by the kirk (church).

The reason behind all this was obvious to any Presbyterian of that time. The development of the printing press meant that Bibles had become abundant. To take advantage of that boys and girls had to learn to read. Knox's original 1560 Book of Discipline had called for a national system of education, but the plan was not implemented. Eighty years later, in 1640, Parliament passed the first statute to this effect. The 1696 act renewed, strengthened and enforced it. The result was that within a generation, nearly every parish in Scotland had some sort of school and a regular teacher (although many had already voluntarily started schools by that time). The education must have been fairly rudimentary in some places: the fundamentals of

---

[9] How the Scots Invented the Modern World: The True Story of How Western Europe's Poorest Nation Created Our World and Everything in it, Arthur Herman, Copyright 1956, p. 22

reading and grammar and nothing more. But it was available and it was, at least in theory if not always in practice, free. [10]

Because of that, Scotland became Europe's first modern literate society. This meant there was an audience not only for the Bible but for other books as well. Even a person of relatively modest means had his own collection of books, and what he couldn't afford he could get at the local lending library, which, by 1750, virtually every town of any size enjoyed. [11] It seems reasonable to conclude that this national push for education is what propelled Scotland to the level of prominence they enjoyed in the late eighteenth century. From 1750 to 1800 and even afterward Scotland and Scottish people were the driving forces behind advances in many different fields. Many notable Scots made their mark at that time. Adam Smith wrote *The Wealth of Nations*, the defining book of modern economics. David Hume was a major source of philosophical concepts still discussed today. Joseph Black did ground breaking work in chemistry. His and James Hutton's friend, James Watt perfected the steam engine, which revolutionized the worlds of manufacturing and transportation. James Lind discovered that scurvy could be cured with citrus fruit, which was a very significant discovery in a seafaring country like Britain. John McAdam devised a cheap and efficient way to build a sturdy roadbed by using crushed stones and gravel. Later developers added tar to the mix, creating tarmacadam, or tarmac for short. Thomas Telford was a construction engineer of epic proportions. He built some of the largest public works projects in the British Isles and their size is matched by their durability. Some of his projects are unique because they required great imagination. Sir Walter Scott and Robert Burns were well known names in literature. George Stephenson used Watt's steam engine to power the first locomotive. The medical school at Edinburgh produced many innovations still used today. The list seems endless. Also, many Scots emigrated to America and helped build that country.

However, by 1700, 140 years after Knox brought Protestant Christianity to Scotland, something called "Natural Religion" had begun to be bandied about by intellectuals in Scotland, England and France. Scotland always seemed to ally itself closer to France than England. The exchange of ideas was at its height in the 17th and 18th centuries. It was common for Scots to attend university in France. Of course, French military aid was sought in seemingly never-ending

---

[10] Ibid, pp. 23 and 23
[11] Ibid, p. 23

skirmishes with the English, and the French complied on more than one occasion.

Natural Religion or "Natural Theology" is a form of religion based upon reason and ordinary experience rather than supernatural revelation (the Bible), although not necessarily denying it. It seems strange that reason was not allowed when studying the scriptures! Proponents of Natural Religion were called "deists." Natural religionists generally used the term, "first cause," for what a Christian would call, "God." They did not believe the first cause was personally involved in the lives of people. They looked at the universe as something that the first cause created before stepping out of the picture and leaving it to run on its own. They accepted the idea of a god but rejected the Bible.

Looking at Natural Religion from a 21st century perspective, one might wonder why they left a god in the equation at all. After all, the god that was left after they robbed him of any power or personality wasn't much use to anyone. They might as well have taken an agnostic or even an atheist approach. I think the answer lies in their recent past, when it was ingrained in almost every Scot that there was a god. They simply could not envision a universe without a god. However, the framers of the concept of Natural Religion did not want to be personally responsible to a God that had rules for life and required an accounting from each person, so they left god in their worldview, but none of his rules or requirements were allowed.

Aside from their psychological leading, there was another very practical reason for not straying too far from God. The Scots had long had a law against blasphemy. In 1695, as a response to the growing influence of English secularism, the law was strengthened with a "three strikes and you are out," provision that called for the death penalty upon the third offence. It also had a special provision that said if a person "not distracted in his wits" railed or cursed against God or persons of the Trinity that also was punishable by death.

In 1696, Thomas Aikenhead was an 18-year-old student at the College of Edinburgh. He and three friends were walking together on a cold day when Thomas said, "I wish right now I was in the place Ezra called hell, to warm myself." [12] The following day someone revealed his remark to the authorities. During interrogation of the other students it came out that Thomas had been

---

[12] Ibid, p. 2

systematically ridiculing the Christian faith throughout the previous school year. He said the whole Bible had been written by Ezra and it was not the literal Word of God. He called Christ "an imposter."

There were many who rose to defend him, the most common argument being his youth. Others were vociferous in calling for his head. His wide ranging comments seemed to reveal more learning than his 18 years would permit. It was as if he had been schooled in these arguments by another more experienced person. There were those who wanted to see an example made of him. This would indicate that other people had recently skirted this law as well, but maybe not in as direct a way as Aikenhead had done.

As he awaited his fate, he made a public apology and promised to change his ways. Appeals were made to the highest authorities, not only in Scotland, but also England. But all was for naught as it seemed all those who had the power to over-ride the presiding judge, Lord Advocate James Stewart, declined to do so.

On December 23, Stewart asked for the death penalty:

> It is of verity, that you Thomas Aikenhead, shaking off all fear of God and regard to his majesties laws, have now for more than a twelvemonth…made it as it were your endeavor and work to vent your wicked blasphemies against God and our Savior Jesus Christ. Having been found guilty, you ought to be punished with death, and the confiscation of your movables, to the example and terror of others. [13]

The sentence was duly pronounced, and Aikenhead was condemned to hang on January 8th of the new year.

His last wish:

> It is my earnest desire that my blood may give a stop to that raging spirit of Atheism which hath taken such footing in Britain…. And now, O Lord, Father, Son, and Holy Ghost, in thy hands I recommend my spirit. [14]

The hangman pulled away the ladder, the body swung, and Thomas Aikenhead, not quite nineteen, was dead.

The Aikenhead case gained notoriety all over Britain, but there were also two witch trials in Scotland that resulted in hangings, and

---

[13] Ibid, pp. 5, 6
[14] Ibid, pp. 8, 9

the 1692 Salem Witch trials in America were also well publicized in Britain. We can look back now and see there was not a lot of grace in the brand of Christianity on display at that time. It seems these trials were an improper response to the very real threat that was at that time being presented by the Natural Religionists. It had been over 100 years since the simple but clear tenets of Christianity had been publicly questioned in Scotland. Then, toward the end of the 1600s the ideas of people like John Locke and Rene Descartes began to make inroads in the thinking of some intellectuals, first in France and England and later in Scotland. Scots began to fear, rightly so, that there was a germ of disaffection growing that would soon lead many people away from their Christian foundation.

Natural Religion was the seed of what would later become full-blown humanism. Because of the fear of the penalty for the crime of blasphemy, deists kept a low profile for many years. The atheist philosopher, David Hume (1711-1776), published all of his works anonymously. Those published after his death were anonymous as well. Even the publisher remained anonymous. Those who knew Hume knew that he was an atheist but he never went out of his way to make that point to anyone, and in fact, made efforts to not offend Christians.

A story related by Hume himself is particularly telling. One day, after he had bought his house in Edinburgh's New Town, he was going home by taking a shortcut across the deep bog left by the draining of the North Loch. As he walked along the treacherous and narrow path, he slipped and fell into the bog. Unable to extricate himself, he began calling for help as darkness began to fall. An old woman, an Edinburgh fishwife, stopped, but when she looked down and recognized him as "David Hume the Atheist" she refused to help him out. Hume pleaded with her and asked her if her religion did not teach her to do good, even to her enemies. "That may well be," she replied, "but ye shall na get out o' that, till ye become a Christian yoursell: and repeat the Lord's Prayer and the Belief [i.e., the Apostolic Creed]." To her amazement, Hume proceeded to do just that, whereupon, true to her word, the old lady reached down and pulled him out." [15]

Hume died in 1776, but people were getting bolder in their willingness to speak out against a totally Biblical worldview. One of the reasons this did not happen any sooner seems to be that, while

---

[15] *Ibid, p. 199*

doctrinal issues might be debated, it was never questioned that the Bible was essentially true. Then, toward the close of the century, one of Hume's friends, a man by the name of James Hutton, threw even that idea into question.

Hutton did not directly confront the Bible. That would have been too risky even at that later date. He put forth a hypothesis that contradicted the Bible's account of origins. Rather than specifically mention the Bible, he conspicuously ignored it. Hutton stated that the earth was "millions of ages old." He famously said that when we look at the geology of the earth, "we find no vestige of a beginning and no prospect of an end." The mountains were worn down and deposited into the sea, and then the earth pushed those landforms back up again, and this process had occurred over and over again countless numbers of times. In addition to his speculations on geology he mentioned that there must have been evolution happening continuously in biology.

Hutton died in 1797. Born later that year was Charles Lyell. Lyell became a geologist, and with his father's leading, became quite fond of Hutton's ideas. It is quite obvious why he liked them when you consider some of the statements attributed to him. He had a deep antipathy toward the first eleven chapters of Genesis and did his best to destroy belief in those foundational chapters of the Bible in the minds of readers in the early 19th century. He said in a letter to George Poulett Scrope:

> I am sure you may get into Q.R. [the well read publication, The Quarterly Review] what will free the science from Moses, for if treated seriously, the party are quite prepared for it. [16]

In a letter to his father-in-law, Leonard Horner, with whom he seemed to have stronger ties as an intellectual sounding board than he had as a father-in-law:

> At the last meeting of the Geological Society, Darwin read a paper of the Connection of Volcanic Phenomena,

---

[16] Life, Letters and Journals of Sir Charles Lyell, Volume I, p. 268, June 14, 1830 in a letter to George Poulett Scrope

and Elevation of Mountain Chains in support of my heretical doctrines. [17]

With a little tongue-in-cheek, Lyell seemed to always be gleeful at proposing "heretical doctrines." In another letter to Horner while Lyell was visiting in America for the first time in 1846:

> Dr King...is a man of thirty years of age, and in an extensive medical practice, who has suffered some persecution, professionally and socially, for believing the world to be more than 6,000 years old, and avowing this at a Lyceum. He has been held up as an infidel by the President of a Catholic College, by some German Calvinists, &c. I have met with other proofs of similar illiberality from persons of all sects, lay and clerical, in the United States, where the subject is much in the same state as in Europe. [18]

In a letter to his friend, George Ticknor, an American, in 1847:

> Making the Bible a school-book here, and setting poor children to read Deuteronomy, is a proof that our Church teaching is not meant to open their minds. People will have education, so they manage thus by sham instruction to evade what they dread, i.e. the making them capable of thinking and reasoning. [19]

In a letter to his friend Principal Dawson after Dawson asked him to review his new book:

> My dear Dawson,
> —I ought to have thanked you sooner for your handsome present of *Archaia*, which I read through with great interest. I thought some parts very eloquent, but you well know I am one of those who despair of anyone being able to reconcile the modern facts of geology and of many other sciences with the old cosmogonies handed down to

---

[17] Ibid, Volume II, p. 39, 40, March 12, 1838 in a letter to Leonard Horner (Lyell's father-in-law)

[18] Ibid, Volume II, p. 102, 103, April 27, 1846 in a letter to Leonard Horner

[19] Ibid, Volume II, p134, 135, September 26, 1847 in a letter to George Ticknor

us by the unknown authors of the early chapters of Genesis. [20]

Discussing with his friend, Thomas Spedding, some of the reviews of his latest edition of *Principles of Geology*:

> I wonder I have been let off with so little serious antagonism; only a few indignant remonstrances on the part of the "Record" and some of the Church reviews for ignoring the Bible, and writing just as if I had never heard of such a book, and could take for granted that the scientific readers were as indifferent as myself at the irreconcilability of my pretended facts and reasonings with Scriptural truths. [21]

Lyell, however, like Hutton, still retained a belief in a first cause. Darwin wasn't sure there was a first cause. Darwin, in addressing Lyell's concerns about a first cause writes in a letter to Lyell:

> I cannot see this necessity, he replied…. I believe Natural Selection will account for production of every Vertebrate animal.

Of course, Darwin's part in the rise of evolution was to publish a book, which was his expansion of his grandfather's ideas of transmutation combined with Lyell's (originally Hutton's) ideas of deep time. Thomas Huxley (1825 – 1895) was really the driving force behind the acceptance of evolution by the scientific community, the public at large, and even by many theologians. Huxley coined a term for himself, "agnostic," which meant, "unknowable." He felt that it was not possible to know god or even to know if there was a god. Huxley was known as "Darwin's bulldog," and his evangelical crusade for evolution continued unabated from 1860 until the time of his death in 1895. His efforts were handsomely rewarded, as noted in the July 1, 1895 edition of the Pall Mall Gazette writing shortly after Huxley's death:

> [*The Origin of Species* and *Man's Place in Nature(Huxley's 1863 book about Human evolution)*], which were anathema to the generation passing away, have become the standards of scientific thought to-day, blessed by bishops, and

---

[20] Ibid, Volume II, p. 332, May 15, 1860 in a letter to Principal Dawson
[21] Volume II, p. 375, 376, May 19, 1863 in a letter to Thomas S. Spedding

quoted by rural deans. The times are changed more than
we can appreciate.

By 1933, when the first formal American document was formed
to promote humanism, agnosticism had changed to full fledged
atheism, as noted in the first tenet of *The Humanist Manifesto*. No
creator is allowed. We should also keep in mind that while modern
humanism includes atheism, it is more than that. In addition to
denying the reality of god, humanism promotes human potential to
solve all the problems we face. We do not need the help of a god.
Humanism has as its goal the glorification of human beings above
everything else.

Even though true philosophical humanists are a minority today
they are aggressively trying to force their worldview onto the public
at large, and are pretty successful at it. Many humanist organizations
operating under deceptive names are very active in promoting the
humanist agenda. How about *People for the American Way*? Sounds
good doesn't it? Isn't Superman one of those fighting for the
American Way? He always helps those who can't help themselves.
But alas, it appears that there are many "American Ways." The one
those from *People for the American Way* are talking about is far
different from the one our country was founded upon, as their self
proclaimed fight against the "Right Wing" indicates.

Or we could examine the *American Civil Liberties Union (ACLU)*.
That sounds pretty good. Who could be against civil liberties? In
fact, I remember that my first contact with that group was when they
forced my high school to hire back a beloved teacher that had been
fired. As a 16-year-old kid I thought they were a pretty cool
organization. It doesn't seem like I've agreed with them about
anything since, however. Rest assured, if there is a chance to tear
down the religious influence in our country, the ACLU will waste no
time getting to work on it.

There are other organizations like People for the Separation of
Church and State, MoveOn.Org, etc. They all have as their goal the
establishment of a humanist nation, and are not much concerned
with whether the majority of the people oppose them or not. By the
way, isn't majority rule part of the American Way? Just wondering.

Leaders of all societies have recognized the fact that if you want
to have your ideas endure, and be the guiding force of future
generations, you need to educate the youth and get them thinking
like the political leaders responsible for establishing that society in
the first place. The Hitler Youth Program could have made Nazism a

lasting concept had Germany won the war. Mao had a similar program in China. Those are negative examples, but we also have positive ones. After instructing the Hebrews in how they should live, God gave instructions about passing that information on to the following generations in Deuteronomy 6:6 -9 and 6:20-25.

> And these words which I command you today shall be in your heart. You shall teach them diligently to your children, and shall talk of them when you sit in your house, when you walk by the way, when you lie down, and when you rise up. You shall bind them as a sign on your hand, and they shall be as frontlets between your eyes. You shall write them on the doorposts of your house and on your gates....When your son asks you in time to come, saying, "What is the meaning of the testimonies, the statutes, and the judgments which the Lord our God has commanded you?" then you shall say to your son: "We were slaves of Pharaoh in Egypt, and the Lord brought us out of Egypt with a mighty hand; and the Lord showed signs and wonders before our eyes, great and severe, against Egypt, Pharaoh, and all his household. Then He brought us out from there, that He might bring us in, to give us the land of which He swore to our fathers. And the Lord commanded us to observe all these statutes, to fear the Lord our God, for our good always, that He might preserve us alive, as it is this day. Then it will be righteousness for us, if we are careful to observe all these commandments before the Lord our God, as He commanded us.

If we go back and revisit those Scottish schools established between 1561 and 1800, we will find that the textbook used to teach the children how to read was the Bible. Many of the teachers were ministers of the church. A normal part of the curriculum was catechism, where students would learn the fundamentals of the Christian faith as well as how to become a Christian. The Church (called the "Kirk" in Scotland) was in charge of education in Scotland until 1872.

In America, the Bible was also used as a textbook until the late 1600s, when the New England Primer became the standard. There were many selections out of the Bible in the Primer. The Primer also had a catechism that discussed such things as obedience to parents, sin, and salvation. In learning the alphabet, many Bible stories were used. Can you imagine that in school today? These were the books that educated many of the framers of the Declaration of Independence and the Constitution of our country. Is it any wonder that God is mentioned in those famous documents?

In 1836, the first of the McGuffey's Readers was published. They began replacing the New England Primers. The McGuffey's Readers had a wider assortment of material, but still had a strong moral tone. There were many stories with a religious or ethical lesson, as well as stories from the Bible. The McGuffey's Readers were extremely popular, and more copies of that book were sold in the ensuing century than any other book, save the Bible.

But the embers of the Natural Religion fire had not been put out. In fact, they were burning brighter and brighter. The Unitarians were becoming a force in New England. Even though they were in the minority they were very aggressive about working to push their social agenda. They sought to get the schools out of private hands. They wanted the government to be in control and for the schools to be supported by taxes. One of their own would see to it that Christianity would get a stiff test. His name was Horace Mann.

Horace Mann was born on May 4, 1796, in Franklin, Massachusetts. He came from a rather meager childhood, learning

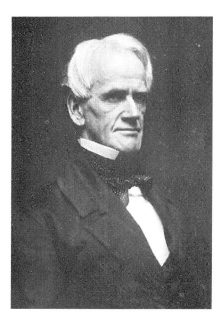

how to be very resourceful and think for himself. He was never able to attend school more than six weeks in a year from the age of 10 until he was 20. He must have really applied himself during those times; however, since at 20 he enrolled at Brown University, and graduated after three years as valedictorian of his class in 1819. The theme of his oration was "The Progressive Character of the Human Race," which gives us a clue about his philosophy of life. From 1821 to 1823 he studied law at Litchfield Law School in

Horace Mann

Litchfield, Connecticut, and in 1823 was admitted to the bar in Norfolk, Massachusetts at the age of 27.

He spent the years from 1827 to 1837 in the Massachusetts state legislature, first as a representative and later as a senator. Eventually he became president of the senate. At the same time, from 1833 to 1837, he was a partner in a law office.

In 1837, he was appointed secretary of the newly created Board of Education of Massachusetts (the first such position in the United States). This placed him in the foremost rank of American educationists. Because that was a paid position, he withdrew from all other professional or business engagements and from politics. This led him to become the most prominent national spokesman for education. He became very absorbed in that position, holding teachers' conventions, delivering numerous lectures and addresses, carrying on an extensive correspondence and introducing numerous reforms. One of the reforms he advocated was the disuse of corporal punishment. Needless to say, at that time it was a very controversial issue, although he won out in Boston.

In 1838, he founded The Common School Journal. One of the six main principles in it was that education should be paid for by the public. Until that time, churches were largely responsible for schools. Mann wanted to take away the influence of the church. In fact, one of the other principles was that education must be non-sectarian. This was a first in America, a country founded upon the Christian religion. But because of the influence Mann had attained by that time, he was successful at getting his curriculum adopted by many school systems.

Some of Mann's philosophies were:

Children should no longer be held responsible for their natural instincts of behavior, but are to be looked upon as innately good. That concept was Unitarian to the core. An elite educational establishment should be organized to "save our society" and manipulate how education should be administered. Man – not God – should be the measure of all things. Children should be taught that there are no absolute values of right or wrong and that one's decisions are always based on particular situations at the time. It might surprise some to find the concept of situational ethics being advocated that long ago in this country.

Horace Mann further stated:

What the church has been for medieval man, the public school must become for democratic and rational man. God will be replaced by the concept of the public good…. The common schools…shall create a more far-seeing intelligence and a purer morality than has ever existed among communities of men. [22] He expanded on that by saying he wanted "a new religion, with the state as its true church, and education as its messiah." [23] He is often called "the father of American public education." [24]

The practical result of Mann's work was a revolution in the approach used in the common [public] school system of Massachusetts, which in turn influenced the direction of other states. Most states had few public schools until that time, but Mann's onslaught was enough to tip the scales in favor of public schools in many states, even though the level of academic performance by their students was just as advanced as that of Massachusetts. They achieved that with private schools and home schooling. At that time, Massachusetts was one of the most populous states. In carrying out his work, Mann met with bitter opposition by some Boston schoolmasters who strongly disapproved of his innovative pedagogical ideas, and by various religious groups, who contended against the exclusion of all sectarian [religious] instruction from the schools.

In 1852 Mann became the president of Antioch College in Yellow Springs, Ohio. He taught political economy, intellectual and moral philosophy, and *natural theology*. I'm sure the moral philosophy and natural theology taught were not from a Christian perspective. The college received insufficient financial support due to denominational infighting; he was charged with nonadherence to sectarianism because, previously a Calvinist by upbringing, he joined the Unitarian Church. The college was founded by the Christian Connexion, a conservative organization, who for obvious reasons, later withdrew their funding completely. [25]

Mann died in 1859, which seems to be an important year in history. Charles Darwin's world-changing book came out in November of that year, and in America a man was born on October 20th that would carry on Mann's demolition of the American educational system, and eventually the American character itself. His name was John Dewey (1859-1952).

---

[22] Home Schooling: The Right Choice, Christopher J. Klicka, 2002, pp. 80-94
[23] The Messianic Character of Education, Rousas J. Rushdoony, 1968, p. 21
[24] *Internet, http://en.wikipedia.org/wiki/Horace 3/12/2010 p. 3*
[25]*Ibid, p. 4*

John Dewey

John Dewey received his Ph.D. from Johns Hopkins in 1884, where G. Stanley Hall was his mentor. Hall indoctrinated him with the vision of a welfare state with the schools serving as the change agent to bring it about in a single generation. [26] G. Stanley Hall's primary interests were in evolutionary psychology and child development. He was heavily influenced by Ernst Haeckel's recapitulation theory, which suggested that embryonic stages of an organism resemble the stages of development of the organism's evolutionary ancestors. That is known to be false today, and it is generally believed that Haeckel intentionally deceived his readers.

Dewey was a self-avowed evolutionist and a big fan of Darwin. He claimed that many of his writings on philosophy were based on evolutionary theory. He read books written by many of Darwin's close friends as well.

Before Dewey became known for his ideas on education, he was mainly known as a philosopher. Dewey assigned the origin of his interest in philosophy to T.H. Huxley and his other scientific reading. [27] One of Dewey's best essays, *The Influence of Darwinism on Philosophy* (1909), exhibits the pervasive influence of evolutionary theory. [28]

When Dewey was on faculty at the University of Michigan he was a member of the "Philosophic Society." He led the first meeting with a talk entitled "Mental Evolution and its Relation to Psychology." [29] Here were the code words of the new scientific philosophers: *Mental* (not spiritual), *Evolution* (not religion), and *Psychology*, (not theology).

While teaching at the University of Chicago, which was a Baptist-supported school, Dewey wrote the following in one of his letters to

---

[26] Restoring the American Dream, Glenn and Julianne Kimber, Part III Institutionalizing Public Education, Horace Mann and Dewey Schools, p. 3

[27] The Education of John Dewey, Jay Martin, p.41

[28] Ibid, p.253

[29] Ibid, p. 90

his wife, which sheds light on how he felt about allowing any religion in the schools:

> President Harper [University of Chicago] has been at some Baptist convention in the east; the speech he made...is enough to give you the shivers; said "secularism" was dechristianizing universities; no professor ought to be allowed who is an agnostic &c; and...if you wanted the genuine thing with patent Christian attachment and guaranteed agnostic automatic cut-off, you better patronize Chicago University. [30]

Dewey's take on morals is interesting. Psychology, of course, replaces abstract theory, since Dewey was intent on demonstrating that morality can be explained naturalistically, in terms of human habits or repetitious human wishes, human needs, and social functions.[31] As these two directions, intrinsic and extrinsic, interact, morals are the result. But since the nature and conditions of the interactions are always changing, so are morals. [32] Dewey's position was that " Morals are connected with actualities...not with ideals, ends and obligations independent of concrete actualities."[33] So, this is the beginning of situational ethics as they are known today. There are no absolutes in Dewey's world.

In a lecture in Scotland called, "The Quest for Certainty," he made the statement that the subject

> was peculiarly interesting to me because it seems to me now that certainty is the last thing that anyone could hope to find. When I was a young man we were all cocksure about most things. But now, all foundations have been shaken... [34]

Dewey started his philosophic career under the influence of supernatural theology. 45 years later, he had become a theologian of the natural. [35]

---

[30] Ibid, p. 206, 207
[31] Ibid, p. 358
[32] Ibid, p. 359
[33] Ibid, p. 359
[34] Ibid, p. 363
[35] Ibid, p.365

It would be hard to think of any one man who has affected this country more than John Dewey. Certainly Benjamin Franklin, George Washington, Thomas Jefferson, Abraham Lincoln, and others have had a big positive effect on America, but Dewey's effect was largely negative. In speaking about Dewey's book, *Democracy in Education*, Robert M. Hutchins, who was the president of the University of Chicago, declared:

> His book is a noble, generous effort to solve...social problems through the education system. Unfortunately, the methods he proposed could not solve these problems; they would merely destroy the educational system. [36]

In May of 1984, W. Cleon Skousen, in The Freeman Digest, wrote an editorial looking back on Dewey's influence on America in the twentieth century.

> Today we are reaping the tragic results of the pedagogical misery that America inherited from Dewey's mis-adventure in experimental education. At the same time we rejoice in the five recent surveys by top professional teachers that recognize the need to divorce Dewey and get back to excellence in American education. [37]

How did Dewey obtain such a hold on the whole American educational system? In 1904, Dewey joined the faculty of the Teachers College of Columbia University. He then partnered with James Earl Russell, the dean of the Teachers College, and they worked for a quarter of a century building this branch of Columbia University into the largest institution in the world for the training of teachers. By 1953, about one-third of all the presidents and deans of teacher training schools in America were graduates of Columbia's Teachers College. [38]

At Columbia, Dewey had god-like status. That, combined with his prolific writing and speaking career, gave Dewey influence over American education unrivaled by anyone else in the twentieth century. In 1901, while at the University of Chicago, before he even started teaching at Columbia, Dewey had placed himself at the

---

[36] *Great Western Books, vol. 1, p. 15*
[37] The Freeman Digest, editorial, May 1984
[38] Restoring the American Dream, Glenn and Julianne Kimber, Part III
Institutionalizing Public Education, Horace Mann and Dewey Schools, p. 4

center of the national movement to reform American education. [39] At that time Dewey made the following very accurate prediction:

> It is my honest and firm conviction that the American University which first sees rightly the existing situation in education and acts upon the possibilities involved, will by that very fact command the entire university situation. [40]

But it went much further than that, because many of those trained in the university went on to teach at the primary and secondary levels. Years later, when many Americans began to complain that Dewey had made a mess of education Dewey begged off and blamed much of it on his former students. But I would ask Dewey, who trained the students? His lectures attracted large audiences, and they were regularly reported in the newspapers. In short, he became the most famous educator in America. [41]

Henry Townsend, Hawaii's superintendent of instruction, summed up the meaning of Dewey's 1899 visit:

> In this session we had the very great privilege of the presence of Dr. Dewey himself, not only on the lecture platform but in our daily discussions. He was our Great High Priest. [42]

Dewey sought change in American society through his involvement with many different organizations that he either started or helped start. Among them were the Progressive Education Association, the National Education Association, the American Civil Liberties Union, and the New York Teachers Union. He also was an original signer of the Humanist Manifesto in 1933.

Beginning in 1929, Dewey proposed and argued for

(1)   a federally planned economy, involving government control or ownership of natural resources, utilities, power, coal, banking, railroads, and credit;

(2)   regulation of the radio and press;

(3)   the taxation of unearned increments in land value;

---

[39] The Education of John Dewey, Jay Martin, p. 206
[40] Ibid, p. 178
[41] Ibid, p. 201
[42] Ibid, p. 203

(4)   higher taxes for higher income brackets;
(5)   the calling of special sessions of Congress to ensure more continuous and more effective government planning to meet people's needs;
(6)   unemployment insurance;
(7)   massive outlays for public works;
(8)   a four-year presidential plan to spend at least $5 million for public works and $250 million for direct relief;
(9)   taxes on corporations;
(10)   taxes on inheritance;
(11)   workers' insurance;
(12)   old-age pensions;
(13)   the abolition of child labor;
(14)   a six-hour workday;
(15)   aid to farmers, including a reduction in tariffs;
(16)   recognition of the Soviet Union; and
(17)   participation in the World Court. [43]

He forecast in *Individualism, Old and New* that the new individual would use the taxing power of the government to effect the redistribution of wealth.[44] It sounds as though he might have fit in well with some of those we call "progressives" in our modern world. Martin, in his biography, talks about Dewey's relationship with the controversial Bertrand Russell:

> In February, 1940, the Board of Higher Education of New York City named the British philosopher, Bertrand Russell, to a special visiting professorship of philosophy.... In this case, Russell had stirred up strife by his previous writings, especially those espousing his views on open marriage, masturbation, religion, and sexual freedom. No sooner had a public announcement been made that Russell had accepted the post than controversy erupted. William T. Manning, the influential, strongly conservative bishop of the Episcopal Church in New York City, immediately sent a letter of protest to the New York Times. Russell, he averred, is "a recognized propagandist against both religion and morality" and a profligate who promotes adultery. Manning's letter was

[43] Ibid, p. 384
[44] Ibid, p. 394

buried inside the paper, but it caught the attention of conservative readers. Responses supporting Manning poured in to the papers. The Tablet, a paper of the Brooklyn diocese of the Catholic Church, announced that at least 84 Catholic organizations had indicated moral outrage at Russell's appointment. Dewey sensed in this, he told Harvard professor W.E. Hocking, "the beginning of a movement" by "this old totalitarian institution," the Catholic Church, "to abolish all municipal colleges in Greater New York." Harvard had offered Russell a visiting position two years hence, and Dewey was also writing to Hocking to make sure that Harvard would continue to support its appointment. [45]

In a later letter of Dewey's to Hocking:

> If men are going to be kept out of American colleges because they express unconventional, unorthodox or even unwise views...on political, economic, social or moral matters...I am heartily glad my own teaching days have come to an end. There will always be some kept prostitutes in any institution." [46]

It appears that Dewey was indignant that there should be any restriction upon what a professor could say or do in the classroom. While he supposedly supported freedom in the classroom, you have to wonder if he would have been as tolerant if the subject of interest had been a professor espousing the Christian religion. As aghast as the Catholic Church had been about Russell, the Catholic journal *America* had stated that a "crude" Russell was not as dangerous as "an insidious Dewey." [47]

Dewey was often at odds with the conservative president of the University of Chicago, Robert Hutchins. In an article entitled, *Rationality in Education*, Dewey states:

> Hutchins undervalues scientific, naturalistic philosophy; he has a static conception of man and human needs; he privileges theoria over praxis and so denigrates vocationalism of all sorts; and, finally, he holds to an

---

[45] Ibid, p. 442, 443
[46] Ibid, p. 447
[47] Ibid, p. 448

absolutist view of Truth, which is "the same everywhere" and at all times. [48]

The scandal of it all! Dewey criticizes the president of a Baptist university for holding to absolute truth.

In 1937 Dewey heard that in a lecture his former student Mortimer Adler, now an ally of Hutchins, had named Dewey "Public Enemy Number One." [49]

Because Dewey was attracting so much attention for his progressive ideas, it was not surprising that he also attracted the notice of the FBI, whose agents periodically wrote and updated their own version of a Dewey biography. [50] The confidential reports of the Martin Dies House Committee on Un-American Activities also paid attention to Dewey, even asserting as "a well established fact" that Dewey was an atheist.

Rev. Walter Albion Squires of the Presbyterian Church in Philadelphia added:

> Dr. Dewey's influence in public education is a matter of no small concern to the religious interests of America [51]

An attack on Dewey by Rev. Geoffrey O'Connell was typical. "Dewey's aims," he told an audience, were "un-American." He and his cohorts at Teachers College had "attempted [the] destruction of Christian aims and ideals in American education." [52]

Dewey was working on one more book, when his death prevented him from finishing it. He began this book as early as 1941, telling Corinne Frost that he would write a "sort of" summation of the history of philosophy to show "how much of our present confusion is due to retention of old ideas after their base and function are gone." It would be a pragmatic methodological critique of where thought had failed to adapt to the news of the day. The main title would be, simply, *Naturalism*. [53] This was a thinly veiled swipe at Christianity. The book was to be organized genetically as the history of a phase of thought, beginning with the Greek

---

[48] Ibid, p. 454
[49] Ibid, p. 456
[50] Ibid, p. 458
[51] Ibid, pp. 458, 459
[52] Ibid, p. 459
[53] Ibid p. 481

"discovery" of human morals.[54] The Greeks were the discoverers of morals? And he doesn't even mention the Bible as being a possible contender for that distinction. The disingenuousness of the man is breathtaking. Edward White, writing in *Science and Religion in American Thought, the Impact of Naturalism*, states:

> He denies essential religious principles because he withdraws from the only realm in which phenomena are truly religious, the realm of the supernatural. His solution, therefore, to the problem of the proper relationship of science and religion is the utter destruction of religion. [55]

Many will wonder why I've chosen to concentrate my efforts on John Dewey. Weren't there others who contributed to our demise? The answer is yes, there definitely were, but I selected Dewey for three reasons. His influence was mostly on young people, and because of that, the effects of his teachings were long lasting. The judges who ruled in the 1965 school prayer case and the 1973 Roe v. Wade decision and all of the other landmark decisions in our times were influenced by Dewey, either by Dewey himself, or more likely, a student of Dewey's or a student of Dewey's students. Even if a teacher was none of the above, the curriculum would have been heavily influenced by Deweyism.

The second reason I chose Dewey was that he came along at a time in America's history that was critical in the formation of modern America. Britain was the unchallenged leader of the world in the late 19th century, and she was turning away from her Christian roots in a big way, helped along by the now respected "science" of evolution that gave people an excuse to look at the world in a different way than their forefathers did. America could choose to follow Britain's lead or she could adhere to the Christian ideals that brought her to the point where she could smell greatness. If someone of Dewey's stature had supported those ideals instead of drawing us toward godlessness, I think it could have made quite a difference in the kind of people we are today.

The third reason I've focused on Dewey is that he quite willingly admits that Darwinism was his inspiration throughout his career, and a focus of this book is to show the destructive social effects that

---

[54] Ibid, p. 482
[55] Science and Religion in American Thought, The Impact of Naturalism, Edward A. White p. 109

are wrought from our acceptance of that insidious doctrine, designed to look scientific but in actuality fundamentally religious in nature.

Let's look at what Dewey and the humanists have built their case upon. Is there something more there than just a desire to eliminate Christianity from the western world? The received wisdom is that science is involved in all of this, but how much science is there and how much of it is philosophy?

CHAPTER 2

THE SEARCH FOR ACCOUNTABILITY

I N building any structure, we must start from the foundation and work our way up to the roof. If part of the foundation is weak and crumbles to the earth, whatever is above it will crumble also. In logic, we learn to build our case on supportable facts that can be demonstrated to be true. It seems that many people today could stand to take a course in logic. They build a case, but alas, many of the underlying arguments are found to be unsupportable, which renders the main argument unsupportable.

The modern humanist mindset is based on the assumption that Christianity is no longer useful, and was never supported by historical reality anyway. Neither one of these assertions is ever supported by any evidence supplied by the humanist. Their mindset also assumes that evolution is true, without any evidence being mentioned. In replacing Christianity with evolution, in order to have a higher authority than themselves to base this on, they say, "we need to listen to our 'smartest people' (those in high positions in academia and government and maybe some of those in the media) to tell us the truth about these things." How often have we heard the ubiquitous "they say" phrase? Whenever I hear that, I always ask who "they" are. And while we are at it, we should ask what motive there might be for why "they" are telling us what they are telling us.

The first two tenets of the humanist manifesto, which set the foundation for that document, state that humanists believe the universe is self-existing, and that man is an evolved creature. So how do they know that? Again, they don't say! To base so much on that document, should they not give us some grounds for why we should believe evolution is true? Since they won't do it, I will take it upon myself to help them along. Maybe their thinking is that Darwin already explained all of this, and all we have to do is go back and read his book. Then we will understand why they did not defend the "truth" of evolution. More than likely, however, their thinking would be along the lines of, "really smart people with impressive sounding degrees have studied this issue and have told us evolution is true." One argument you hear from time to time is that evolution is a "theory," therefore it has just as much validity as any other theory, like gravity, etc. Those people are then relying upon the authority of those scientists who designated evolution as a theory, to make their case.

And if we still have a few questions, we can read Darwin's second book, and some of Huxley's writings, and maybe a few others, including John Dewey. Surely after all of that, we will agree with their first two tenets, and we will understand why they assumed them to be self-evident when they wrote the Humanist Manifesto.

Taking their advice, we find that Thomas Huxley seldom defended the truth of Darwin's ideas. He expected his listeners to believe them without having to prove each one. In fact, he disagreed with many of Darwin's ideas, but he kept that between Darwin and himself. He would never reveal that in public, because Huxley was a smart man and he knew that the X Clubbers [his group of nine cronies who had common interests] had to keep a united front in order to make headway with the public. He was a master at explaining Darwin's ideas and telling stories that would allow the imagination of the listener or reader to create a picture in their mind of that misty world of long ago. He was also very good at twisting the Bible to make it appear inconsistent and self contradicting. I'm sure he thought that if he could take away the only alternative (the Biblical account of origins), people would naturally be more inclined to believe evolution, since that was their only remaining choice. Of course, much like the modern evolutionists, he told his just-so stories as if there was absolutely no doubt about whether they were true.

Charles Darwin didn't claim that his version of the past was without inherent difficulties. Numerous times he invited his readers to find fault with his theory. Before he died, he may have deserted the idea of natural selection himself. His ideas of transmutation were borrowed from his grandfather, Erasmus Darwin (1731- 1802), who got at least some of them directly from James Hutton, and who wrote a book in 1796 called *Zoonomia,* which Charles read at an early age. *Zoonomia* lacked the details that Charles eventually came up with, and was mainly conjecture about physiological processes, but a section of it dealt with how different species may have evolved.

Darwin was also very interested in a book anonymously written in 1844, called *Vestiges of the Natural History of Creation* (it was later found out the actual writer was Robert Chambers, a Scotsman). David Herbert writes in his book, *Darwin's Religious Views,*

> Charles Darwin, who already believed in evolutionism, recognized the book as "a grand piece of argument against immutability of species" and read it "with fear and trembling." [56] In the "Historical Sketch" of his *Origin,* Darwin pointed out that one of the major weaknesses of Chambers' theory was its lack of a mechanism of change.[57]

Darwin could be forgiven for thinking that species were mutable (able to change into another species). The field of genetics had not been discovered yet, and high-powered microscopes were still in the future. The cell was thought to be just a blob of protoplasm with limited complexity. He was smart enough to know that for one species to turn into another there had to be some mechanism to cause that to happen. Anyone could see that it wasn't happening in the present, at least not at a rate that was detectable. When traveling on the *Beagle,* he devoured Charles Lyell's book *Principles of Geology,* which gave him the vehicle for those changes: enormous periods of time. So, he thought deep time was the lynchpin that allowed it to happen.

It is important to remember that Charles Darwin was a geologist before he was ever known for his biology. On the voyage of the *Beagle,* the vast majority of his observations were geological in nature, not biological. His thoughts on geology came from Lyell and Hutton.

Charles Lyell (1797- 1875) was a self-trained geologist. Early on, he became a big supporter of James Hutton's concept of long eons of

---

[56] Charles Darwin's Religious Views, David Herbert p.87 2009 2 2 2 Ibid, p. 89

time, essential for the changes they saw in the earth. In 1830-1833 he wrote his *Principles of Geology* in three volumes. That book and the Bible were the two books Charles Darwin took on his five-year voyage on the *Beagle*. They were both given to him by Captain Fitzroy, who in turn had been given the books by Darwin's old Cambridge professor, John Henslow, for Darwin's perusal. Lyell popularized the theory of uniformitarianism, the idea that present geological processes are adequate for the development of all we see in the natural world. Lyell, however, does not take credit for originating the theory, as he states in an 1839 letter to his friend, Dr. Fitton:

> The mottos of my first two volumes were especially selected from Playfair's Huttonian Theory [John Playfair, a friend of Hutton's, wrote a book in 1802, which discussed Hutton's theory, but was much more readable than Hutton's previously written book], because although I was brought round slowly, against some of my early prejudices, to adopt Playfair's doctrines to the full extent, I was desirous to acknowledge his and Hutton's priority, and I have a letter of Basil Hall's in which after speaking of points in which Hutton approached nearer to my doctrines than his father, Sir James Hall, he comments on the manner in which my very title-page did homage to the Huttonians, and complimented me for thus disavowing all pretensions to be the originator of the theory of the adequacy of modern causes. [58]

Modern humanists base their beliefs on evolution, but they don't bother to provide any evidence for the validity of the evolutionary theory.

Huxley, who was most responsible for advancing the concept from an interesting idea to a dominant societal worldview, affecting how people view not only science, but also religion, history and many other fields of endeavor, did not defend its scientific accuracy, but viewed it as self-evident.

Darwin, even though he admitted there could be errors in his theory, relied upon the long ages proposed by Lyell to make it work. Lyell did not claim to be the originator of the long ages, but merely stated that he was following up on the work of Hutton. So, it appears

---

[58] Life, Letters and Journals of Sir Charles Lyell, Volume II, p.49 1839

the buck stops at James Hutton. Hutton is universally claimed to have "discovered" deep time. Historical authors Donald B. McIntyre and Alan McKirdy state that

> Hutton provided unequivocal evidence that the earth was far older than generally believed. His theory, based on extensive field experience, was confirmed from further observations made specifically to test it. Recognising the vast extent of past time, he saw the possibility of evolution, not only of the physical world, but also of living creatures. Fifteen years before Darwin was born, Hutton saw *natural selection* as a "beautiful contrivance" for adapting animals and plants to their changing environments. His understanding of "deep time" allowed his successors to discover that, in the words of Nobel laureate George Wald: "We live in a historical universe, one in which not only living organisms but stars and galaxies are born, mature, grow old and die." [59]

Again, in the same book:

> Scientists currently think that the earth is four and a half billion years old. Our present knowledge is the culmination of two centuries of research, started by James Hutton, an Edinburgh man, who demonstrated that the earth was immensely old. [60]

From author Jack Repcheck, who wrote a biography of Hutton, we read:

> James Hutton, a Scottish natural philosopher, boldly confronted this centuries-old wisdom [that the earth was around 6,000 years old]. Writing in 1788, he formally presented proof that the earth was significantly older than 6,000 years. In fact, its age was incalculable—it could be hundreds of millions of years old, it could be billions. Hutton reached his conclusions about the age of the planet through his revolutionary *theory of the earth*, which recognized the importance of the glacially slow process of

---

[59] James Hutton, The Founder of Modern Geology, 2001, Donald B. McIntyre and Alan McKirdy p. xi
[60] Ibid, p. 1

erosion coupled with the dynamic movements of the earth's surface caused by intense underground heat.[61]

Also from Repcheck's book:

> For Darwin, the key insight in Lyell's book was that the earth is profoundly old—geologists now believe that it is 4.6 billion years old—an idea that Lyell properly credits to James Hutton in the first pages of his book…. If Darwin had not been jolted by Hutton and Lyell into appreciating the age of the earth, it is arguable that he would not have deduced the theory of evolution…. In addition to giving geology, as Stephen Jay Gould stated, its most transforming idea—that the earth was ancient—Hutton devised the first rigorous and unified theory of the earth.[62]

Quoting from Stephen Baxter's *Ages in Chaos*,

> James Hutton proved that the earth is not as young as mankind, but vastly older. As early as 1788, this Scottish amateur scientist perceived revolutions in the Earth, and declared that the geological record revealed 'no vestige of a beginning, no prospect of an end.' The demonstration that we are as lost in time as in Copernicus' space has surely been the most extraordinary upheaval of all in modern human thinking – as well as the most essential, for without it the work of Darwin would have no context; there would have been no time for evolution to do its work. [63]

From all of the previous quotes, it sounds as though when Hutton was out exploring, he must have come upon a rock that had a date of four billion BC stamped on it! In all the talk about Hutton "discovering deep time," being the "father of geology" and hence the progenitor of evolution, I have never run across any close examination of his methods or his motives. For all of the hypotheses that are based upon his ideas or at least involve his ideas you would think someone might have done that. We will do that in the succeeding chapters.

---

[61] The Man Who Found Time, 2003, Jack Repcheck, p. 4
[62] Ibid, pp. 6-8
[63] Ages in Chaos, Stephen Baxter, 2003, p. 7

We will see if the foundation upon which the humanists have built their case is solid. We will again give them a chance to build a foundation for their later arguments, even though they have neglected to do it on their own. After all, they said in several places that Hutton had _proof_ of the long ages. If that is so, it shouldn't be too hard to find, should it?

CHAPTER 3

JAMES HUTTON

J AMES Hutton was born in Edinburgh, Scotland on June 3rd, 1726, 19 years after the union of England with Scotland. He had three sisters. He also had an older brother who died at an early age. His father was a successful merchant, and treasurer of the city of Edinburgh. He died when James was only three years old. His mother was apparently a very strong woman and saw to it that James got an education. There is no mention in any of his remaining correspondence whether he regularly attended church during his childhood, but in a Scottish school of that era, he would have received quite a bit of religious instruction. John Playfair states in his biography of Hutton and Hutton's friend, Joseph Black, making a comparison of the personalities of the two men, "that of Dr. Black was correct, respecting at all times the prejudices and fashions of the world; that of Dr. Hutton was more careless, and was often found in direct collision with both." [64]

He went to Edinburgh High School. He had trouble accepting authority throughout his life, which may have caused him some problems in school, although we know of no major difficulties. According to one author, "We can infer from his later career that he

---

[64] Playfair, John, James Hutton & Joseph Black, Biographies by John Playfair and Adam Ferguson, from Volume V of *Transactions of the Royal Society of Edinburgh*, 1805, Publish by the RSE Scotland Foundation, p. 96

was sociable and clever, and that he possessed a lively but restless and undisciplined mind. He probably had a distaste for protocol and authority…. At Edinburgh High School, the schoolboy Hutton must have been a handful for his masters."[65]

James Hutton

It didn't seem to prevent him from doing well enough in school to enter the University of Edinburgh at the age of 14, which was not an unusual age at that time for entering university. He spent three years there, graduating at 17. He then got a job as a writer, copying forms and legal proceedings, but he spent too much time while on the job doing other things, such as chemical experiments, and was fired.

Hutton's interest in chemistry was something he wanted to pursue further, but at that time there was no college major for chemistry alone. Chemistry was, however, a significant part of the training required in medical school, so Hutton went back to Edinburgh University for three more years, from 1744 to 1747, to study medicine.

Hutton's life then grew much more complicated. In 1747, at the age of 21, he became the father of a child out of wedlock. Even though such an occurrence was rare in that culture, there was a customary protocol for it. The father would move away for at least a few years. Hutton complied by moving to Paris, and while there, attended medical school for two years. The mother of the child apparently moved with the child to London, where they lived out their lives. Knowing the harsh treatment other people received from the church in Scotland for violating Christian teaching, Hutton undoubtedly suffered some pretty severe judgment from all those who were aware of his indiscretion with the young lady. Hutton may have been bitter about that, and Paris was even then beginning

[65] Baxter, Stephen; Ages in Chaos, James Hutton and the Discovery of Deep Time, 2003, p. 16

to produce the philosophers who could assuage his hurt. Voltaire was beginning to get into trouble for his polemics against the church. Did Hutton identify with Voltaire's writings? Certainly he was aware of them. Denis Diderot was gaining fame for several works, among which was one on natural religion and another on the excesses of the Catholic Church.

Hutton moved from Paris to Leyden in Holland, receiving his medical doctorate there in 1749. He moved from there to London in 1750, but he was not motivated to become a medical doctor. Did he make an attempt to reconcile with the mother of his child? We will never know. It is not clear what occupied his time between 1750 and 1752, but we know he was in Edinburgh in the summer of 1750.

Before he had left Edinburgh the first time, he and his friend, James Davie, had discussed their mutual interest in making sal ammoniac out of coal soot, which there was plenty of in Edinburgh. At that time sal ammoniac, which is a white salt, was used in the cloth dyeing business and for working with some metals. They reached an agreement whereby Davie would run the business, but Hutton shared in the profits. Presumably, Hutton provided some financial assistance. It probably took a few years to produce sizeable profits, however.

His father had left him a small farm in Berwickshire, about 20 miles southeast of Edinburgh, and Hutton began to like the idea of farming for a living. Before he took over the farm, called Slighhouses, he went to Norfolk County in England to stay with a successful farmer there and learn the business. Those were enjoyable years for Hutton. He finally got around to working his own farm in 1754. He adopted some of the farming methods he observed in both Norfolk and on a visit to the continent. One of his neighbors at Slighhouses was a man a little older than him named Sir John Hall, a man whom he came to know very well over the years, and he respected him very much. Hutton did well with the farm but it seems that by 1768 the sal ammoniac business was starting to return some profit, so he rented the farm out and never worked again. He moved to Edinburgh and lived there until his death in 1797.

Theory of the Earth Falls Flat

Hutton began developing what became his "theory of the earth" in the 1760s, but he did not tell others the details of it except his closest friends, Joseph Black and John Clerk of Eldin. Many of his friends in the Royal Society of Edinburgh had known for years that he had been working on a theory of the formation of the earth. In 1785, he was induced to give a two-part presentation to the society to explain it. For some reason, maybe nerves, he was too sick to give the first presentation on March 7. Since he had been required to have the material in writing as well, his friend Joseph Black read it. For the second talk on April 4, Hutton was well enough to deliver it in person. The society fellows were certainly not overwhelmed. Playfair states,

> It might have been expected, when a work of so much originality as this Theory of the Earth, was given to the world, a theory which professed to be the result of such an ample and accurate induction, and which opened up so many views, interesting not to mineralogy alone, but to philosophy in general, that it would have produced a sudden and visible effect, and that men of science would have been every where eager to decide concerning its real value. Yet the truth is, that it drew their attention very slowly, so that several years elapsed before any one shewed himself publicly concerned about it, either as an enemy or a friend [66]

There could be several reasons for this. The first one might be that Hutton's writing was notoriously poor, and as he was presenting from written notes a large amount of material that was probably unfamiliar to most of them they could not absorb it all. But the accepted cosmology of that time stipulated a 6,000 year age for the earth and the destruction of the earth by a global flood 1600 years after the creation. Not too many people questioned those things, and here Hutton was, annihilating both of them in one fell swoop! And he did so without providing any experimental evidence for his theorizing. I'm sure they wanted some time to think about something so radical. Also, there were probably many who did not *want* to consider his theory because of the obvious contradiction to the Scriptures. Some of them were conscientious Christians following their good senses. Others were probably fearful of the political consequences if they were, as a body, to accept Hutton's theory.

---

[66] Playfair, John, James Hutton & Joseph Black, Biographies by John Playfair and Adam Ferguson, from Volume V of *Transactions of the Royal Society of Edinburgh,* 1805, Published by the RSE Scotland Foundation, pp. 60 & 61

It was three years before there were any written reviews of it, and then they weren't very flattering to Hutton. Hutton, aware of his shortcomings in presenting the material before the society, went into the field to look for the evidence that would exonerate him. But three years after presenting his theory before the Royal Society of Edinburgh, his health began to fail and he was no longer able to do field work. He made up for it by doing a prodigious amount of writing in the last nine years of his life. In fact, his published works during that period dwarfed everything else he had written up to that time. It seems that he had already written notes on all the subjects he wrote about; he simply compiled them in an organized manner and edited them for publication. The subjects were diverse. In 1792, he published *Dissertations on Different Subjects in Natural Philosophy*. In 1794 he released the 2100-page, three-volume, *An Investigation of the Principles of Knowledge and of the Progress of Reason from Sense to Science and Philosophy*. He still had not published a book that gave a full accounting of his theory of the earth, but in 1795 after a verbal attack by the Irishman Richard Kirwan, on his theory and on him personally he quickly published the book *Theory of the Earth*. After that and up to the time of his death he was working on a book about agriculture.

Theory of the Earth Revived by two young friends

Hutton never saw any appreciable amount of acceptance of his geology during his lifetime. His peers in Edinburgh listened to his arguments, and some of them tacitly agreed with his conclusions, but there was no enthusiasm to help him spread his ideas. He was on good terms with all of them, and they were polite but unconvinced. Two notable exceptions were the saviors of his system. John Playfair was 22 years younger than Hutton, and it is obvious from his writing that he almost worshipped Hutton. One can imagine that he would have been impressed by Hutton's acceptance in the professional circles of Edinburgh, and being his junior by a couple of decades made Hutton bigger than life to Playfair. Then, there was the matter of Hutton's personality. Several times in Playfair's biography of Hutton, he notes what a marvelous personality Hutton had. He must have been very funny and engaging. On top of all that, in Hutton's later years he selected Playfair to go out in the field with him. It certainly makes sense that Playfair would be impressed by Hutton. The problem is that all of the above factors have nothing to do with geology, but Playfair was oblivious to that fact.

The other person who played a big part in furthering the Huttonian theory of the earth was young Sir James Hall. Hall's father, Sir John Hall, was that same man who befriended Hutton years before when Hutton was farming at Slighhouses. I'm sure it impressed Hall that he was now keeping company with the same man his father knew as a personal friend. Hall was 13 years younger than Playfair, and 35 hears younger than Hutton. But Hall seems to have been a little more discriminating than Playfair when it came to accepting Hutton's theory. He needed to do some experiments of his own to verify some of Hutton's conclusions. Hutton objected to that type of thing because he thought there could be nothing gained from it, and it could even damage their cause. It would be impossible to duplicate what was going on down in the bowels of the earth by doing an experiment on top of the earth, and the experiment could appear to contradict the theory when the real reason it did not work was that the subterranean environment could not be duplicated. Out of respect for Hutton, Hall did not perform any experiments while Hutton was alive, but once he was gone, Hall, with the approval of Playfair, did some experiments in order to verify some parts of the theory. One of the perceived problems of Hutton's theory was that in his recourse to heat as the driving force for the changes appearing in the earth, it seemed that basalt did not conform the way it should. The naturally occurring basalt on the earth is in a crystalline form. If basalt is heated in the lab to the point that it melts, the cooled mass takes on the appearance of glass with no crystals. So, it looked as if Hutton could have been wrong about heat melting the basalt. Hall figured maybe the problem was the rate of cooling. After a number of experimental tries, he was able to slow the cooling to the point where the final result looked like natural crystalline basalt. This was a eureka moment for Hall. I think his view of Hutton went up several more notches at that point.

Another experiment was aided by James Watt, Hutton's friend, and perfector of the steam engine, who had access to many different types of furnaces. Hall put limestone inside gun barrels with a little water. The ends were sealed shut with metal, and then the barrels were heated to very high temperatures. The object was to try to determine what happens to a substance when heated under very high pressures such as those that exist deep within the earth. He also did the same experiment with wood. The wood turned to a type of coal, and the limestone appeared to melt into a type of marble. These experiments seemed to verify Hutton's predictions. Now, it really looked as though maybe all the other unproven assumptions of Hutton's were true also. Or so Hall must have thought.

Playfair, however, was the straw that stirred the drink when it came to reviving Hutton's image. In 1802, he reformed Hutton's ideas, so woefully conveyed in *Theory of the Earth*, into a book called *Illustrations of the Huttonian Theory*. Finally, Hutton's ideas were comprehensible in a written form. Playfair had much more talent as a writer than did Hutton. In 1803 he presented his biography of James Hutton to the Royal Society of Edinburgh. Two years later that was combined with a short biography of Joseph Black and became a small book. Also in 1803 a club was formed specifically to battle the opponents of Hutton's theory, and to attempt to popularize it with the public. Playfair, Hall, Sir Walter Scott and Francis Horner were involved. Francis Horner was the brother of Charles Lyell's father-in-law, Leonard Horner. Small world, huh? Scott was the great writer and poet. The Friday Club, as they called it, met (predictably) on Fridays at a local tavern. The club continued until 1818, when Playfair became too ill to take part in the meetings. Playfair died in 1819. The effort of the young Huttonians was seemingly not accomplishing its purpose. However, something happened in 1824 that would change all of that.

A 26-year-old Charles Lyell had been doing some geologizing in the north of Scotland. He decided that since he would be going near the Dunglass estate of Sir James Hall on his way back to London, he would pay Mr. Hall a visit. The 63-year-old Hall enjoyed Lyell, and took him to see Siccar point. Ironically, when Hutton took Playfair and Hall there in 1788, Hutton was 62, and Hall was 27. Lyell was just as captivated as Playfair and Hall had been in 1788, though it may have been just as much because of the person who took him there as it was what they were looking at. Lyell was already a proponent of the Huttonian theory, but his enthusiasm for it must have increased exponentially with this experience.

Lyell, a truly gifted writer, began carrying the torch for Hutton's ideas and after his publication of *Principles of Geology* in 1830-1833, the battle began to turn decidedly the Huttonian's way. We'll discuss that in more detail in the next chapter.

Eighteenth Century Edinburgh

From the time Hutton moved to Edinburgh in 1768, his efforts were primarily devoted to geology. At the age of 42, he had plenty of income, and his three sisters, with whom he lived, took care of his domestic affairs.

Edinburgh was a very enjoyable place for Hutton to live in the last half of the 18th century. It was highly suited for the life of a professional. There was a club for every purpose, and others that had no purpose at all except to provide a good time to all who attended. Hutton, who had a magnetic personality that drew people of many different persuasions to him, must have been in seventh heaven. John Playfair writes, in his biography of Hutton, that

> he was in the midst of a literary society of men of the first abilities, to all of whom he was peculiarly acceptable, as bringing along with him a vast fund of information and originality, combined with that gayety and animation which so rarely accompany the profounder attainments of science.[67]

Later in the same book he provides a description that makes me wish I could have known the man personally:

> Though extreme simplicity of manner does not infrequently impart a degree of feebleness to the expression of thought, the contrary was true of DR. HUTTON. His conversation was extremely animated and forcible, and, whether serious or gay, full of ingenious and original observation. Great information, and an excellent memory, supplied an inexhaustible fund of illustration, always happily introduced, and in which, when the subject admitted of it, the witty and the ludicrous never failed to occupy a considerable place. — But it is impossible by words to convey any idea of the effect of his conversation, and of the impression made by so much philosophy, gaiety and humor, accompanied by a manner at once so animated and so simple. Things are made known only by comparison, and that which is *unique* admits of no description.[68]

---

[67] Ibid, p. 46
[68] Ibid, p. 94

Hutton made many friends in Edinburgh, but his best friend was the chemist, Joseph Black. He also became close with the famous author of "Wealth of Nations," Adam Smith. He was acquainted with David Hume, the famous atheist philosopher; Hutton's writing on philosophical subjects echo the writing of Hume, and Hutton's friend, Smith, was known to be a good friend of Hume's. Before Hume died he named Smith his executor. Together with Black and Smith, Hutton started the Oyster Club in 1778.

> At its weekly meetings, over tankards of porter and feasts of Oysters – a fashionable delicacy – 'the conversation was always free, often scientific, but never didactic or disputatious; and as this club was much the resort of the strangers who visited Edinburgh, from any object connected with art or with science, it derived from thence an extraordinary degree of variety and interests.'"[69] [70]

While the clubs usually had a stated purpose, the unstated purpose was the opportunity for men to socialize without the presence of women and to drink. According to Stephen Baxter,

> Enlightenment Edinburgh was awash. The drink of preference was claret, a legacy of Scotland's historical ties to France...The quantities consumed could be heroic. A gentleman would be labeled a "two- or three-bottle man," depending on his consumption over dinner. Then after the meal, the protocol was for the host to toast each guest in turn – and then each guest toasted his host, and each of the other guests. A little mathematics shows that even a modest gathering of, say, five people would require a total of twenty toasts to be raised. But the booze wasn't restricted to dinner. Drinking, according to one account, "engrossed the leisure hours of all professional men, scarcely excepting even the most stern and dignified."

---

[69] Baxter, Stephen; Ages in Chaos, James Hutton and the Discovery of Deep Time, 2003, pp. 120, 121
[70] Playfair, John; James Hutton & Joseph Black, Biographies by John Playfair and Adam Ferguson, from Volume V of *Transactions of the Royal Society*, 1805, p. 98

People would drink over business deals and legal matters, even preparing for a day's work on the bench. [71]

One of the more notorious clubs of Edinburgh was the Beggar's Benison. Baxter goes on:

> The club would become infamous for the obscenity of some of its activities, not least the hiring of "posture girls" for the edification of its gentlemen…One historian would claim that "it is difficult to say who, of any prominence in literature or society, at that time, was not a member of the Beggar's Benison." The Benison even granted an honorary membership to the Prince of Wales – later George IV – a notorious socialite who gorged, drank and flaunted his mistresses in public.
>
> It is not known whether Hutton was a member of the Benison, but as far back as 1741, his good friend Sir John Clerk had been a correspondent of the Benison's "sovereign" over a Roman phallus that had turned up in Scotland (Clerk was a noted antiquarian)…
>
> Of course, there was a down side to all of this. In the 1780s, William Creech, eventually Hutton's publisher, would satirically portray a dark mirror of the gentlemen's clubs – the "Jezebel Club," a society for the prostitutes whose numbers had multiplied during the years of the Enlightenment. The Jezebel Club had ongoing vacancies, Creech said harshly, for many of its members were dying, "decayed," before they were twenty.
>
> In this milieu Hutton lived his life to the full."[72]

One of Hutton's friends was James Watt, the person most responsible for developing a working steam engine. To do that work, however, Watt had to move to Birmingham, where he was financed by the industrialist, Matthew Boulton. The letters between Hutton and Watt provide a rich source of information about both of them. Watt joined the Lunar Society in Birmingham, along with such people as Josiah Wedgwood, the man who started the still-famous Wedgwood pottery company, and the maternal grandfather of Charles Darwin, Joseph Priestly, a noted theologian and inventor, and Erasmus Darwin, the paternal grandfather of Charles Darwin

---

[71] Baxter, Stephen; Ages in Chaos, James Hutton and the Discovery of Deep Time, 2003, pp. 93, 94
[72] Ibid, p. 94

and a very successful medical doctor and writer. Darwin, at one time, was offered the position of being the royal doctor, but turned it down. The Lunar society met once a month on the full moon, and they were known as Lunaticks. They met at about 2:00 PM and usually adjourned about 8:00PM. They met near the full moon so they would have light to walk home by in the greater part of the year when it was dark at that time. Their purpose was ostensibly to advance the arts and sciences.

Hutton made a trip to Birmingham in 1774 on his way to Wales to study some geological formations firsthand. He met most of Watt's friends who, a year later, comprised the Lunar Society. That was the beginning of a 20-year friendship between Hutton and Darwin. The two of them performed some experiments using an air gun to fire at the bulb of a thermometer in order to determine the effects of expansion.

Hutton Not a Pious Man

Besides his letters to Watt, Hutton also wrote to George Clerk-Maxwell and John Clerk of Eldin. We learn much from these letters, but the reader should be warned that there is material in these letters that could be offensive to some. Quotes from these letters are included because they speak volumes about who this man is that we are attempting to understand. Not only do we have to deal with the difference in writing the English Language 235 years ago, we also have to decipher their slang. Fortunately, there are those who have done that. On his trip to Wales, he wrote to Clerk-Maxwell,

> with my arse to the east & face to the Irish channel being willing to see through Wales or at least look at it; it will cost me some leather no doubt...I have eat green goose, but notwithstanding the weather would seem to favor spontaneous generation a slice of cucumber is all I have got in the vocable of C, and that you know is no provocative I have just muddled with brandy & water & so to bed. [73]

Baxter explains the passage,

---

[73] Letter of Hutton to Clerk-Maxwell in Edinburgh, July 1774

This is bawdy stuff, two centuries out of date, takes a bit of translating. Hutton is really telling Clerk-Maxwell about his amatory adventures. The 'C' probably means "cunt." "Green goose" was slang for a bird of less than four months old, probably meaning here a young girl. But all that seemed to be on offer in Bridgnorth [Wales] was "a slice of cucumber," meaning a married woman, which he didn't find quite so stimulating. [74],[75]

He finished one solitary evening, as he wrote to Clerk-Maxwell, by drinking the last of his "sixpenny'th of toddy to omnibus friendibus concubinibus ubicumque" – his pidgin Latin meaning "Here's to all concubines wherever they are."[76]

In the same letter, Hutton joked about growing homunculi "as eggs in turkey & fir trees in a nursery," and developed elaborate metaphors concerning machinery and sex. This kind of stuff was common in lewd writings of the time. The Beggar's Benison members were fond of the idea of "Merryland," an imaginary island that derived from English pornography, a marvelous place whose hillocks, shrubs and grottoes provided plenty of resource for sexual illusion. Hutton's letters show he was thoroughly immersed in his era's culture of sensuality: again, so much for Playfair's upright citizen."[77]

Playfair's writings about Hutton always painted Hutton as a very respectable and morally upright man. In the same letter Hutton writes,

> In despair I made a violent struggle but geting out upon the wrong side I went to Buxton [presumably to see Erasmus Darwin, who lived there] as the likest place to Scotland; there I had the mortification to find that had I not been so engrossed with the beastlyness of gluttony

---

[74] Baxter, Stephen; Ages in Chaos, James Hutton and the Discovery of Deep Time, 2003 p.111

[75] For further reading about the lewd writings of the day see Smollet in his poem *Advice* (1746) and tracts by Sir John Hill, Richard Roe, and Vincent Miller and Porter, R., *The Sexual Underworld of the Enlightenment* (London, 1982), p. 60-64; *Sexuality in Eighteenth Century Britain, edited by P.- G. Bouce (Manchester, 1982)*

[76] Baxter, Stephen; Ages in Chaos, James Hutton and the Discovery of Deep Time, 2003 p. 112

[77] Ibid, pp. 114 and 115

and the manliness of drinking I might have met my friends at Buxton with Omiah [a Tahitian that had come back to England with Captain James Cook on his second voyage to the South Pacific] who was there only 8 days before – having my dear native country in view I have undergone the most amazing hardships all last summer & harvest but at last thank God surmounting every difficulty that the divel [devil] had accumulated in the way I arrived at the blessed place of my nativity where I had not turned around to look about me when I received an incendiary letter from Madame Young you know how needless it would be to think of refusing her demands so away I set out to the north of Perth and lived at the root of the Grampians [mountain range in Northern Scotland] till just now…"[78]

We don't know who Madame Young was, but she must have had quite a pull on Hutton, since there was at that time an experiment regarding gravity being done nearby at Mt Schiehallion by the Astronomer Royal, Neil Maskelyne. People were coming from near and far to observe. He was trying to determine if the mountain itself creates gravity. That would ordinarily be something that Hutton would be quite interested in, but he shunned it to go spend some time with this woman!

The last crude comment in that letter by Hutton shows that he is perfectly comfortable with the slang of the time:

A smith here has been consulting me about taking out a patent for some improvement of a bed; I'm thinking of adding to it a machine which shall be called the muscular motion whereby all the several parts shall be performed of erection, intrusion, reciprocation and injection…[79]

What was Hutton's Thinking about Religion?

I think we can see that Hutton did not live a life of piety. If he had been accused of being a heathen at the age of 21, when he had his trying moments regarding the unwanted pregnancy, I'm sure the same would have applied as he approached 50. He was, however, a deist for sure and a classic one at that, as we will learn when we get

---

[78] Ibid
[79] Letter of Hutton to James Watt in Edinburgh, October 1774

into his personal writings. He believed there was a God, or "first cause," and curiously, he and almost all of the deists believed in a "future state," of existence after death that might be analogous to what a Christian would call heaven.

The atheist, David Hume, was a very important person in Hutton's thinking. While Hutton was not an atheist, his thinking reflects Hume at its finest. Writes Baxter regarding the relationship between the two,

> Hume's work was very important for Hutton – who was dealing, in his geology, with remote realms like the depths of the Earth, or distant ages past, of which we can have no direct knowledge. How, then, is it possible to know anything about them at all? He would find tentative answers in Hume's thinking.
>
> More controversially, Hume also asked very hard questions about God. In his *Dialogues Concerning Natural Religion*, he asked why we should look for "mind" as the organizing principle of the universe. Maybe the order we perceive just *emerged*. "For aught we know a *priori*, matter may contain the source, or spring, of order originating within itself, as well as the mind does." This sentence was written a full century before Darwin came up with a way to show how the organized complexity of life could indeed emerge from "matter itself," without the need of any guiding mind.
>
> Hume could at times be very harsh about institutional religion: "Survey most nations and most ages. Examine the religious principles which have in fact prevailed in the world. You will scarcely be persuaded they are anything but sick men's dreams." No wonder the popular take on Hume's work was that he was denying God. This led to him being refused university posts. Hume and Hutton, in fact, were the most significant figures of the Scottish Enlightenment *not* to hold formal academic positions." [80]

At this point it should be said that the vision of all of the detractors of the Christian religion at that time and after was very narrow sighted. If they had been objective they would have seen that the Christian religion was directly or indirectly responsible for almost all of the good that was occurring in that part of the world.

---

[80] Baxter, Stephen; Ages in Chaos, James Hutton and the Discovery of Deep Time, 2003 pp. 91, 92

Hume and Hutton may have never received any schooling if not for the schools that were run by the Church in Scotland. Later, hospitals and orphanages were exclusively enterprises of the Church. These are just a small sample of the organized responses of the Church to the needs of the world around it, but the changed lives of individuals more than likely had an even bigger effect.

Hutton was not just a casual deist. He was so passionate about it that the third volume of his *An Investigation of the Principles of Knowledge, and of the Progress of Reason, from Sense to Science and Philosophy*, which was 755 pages long, were devoted to undermining Christianity, while building a case for Natural Religion. And what better way to do that than by destroying the first 11 chapters of Genesis, which provide the foundation for the rest of the Bible? The scriptures that tell us who we are, who God is, and what our relationship with God should be are to be found there. The origin of sin is found there. God's purposes for the earth and His love for His creation are described there. The result of sin is described there. The whole New Testament, which has the remedy for sin, would be unnecessary without Genesis.

Many people die suddenly and don't have time to prepare for it. Hutton had the advantage of knowing several years in advance that his time was growing short. In 1791 he began suffering from retention of urine. His best friend, Joseph Black, a medical doctor by degree, operated on him, and was somewhat successful in restoring some of Hutton's health, although Hutton was never able to go out into the field again. In 1793, he lad a relapse but again improved with the help of Dr. Black. It is interesting to note that even though his friends were urging him to publish his *Theory of the Earth* he put that off until he could publish *Principles of Knowledge* first. *Principles* had all of his ideas regarding Natural Religion and Christianity in it. Evidently, it was more important to him that the world know his views on those things than on geology.

What is a natural religionist or deist?

What exactly did Natural Religionists (Deists) believe? They believed in one god (first cause, as it was known to most of them). They believed that all that was necessary to know about God could be known through observing the world around us; divine revelation (the Bible in the Christian religion) was not needed. They believed that morals, virtue and ethics were socially derived qualities that had nothing to do with religion. The highest goal of humanity should be the happiness of all but more particularly one's own happiness. Hence, with Franklin, Jefferson and Madison, known deists, involved in drafting the Declaration of Independence, that document contains a phrase regarding, "the pursuit of happiness," right near the start of it. Deists dwelt on the positive aspects of their "future state," a condition of peace and happiness after death, but unlike Christians, deists didn't seem to have a hell for the unrepentant in their cosmology.

Interesting is the fact that most of these concepts are obviously derived from the Bible, but once they adopted the concept, they said it had nothing to do with the Bible. A fiery preacher by the name of Abraham Taylor noticed the same thing, and in 1755 came against the Natural Religionists in the strongest manner:

> Therefore, in our day, natural religion is decked in plumes borrowed from scripture, and then held up in opposition to it, as a perfect rule, and as such not needing the assistance of revelation. This is scandalously base and unfair. For instance: no one mere rational writer ever gave a tolerable account of a future state; and none of the delineators of the religion of nature … ever did it, without leaving the plainest traces of his having aid from Scripture; and yet these sketches, which are drawn by the help of Scripture, must be palmed upon the world, as the doctrines of mere reason unassisted by the light of revelation. Thus Scripture is pillaged, in order to its being represented as a needless useless thing…[81]

Before going any further, we should identify the meaning of the terms used by Hutton. He uses the word *philosophy* to refer to Natural Religion or Deism. *Superstition* is the deist word for organized religion, usually referring to Christianity. The doctrines of Christianity are referred to as *prejudices*. We will see these terms used in the following quotes.

Against the backdrop of Abraham Taylor's statement, let's see how Mr. Hutton's thoughts compare. Regarding the Bible, writing in *Principles of Knowledge*, he states:

[81]http://us.mc324.mail.yahoo.com/mc/welcome?.gx=1&.tm=1251866771&. rand=5auahp2dec8vp, accessed 08/03/2010

The Christian religion was formed in Judea; and it was founded on one which the Jewish nation then possessed. But, the Jewish religion had its origin among some ancient tribes, before the code of laws, which Moses is said to have given that nation, had been devised. Now, though we cannot know, from history, the particulars of that religion which among the Hebrews was reformed by their enlightened lawgiver, we have reason to believe that it was, like the religion of all barbarous nations, founded on superstitious notions, and suited to the ignorance and inhumanity of rude ages." [82]

Regarding the future state, he states:

It is thus that a future state in which virtue is rewarded and vice punished, at the same time that this is a philosophical truth, it is a part of most religions which have been contrived in this world. [83]

Like most deists he believes religion is contrived or made up by ignorant savages of the ancient past to deal with the uncertainties of life.

There are for us two sources of religion, viz. philosophy [deism] and superstition [Christianity] [84]

This statement reveals his mindset regarding Natural Religion versus Christianity.
Regarding his view of Christians,

there is nothing so incredible but what will be believed, if coming from an authority that is not suspected, and if not opposed by the prejudice of the person, whose faith is thus to be formed in superstition, and not in science [philosophy or Natural Religion]." [85]

---

[82] Hutton, James, M.D. & F.R.S.E.; An Investigation of the Principles of Knowledge, and of the Progress of Reason, from Sense to Science and Philosophy, In Three Volumes; vol. III, 1794 p.661

[83] Ibid, pp. 622,623
[84] Ibid, p. 623
[85] Ibid, p. 626

Hutton despised authority, as was noted on several occasions by Playfair. Hutton also affirmed this trait of his in several places in his *Principles of Knowledge.* We must remember that at that time in Britain and in most of the European countries, probably as a residue of the past centuries of Catholicism, people viewed their relationship to God as controlled by the authorities in the church. The modern concept of doing "your own thing" and not depending on someone else to tell you how and what to think was unheard of in that age. Many people resented it, but their overt behavior was muted because of the severe consequences of public disapproval. A couple of generations later, Charles Lyell was in the same position.

Hutton's relationship to his god is certainly a convenient one. In *Principles of Knowledge* he comments:

> It is impossible to refuse giving adoration to a God, who asks no more of man — than that he should learn to make himself most happy." [86]

He certainly did not venerate the Patriarchs of the Old Testament or anything that went before them.

> In this inferior state of man [the savage state of the founders of the Hebrew nation], he never can look up in contemplation of a *first cause*; for, his views are limited to the particulars, the more immediate object of his knowledge. In this rude state of the savage, he seldom generalizes, so as to arrive at universals; and, when he reasons beyond the more immediate objects of his knowledge, or what is generally termed common sense, he falls into the grossest error and delusion.
>
> Such we may suppose to have been the original of every nation. But, in the dark ages of their barbarism, nations have had religious opinions, and certain rites or forms of worship. It is then that many gods have been acknowledged; that the most absurd rites have been complied with; and that most cruel sacrifices have been offered to their idols and their demons.
>
> Such had once been the state of the Hebrew nation; superstition, cruelty, and idolatry, derived from the savage or barbarous state, had pervaded their opinions and their worship. This then is the natural state of their

---

[86] Ibid, p. 666

national religion, considered as in its barbarous and unreformed state.

It is unnecessary to inquire more particularly into the state of that original religion of the Hebrews, which in the advancing light of human science is to be reformed. It is enough to see that their original religion must have been erroneous; and now we are to look for the first epoch of its reformation." [87]

The great truth which was retained in the Hebrew code was this: That there is but one God, the cause of all things, a Being unlike to any thing which may be imagined by man. In other respects, their opinions were erroneous, and their worship was still barbarous. They represented their god as partial, jealous, and revengeful; and they sacrificed animals, as an atonement for the sins they had committed, and to appease a being, who had the inconstancy to change his purpose like a man.

How long they had continued in that corrupted state perhaps cannot be known. At last, however, science flourished in Greece; and from thence we have authentic records, with regard to the progress of philosophy in that quarter of the world.

We know, that then the purest system of morality appeared among the various speculations of philosophic men; and, it is upon the purest morality, as well as philosophic principle, that the Christian religion reformed that of the Jews, in abolishing their abominable and absurd rites, and in justifying the character of the *one God*, in representing that perfect Being, not as the partial and revengeful despot, but as the benevolent Father of mankind. [88]

Like other deists, Hutton will throw a bone to the Christians if it means demeaning the Jews, but remember he was living in a Christian country that didn't take kindly to heretics. What you won't hear is a deist talking about Christ himself or talking about the atonement. Anything good they have to say about Christianity is in reference to Jesus' teachings about loving others, doing good, and other general doctrines that most anyone would agree with.

Hutton despised the miracles and mysteries of the Bible. Like many of the teachings in the Bible, they are too specific and don't lend themselves to the generalizing that the deist likes to do.

---

[87] Ibid, pp.662 & 663
[88] Ibid, pp. 664 & 665

Miracle and mystery have been employed, to the disgrace of human reason; and thus religion, which, (after understanding morals,) is in its nature the plainest of propositions, and in its natural tendency the most agreeable of informations, has been made to puzzle the minds of reasoning men, and to fill the superstitious with dreadful apprehensions. [89]

He believed that

morality is that science, with regard to happiness, in which a mind forms opinions from its former knowledge; and it is that system in which mind determines consciously its present action, in foreseeing future events, by which its happiness or misery is to be affected." [90]

It will thus appear that man, who, according to our theory, is both a moral and a scientific agent, has two purposes in speaking truth. One of these is to gratify the intellectual satisfaction of his mind, which is always, or in general, pleased in knowing truth. The other is to obtain some particular good, or attain some end, which is then the object of his intention." [91]

In his next statement he gives us a different and somewhat unexpected source for morals:

Thus, though in nature there are laws of morality to which the species are in wisdom necessarily led, yet, practically among men, morals, in general, are founded upon manners. How important, therefore, must it be, to have manners directed wisely for that valuable purpose." [92]

Let's see what he thinks about virtue, which is closely connected to morals.

Man, who is affected with sympathetic as well as with immediate feelings, being educated in society, forms his notions of virtue and vice from that approbation and

---

[89] Ibid, p. 668
[90] Ibid, p. 221
[91] Ibid, p. 409
[92] Ibid, p. 502

disapprobation of others which he meets with in pursuing his own inclination. Thus it will appear, that man first learns virtue instinctively, that is to say, he knows virtue first before he understands it. The understanding of virtue is the science of morals; and properly belongs to philosophy, which is the most general reasoning of a scientific mind. [93]

In this case, it belongs to the wisdom of the community, and is a public duty in the council of the state, that of making men see their proper interest in public virtue. Now, this salutary purpose is affected by the hopes of honour, which should only be attained in promoting public good, and by the apprehension of disgrace, which should follow the neglect of duty with no less certainty than misery pursues crime." [94]

Finally, regarding virtue,

In this career man sees what is truly virtuous; and he makes himself virtuous, not in loving virtue above all things, but in wishing above all things to be loved of men. [95]

So, did Hutton apply this to himself? Is this why he came up with his groundbreaking and startling geological theory... to be loved by men? All of the above comments by Hutton refer to a motivation for actions that is tied directly to rejection or acceptance by others.

We've had three comments on morals and three comments on virtue without ever discussing the concept of God or Christianity. Nor did a deist ever cross that line, because their worldview didn't admit of a need for revelation from God.

Why did Hutton develop deist views? In studying the life of James Hutton, there is scant information available about his childhood. But we can discern some influences upon his life that could have steered him in the direction of Natural Religion. Attending Scottish primary schools, he would have received a healthy dose of Bible teaching, and given the fact that he had a rebellious streak, his desire for something other than Christianity

---

[93] Ibid, p. 349
[94] Ibid, p. 441
[95] Ibid, p. 488

could have started at a young age. Maybe he was bitter that his father died when he was so young.

He started his matriculation at Edinburgh College at the age of 14, which was not an especially young age at that time for starting college, but it was an impressionable age. His teacher there for Natural Philosophy was Colin MacLaurin (1698-1746). MacLaurin had come to know Isaac Newton (1643-1727) late in Newton's life. Newton was so impressed with the young lad that he wrote a letter of recommendation to Edinburgh University when they were considering hiring MacLaurin as a professor. Newton even agreed to pay a portion of MacLaurin's salary.

MacLaurin took much from the learning of Isaac Newton and went on to become one of the most renowned professors in the history of Edinburgh University. Today, they still publish the MacLaurin series of Mathematics texts that are used in schools in the U.S. and Britain. Even while he was still teaching at Edinburgh he was a towering figure that must have inspired awe in an impressionable teenager like Hutton.

Newton wrote more on theological topics than he did on science or mathematics. He wrote much about design in nature and how it revealed a benevolent God who designed it in such a way that it benefits mankind. His personal views on the doctrines of Christianity are not well known. MacLaurin, on the other hand, was a vocal deist. MacLaurin was probably influenced by some of the other philosophers who were beginning to have their voices heard, such as John Locke in Britain and Rene Descartes in France, both strong advocates of deism. We can be sure MacLaurin's deism made quite an impression on the youthful Hutton. Playfair writes:

> Of the masters under whom he [Hutton] studied there [Edinburgh], MacLaurin was by far the most eminent, and Dr. Hutton, though he had cultivated the mathematical sciences less than any other, never mentioned the lectures of that celebrated professor but in terms of high admiration. [96]

MacLaurin was also responsible for starting the Philosophical Society in 1737, which later became the Royal Society of Edinburgh.

---

[96] Playfair, John; James Hutton & Joseph Black, Biographies by John Playfair and Adam Ferguson, from Volume V of *Transactions of the Royal Society of Edinburgh*, 1805, Publish by the RSE Scotland Foundation, p. 39

If Hutton did not adopt deism wholeheartedly while at Edinburgh University, he certainly gained the motive for it several years later, when, at the age of 21, he found himself the unmarried father of a child. This is one more confirmation of his rebellious attitude toward the morals of the society that he was a part of, and also specifically tells us of the disregard he had for the teachings of the Bible and the Presbyterian Church of Scotland, which taught morals in the schools. Undoubtedly, there were accusations against him about his loose morals by those of professed Christian belief, and there must also have been some guilt on his part as well. Then, to remove himself to Paris, of all places, would be just the recipe to ensure that he would find a godless answer to his problems. France, in the middle of the 18th century, was starting to feel the rumblings of revolution. A major part of that revolution entailed a rebellion against the Roman Catholic Church, which represented Christianity to most French people. What better place than in a university setting in Paris to hear the anti-Christian ideas of Voltaire, Diderot, and Rousseau? The dominoes were all beginning to fall in the same direction, and unfortunately, it happened in a relatively short period of time, and at an impressionable age for Hutton. He was more than likely by that time a confirmed deist. Deism offered him an escape from the guilt associated with the teachings of the national Church of Scotland.

It is not known why Hutton became interested in geology, but it is likely that, while in France, he came across the writings of the natural philosopher and geologist Comte De Buffon, or other similar works delving into natural history, and in France, those writings did not glorify God, but instead, disregarded the Bible in every respect. Many philosophers have often reflected that Hutton's writings more closely resembled those of Buffon than any other geologist of that time. Buffon, for example, ignored the Bible in his musings and speculated that the earth could be as old as 70,000 to 80,000 years. When the church leaders became aware of that, they demanded a recantation, which Buffon did. Then, he went right about writing the same things again that got him in trouble the first time, implying errors in the Bible. We need not even suppose that Hutton was only influenced while in France, because communication between Britain and France had grown quite fluid and Scotland seemed to have even stronger ties to France than England had. For example, when a lad of means graduated from university in Scotland an almost expected ritual was to visit the continent on an extended vacation, sometimes lasting a year or two. France was always one of the main countries on the itinerary. Those trips were an extension of the education obtained at the university.

Later, when Hutton became a farmer, he had ample opportunity to view the surface features of the earth and make observations about the cause of things, to formulate his ideas that would support his geology, which in turn would support his theology. He must have thought quite a bit about these things, because in 1764, ten years after moving to the farm at Slighhouses, he abruptly left, presumably in the summer, when he should have been hard at work on the farm, and made an extended geological excursion to the north of Scotland with Sir George Clerk. They cut a wide swath, and the land they were looking at is noted for its chaotic formations and unusual features that a geologist would love to speculate about.

In 1765 he entered into the partnership with James Davie for the sal ammoniac business. It may be that Hutton was able in some way to come up with money from one of the two

Siccar Point 1: This is Hutton's much-talked-about contact point where the tilted strata meet the horizontal strata.

farms in Berwickshire to put into the business because Davie provided complete management of the business but shared the profits with Hutton. In 1768 he was able to rent out the farm that he had personally farmed, which provided further income for him.

We have seen that Hutton was a deist, and had an antipathy for organized religion and Christianity in particular. We have seen that he had a firm grounding in Natural Religion and a reason to be bitter toward those who viewed their relationship with God in a more traditional way. We have not looked at his actual geology to see if what he came up with to support his views had any merit.

Was Hutton's Geology Valid?

The number one evidence supporting Hutton's geology would be the unconformity at Siccar Point. Siccar Point is a headland sticking out into the North Sea just about 30 miles due east of Edinburgh. The feature that distinguishes it from most land forms is that there are strata that

Siccar Point 2: A close-up view of the contact point between the two different strata.

were originally laid down horizontally, but have been tilted so that the plane of the strata is almost vertical. Sitting on top of that are more strata that are nearly horizontal, perpendicular to the previously mentioned strata. The following is Playfair's account of that day in 1788 when Hutton took Playfair and the young Sir James Hall out to Siccar Point. Note the almost worshipful tones when he talks about Hutton. Also, note that there is absolutely no indicator of age in this formation, only evidence that different parts of it were laid down at different times.

> Dr Hutton wished particularly to examine the latter of these [Siccar Point], and on this occasion Sir James Hall and I had the pleasure to accompany him. We sailed in a boat from Dunglass, on a day when the fineness of the weather permitted us to keep close to the foot of the rocks which line the shore in that quarter, directing our course southwards, in search of the termination of the secondary strata. We made for a high rocky point or headland, the SICCAR, near which, from our observations on shore, we knew that the object we were in search of was likely to be discovered. On landing at this point, we found that we actually trode on the primeval rock, which forms alternately the base and the summit of the present land. It is here a micaceous schistus, in beds nearly vertical, highly indurated [hard], and stretching from S.E. to N.W. The surface of this rock runs with a moderate ascent from the level of low-water, at which we landed, nearly to that of high-water, where the schistus has a thin covering of red

horizontal sandstone laid over it; and this sandstone, at the distance of a few yards farther back, rises into a very high perpendicular cliff. Here, therefore, the immediate contact of the two rocks is not only visible, but is curiously dissected and laid open by the action of the waves. The rugged tops of the schistus are seen penetrating into the horizontal beds of sandstone, and the lowest of these last form a breccia containing fragments of schistus, some round and others angular, united by an arenaceous cement.

Dr. Hutton was highly pleased with appearances that set in so clear a light the different formations of the parts which compose the exterior crust of the earth, and where all the circumstances were combined that could render the observation satisfactory and precise. On us who saw these phenomena for the first time, the impression made will not easily be forgotten. The palpable evidence presented to us, of one of the most extraordinary and important facts in the natural history of the earth, gave a reality and substance to those theoretical speculations, which, however probable, had never till now been directly authenticated by the testimony of the senses. We often said to ourselves, what clearer evidence could we have had of the different formation of these

Siccar Point 3: Sir James Hall's drawing of the Siccar Point unconformity

rocks, and of the long interval which separated their formation, had we actually seen them emerging from the bosom of the deep? We felt ourselves necessarily carried back to the time when the schistus on which we stood was yet at the bottom of the sea, and when the sandstone before us was only beginning to be deposited, in the shape of sand or mud, from the waters of a superincumbent ocean. An epocha still more remote presented itself, when even the most ancient of these rocks, instead of standing upright in vertical beds, lay in horizontal planes at the bottom of the sea, and was not yet disturbed by that immeasurable force which has burst asunder the solid pavement of the globe.

Revolutions still more remote appeared in the distance of this extraordinary perspective. The mind seemed to grow giddy by looking so far into the abyss of time; and while we listened with earnestness and admiration to the philosopher who was now unfolding to us the order and series of these wonderful events, we became sensible how much farther reason may sometimes go than imagination can venture to follow." [97]

Might I suggest that Hutton's imagination is *all* we have in that statement? Reason was tossed out the window long before.

There seems little doubt that Hutton was correct in surmising that the two sections of strata were laid down at different times, but jumping to the conclusion that they had to be separated by eons of time is an unwarranted assumption. They could just as easily have been separated by only a few hours or days if their formation was achieved by a catastrophic process. Playfair's and Hall's willingness to accept the vast age proposed by Hutton rests on nothing more than their naivety and Hutton's status as an Edinburgh elite. They were accepting his authority instead of letting the evidence speak for itself and coming to their own conclusions. The fact that Hutton did not even mention the reigning paradigm of a catastrophic world flood in his *Theory of the Earth* is suspicious at best and devious at worst. He was not highly regarded by the diluvialists during his lifetime. It would seem that if he really intended to persuade them to his system he would have been well advised to at least address their views about the subject at hand. For him to act as if nothing more was necessary than to wave his hand and say there must have been a long interval between the laying down of the different strata displays an arrogance that will present itself on more than one occasion. There is a saying that the hardest thing to get someone to believe is that which it is not in their best interest to believe. This is exhibit "A" of that rationale.

Dr. Tas Walker of Creation Ministries International has written an excellent paper on Siccar Point, showing it to be one of the best evidences that there was a worldwide flood. The creation of Siccar Point was definitely a result of a catastrophic process. The particles of sand and silt were transported so rapidly they didn't have time to sort into different sizes as they do under gradual processes. The

[97] Ibid, pp. 71,72&73

grains of sand are jagged, not rounded as they would be if they were deposited over a long period of time.

The layers comprise very large surface areas in most cases, indicating that it was a very large body of water that accomplished its work all at once. The lower rocks were folded but not cracked, indicating they were soft and full of water when they were laid down.

Regarding the upper layer of sandstone Walker says:

> The upper sandstone beds (the "Old Red Sandstone"...) also shout catastrophe. A 1-m-(3-ft-) thick layer at the base consists of broken rocks, called a breccias (below) — evidence that fast flowing water eroded the contact. The large clasts (broken pieces) of greywacke tend to face the same direction (imbricate) indicating strong currents. The broken rock is still angular, showing it was transported rapidly. The catastrophe was vast because the Old Red Sandstone covers a huge geographical area---400 km (250 miles) from Siccar Point to Northern Ireland in the west, and 100 km (60 miles) from the Southern Uplands to the Grampian Mountains in the north. Although it is more than 7 km (23,000 ft) thick, the beds are amazingly uniform and parallel over huge distances. It was no normal river that deposited these sediments. [98]

Walker goes on into many other details of the peculiar outcrop known as Siccar Point that we don't have space here to enumerate, but it is obvious that he has a whole lot more ammunition for his point of view than Hutton had for his.

There was a very revealing letter from Playfair to Hall that depicts their almost reverent attitude toward James Hutton. Playfair visited the Isle of Arran soon after Hutton's death. Some of Hutton's most important field work had been done there in 1787. Playfair writes:

> The junctions I saw were I believe all visited by Dr. H. At one of them I could see the marks of his hammer (or at least I thought so), and could not without emotion think of the enthusiasm with which he must have viewed it. I was never more sensible of the truth of what I remember you

---

[98] Internet, www.CreationOnTheWeb.com, Siccar Point Scotland, Unmasking a Long Age Icon, Tas Walker, Ph.D., accessed June 2010

said one day when we were looking at the Dykes in the water at Leith since the Dr.'s death, "that these phenomena had now lost half their value." [99]

Let's look at some of the other excursions Hutton made, and see if there is more substance to those. Hutton had a strong suspicion that

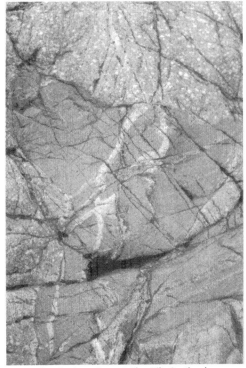

Granite Intrusions at Glen Tilt, Scotland

granite was not the oldest of rocks, as had been generally believed, and he felt he could make his point if he could document a place where granite had been extruded in a liquid form into other rocks. John Clerk of Eldin had told him about an area in the north of Scotland where he had seen that, so, at the invitation of the Duke of Atholl , he embarked on a combination hunting/ geology trip, with the Duke doing the hunting and Hutton and Clerk doing the geologizing. They hadn't gone far, just seven miles up the Glen Tilt River, before Hutton found what he was looking for. There, above the riverbed, they saw where the granite had extruded itself up into the schist. The obvious deduction is that the granite had at one time been in a liquid state. He said it proved that the granite was younger than the schist, and that, therefore, granite is not the oldest rock. Well, certainly the granite that ran up into the schist was younger, but it would make sense that the underlying granite would be older than what lies on top of it. The heat, which Hutton was so noted for, could have melted the granite right where it was and then the pressure would have forced it up into the overlying layer.

[99] Repcheck, Jack; The Man Who Found Time, 2003, p.168

The main component of Hutton's system that sets him apart from the diluvialists is his inclusion of heat in the system. Hutton had known the Clerk family for many years, perhaps all his life. The Clerks were wealthy, and owned a considerable amount of land, much of it with mineral wealth. They owned coal mines not too far from Edinburgh. You don't have to descend very far into a coal mine before you notice that the deeper you go, the warmer it gets. The Clerks may have mentioned this to Hutton, or maybe Hutton went into some of those mines himself. Extrapolating that data to greater depths, one could see that it might get very hot deep within the earth, especially with no mine shafts to release the heat. The diluvialists did not comprehend that the pressure inside the earth creates heat. They were looking for the heat to come from the combustion of coal, or some other substance in the case of volcanoes. Therefore, they concluded that sources were inadequate for the heat that Hutton described. This only made them look foolish. Hutton didn't really understand where the heat came from, either, but he was sure heat was involved.

There were other instances where the diluvialists were easy targets for Hutton because they didn't follow a strictly biblical approach. It was when they went beyond scripture that they were most vulnerable. On the other hand, if they had taken some scriptures more seriously, they might have come up with more credible models than they did. For instance, when Genesis 7:19 describes the beginning of the flood it talks about the water covering the *high hills.* At the end of the flood in Genesis 8:5 it talks about the *mountains* being covered. The implication is that the hills (mountains) were much higher at the end of the flood than they were at the beginning. It is a subtle difference, the significance of which most people miss, but if the diluvialists had explored a model whereby parts of the earth were pushed up and other parts sank down during the flood or soon after, it would have given them a much more defendable cosmology. As it was, they had to come up with ways for water to have covered the highest mountains at nearly the height they are now.

As he appeared to be correct about the two formations at Siccar Point, he also looked competent in regard to the heating of granite. To those around Hutton, especially the younger, more impressionable men, he appeared to have it all figured out. Never mind that he also thought that limestone and flint were products of heat (we now know they were formed by water). They should also have asked Hutton how it is that many strata are bent, not cracked, in the same way from the top of the formation all the way to the bottom, if these processes took place gradually over eons. In the Grand Canyon there is a layer that is 4,000 feet thick, bent the same way from top to bottom. This means the whole mass had to be soft and pliable at the same time. It could not have remained that way for millions of years. If one 4,000-foot-thick formation was in such a state, is it too much of a stretch to believe all of the strata under our feet were formed in the same way, just the way the Bible says they were? Hutton never saw the Grand Canyon, but he had numerous similar smaller scale replicas in Britain and on the continent that should have put some question marks into his mind about his theory of the earth.

In 1786, Hutton went with John Clerk of Eldin to Galloway, which is in the southwest corner of Scotland. They found further evidence of the schist having been penetrated by the granite. So, once again we know that the schist that was penetrated had to be older than the liquid that penetrated it, but nothing more than that. We have no information on their *relative* ages.

In 1787 Hutton made two more forays into the field before the grand finale in 1788 to Siccar Point. Remember, he was doing all of this because when he had presented his theory before the Royal Society in 1785, they said he had no evidence, only conjecture, for his ideas. He went to the Isle of Arran with the son of John Clerk of Eldin (whose name was also John). They found basalt dykes sticking out of the ground in various places, but in some places the basalt had taken on the appearance of black glass, which meant that it had cooled faster than in other places. Hutton was happy with this discovery, because it showed that the origin of the dykes was igneous, but it seems he should have contemplated why some of those areas cooled so fast. Could they have been under water? Another one of his observations that he made as a result of that trip was:

> No proposition in natural history, concerning what is past is more certain. Pladda [a little island off the coast of Arran] is the intermediate step by which we may remount to this view of high antiquity. We see the destruction of a high island in the formation of a low one; and we may perceive the future destruction, not of the little island only, but also of the continent itself, which is in time to disappear. Thus Pladda is to the island of Arran what

Arran is to the island of Britain, and what the island of
Britain is to the continent of Europe. [100]

Note the authority with which he speaks, without providing any
sort of evidence. This was typical Huttonese. But when you have
young, impressionable assistants who might be a little in awe of
Hutton's standing as an Edinburgh elite, it carries the day and
appears to be fact.

That same year, he visited a friend near the town of Jedburgh and
was told about an unconformity that was a forerunner of what was
later to be found at Siccar Point. At Jedburgh there is schist that has
been turned so that the layers are vertical and the edges of those
layers are sitting under horizontal layers of red sandstone. Very
interesting, but it proves nothing as far as time is concerned.

That brings us back to 1788, when he was 62, and made his trip to
Siccar Point with Playfair, who was 40, and Sir James Hall, who was
27. He had proven nothing except that there are places where a time
sequence can be shown, although we have no idea how much time
was involved; and there are other places where it can be shown that
granite extruded itself in a liquid form into other rocks, usually
schist or basalt.

There seems to be a question of whether Hutton had lost his
enthusiasm for his theory of the earth, based on the fact that he
wrote several books dealing with other subjects in the 1790s, when
he knew his time on earth was growing short. He only got serious
about publishing *Theory of the Earth* in 1795, when Richard Kirwan,
an Irish geologist and writer on many subjects, attacked his theory.
The same day he read Kirwan's assault; he determined to get *Theory
of the Earth* published and did so in a few months. Maybe he felt it
was not going to be possible to convince very many people of the
truth of his theory.

In 1802, when Playfair wrote his book, *Illustrations of the
Huttonian Theory of the Earth,* there were a number of arguments for
the theory put forth that deserved examination. Presumably, most of
them originated with Hutton. Hutton noticed that rivers almost
always show signs they are occupying a channel that is just a small
part of what was once a much larger channel. In many cases the
previous "channel" was actually a lake. Playfair writes:

---

[100] James Hutton, The Founder of Modern Geology, Donald B. McIntyre and
Alan McKirdy, 2001, p. 37

The courses of many rivers retain marks that they once consisted of a series of lakes, which have been converted into dry ground, by the twofold operation of filling up the bottoms, and deepening the outlets. This happens, especially, when successive terraces of gravelly and flat land are found on the banks of a river. Such platforms, or *haughs* as they are called in this country, are always proofs of the waste and *detritus* produced by the river, and of the different levels on which it has run; but they sometimes lead us farther, and make it certain, that the great mass of gravel which forms the successive terraces on each side of the river, was deposited in the bason of a lake. If, from the level of the highest terrace, down to the present bed of the river, all is alluvial, and formed of sand and gravel, it is then evident, that the space as low as the river now runs must have been once occupied by water; at the same time, it is clear, that water must have stood, or flowed as high at least, as the uppermost surface of the meadow. It is impossible to reconcile these two facts, which are both undeniable, but by supposing a lake, or body of stagnant water, to have here occupied a great hollow (which by us must be held as one of the original inequalities of the globe, because we can trace it no farther back), and that this hollow, in the course of ages, has been filled up by the gravel and alluvial earth brought down by the river, which is now cutting its channel through materials of its own depositing. There is no great river that does not afford instances of this, both in the hilly part of its course, and where it descends first from thence into the plain. Were there room here for the minuter details of topographical description, this might be illustrated by innumerable examples.

It is said above, that the water must have run or stood, in former times, as low as the present bottom of the river; but there is often clear evidence, that it has run or stood much lower, because the alluvial land reaches far below the present level of the river. This is known to hold in very many instances, where it has happened that pits have been sunk to considerable depths on the banks of large rivers. By that means, the depth of the alluvial ground, under the present bed of the river, has been discovered to be great; and from this arises the difficulty, so generally experienced, of finding good foundations for bridges that are built over rivers in large vallies, or open plains, the ground being composed of travelled materials to an unknown depth, without any thing like the native or solid strata. In such cases, it is evident, that formerly the water must have been much lower, as well as much higher, than its present level, and this is only consistent with the notion, that the place was once occupied by a deep lake." [101]

This is a classic case of evidence for a worldwide flood staring them in the face, but they will invent any kind of convoluted explanation of the events they see that will prevent them from accepting a global flood. If there were lakes there, they would have been tranquil ones. Lakes don't tear through rock and create new channels for water. And, if as Playfair says, this is a phenomenon found all over the world, wouldn't a worldwide flood explain that? In fact, if one were looking for "proof" of the flood this would be one of the best examples imaginable.

On page 89 of Playfair's *Illustrations* he expounds one of Hutton's major points:

With the granite, we shall consider the proof of the igneous origin of all mineral substances as completed. [102]

Well, he and Hutton can consider it completed, but no one today does. Limestone predominates in strata all over the earth, and no one today would argue against the idea that limestone is created by the action of water. He is talking here, of course, of the cases where Hutton exposed the extrusion of granite in a liquid form into adjacent materials.

Just as confidently he says,

Now, if it be granted that the strata were at any time soft and flexible, since their complete formation, it will be found impossible to deny their having been softened by the application of heat. [103]

Hutton was the first geologist to recognize the fact of the earth's internal heat, but like all good things, sometimes we over-use them. It has become apparent that Hutton's ability to convince Playfair that

[101] Playfair, John; Illustrations of the Huttonian Theory of the Earth, 1802, pp. 355- 357
[102] Ibid, p. 89
[103] Ibid, pp. 225, 226

heat was involved in the formation of the earth on a large scale, in opposition to prevailing theories of that time, impressed him immensely. By that time Playfair was ready to accept Hutton's conjectures about the age of the earth, although Hutton provided no evidence for that idea. In other words, Playfair had elevated Hutton so high in his respect that Hutton no longer needed to provide evidence for any of his geological ideas. In this case though, Playfair and Hutton could not have been more wrong, as the vast sedimentary layers of limestone throughout the earth were formed by watery events, not heat. Shouldn't this seal the deal as far as Hutton's credibility goes? Bent strata today is universally accepted as evidence of its original pliability, so Hutton was really out to lunch with his heat thing on this one, but the historians of science still have him up on that pedestal as if he is infallible.

Another often overlooked aspect of the growing acceptance of Huttonianism at that time was the fact that none of the diluvialists really supported the strict biblical account of the formation and development of the earth. There were some similarities to the biblical account, mainly the acceptance of at least one worldwide flood, but it was a loose connection. Prior to about 1850 the diluvialists were called neptunists. By far the best known geologist of that day was the "neptunist" Abraham Werner (1749 – 1817) of Germany. But Werner believed in many past worldwide floods. He thought the Genesis flood was a tranquil event that by itself could not account for the phenomena seen in the crust of the earth. Though he didn't broadcast it, he believed the earth was millions of years old. Werner didn't recognize any involvement of heat in the creation of the strata, but credited it all to the action of water. But his geology revealed his true beliefs. Usually, Hutton was only attacking the neptunists; he was not directly attacking the Bible, but by doing that he was given credit for disproving the Bible. It was a "straw man" argument. As Hutton's theory grew more popular, Werner had great difficulty defending the idea that no heat was involved.

Deodat de Dolomieu was one of the few geologists to whom Hutton paid any attention. Playfair's biography of Hutton lists Dolomieu along with Ferber, Bergman, Saussure and Deluc as the other geologists that affected the formation of Hutton's system. Playfair tells about Dolomieu's findings in Italy:

> Near Vizini, in the Val di Noto, Dolomieu tells us, that he counted eleven beds, alternately calcareous and volcanic, in the perpendicular face of a hill, which at a distance

appeared like a piece of cloth, striped black and white; *ubi supra*. In another instance he saw more than twenty of these alternations. He has since made similar observations in the Vincentine and in Tirol. [104]

So what we have is a situation where the strata shows alternate depositions of black, white, black, white, etc. with 20 layers; the black being basalt and the white being limestone. The limestone was laid down by water. The basalt may have been moved in by water, but was in a liquid state due to its heat. This is a case where the whole sequence would have to have been performed quite rapidly for it to have happened at all. Playfair believed that limestone was created by heat; however, so it didn't create the problem in his mind that it should have.

Dolomieu also believed that the sea had once been 3,000 to 3,600 feet higher in the past. That would seem to have been an idea that might have caused one to wonder if maybe the diluvial system might have some merit.

Playfair, and by extension, Hutton, show faulty reasoning, which comes about by their lack of knowledge of cavitation. Cavitation takes place in large volumes of water moving at high speeds. An analogy would be the work of air in a tornado where you see such things as straws sticking in tree trunks. A good example of cavitation exists in the scablands of Eastern Washington. An ice age dam broke in the vicinity of what is now Missoula, Montana. It released about 500 cubic miles of water that came rushing westward toward the Columbia River at the rate of about 60 miles per hour. At the bottom of that mass of water, cavitation occurred on a grand scale. The rock was ripped away as if it were nothing more than silt, leaving a most unusual-looking landscape complete with huge potholes and rock erratics. But Playfair declares,

> again, if we consider a valley as a space, which perhaps with many windings and irregularities, has been hollowed out of the solid rock, it is plain that no force of water, suddenly applied, could loosen and remove the great mass of stone which has actually disappeared. The greatest column of water that could be brought to act against such a mass, whatever be the velocity we ascribe to it, could not break asunder and displace beds of rock many leagues in length, and in continuity with the rock on

---

[104] Ibid, p. 272

either side of them. The slow working of water, on the other hand, or the powers that we see every day in action, are quite sufficient for this effect, if time only is allowed them." [105]

Playfair and Hutton could not have been further from the truth. The exact opposite to what they believed was the only thing that could cause water to eat through hard, solid rock.

The following quote of Playfair's shows the lengths that people will go to convince others of their ideas:

> The Yellow Sea, which is a large gulf contained between the coast of China and the peninsula of Corea, receives so much mud from the great rivers that run into it, that it takes its colour, as well as its name, from that circumstance; [106]

Whatever you may think of the two men as geologists, this shows they are not etymologists (people who study the history of words). The word rendered *yellow* in English is also given as *yalo* or *yolo* in other languages, and has nothing to do with color. We only spell it the way we do because *yellow* is the most familiar English word that sounds somewhat the same as the local word ascribed to that sea. The English "y" sound followed by a vowel, then by an "l," then by another vowel is a combination that has been used in languages around the world from time immemorial, but most of those words would not be recognizable to an English-speaking person. Hutton and Playfair pushed the envelope on the credulity of their readers, all the while knowing that many of their points were very speculative.

On page 430 of *Illustrations*, Playfair shows that he has seen evidence of the worldwide deluge but because of his myopia caused by his adherence to Hutton's system, he can't accept the obvious explanation of a worldwide flood.

> The animal remains of the second class [that is, those found in the sedimentary rock layers], are generally found in the neighbourhood of limestone strata, and are either enveloped or penetrated by calcareous, or sometimes ferruginous matter. Of this sort are the bones found in the

---

[105] Ibid, pp. 401, 402
[106] Ibid, p. 416

> rock of Gibraltar, and on the coast of Dalmatia. The latter
> are peculiarly marked for their number, and the extent of
> the country over which they are scattered, leaving it
> doubtful whether they are the work of successive ages, or
> some sudden catastrophe that has assembled in one place,
> and overwhelmed with immediate destruction, a vast
> multitude of the inhabitants of the globe. [107]

He is saying that from appearances, at least in those instances cited, there appears to have been a cataclysmic flood that buried those animals. You would have thought that evidence would have made a creationist out of him, but he still clung to Hutton's "millions of ages." The obvious conclusion seems to be just too much for him to bear. If he won't even consider a flood in this circumstance, what would it take to convince him of that reality?

There are countless examples of sequential deposits of strata, of liquid rock being extruded into other rocks, and many more less spectacular examples of geological phenomena, but the strongest evidence we have for the age of anything studied by Hutton is a wave of his hand and a statement that "these rocks must be very old." That, according to uniformitarian geologists, is, as nearly as I can tell, the best proof of their age and it is plenty good enough for them!

Modern methods for dating the earth are no better. Geologists still use the geologic column as their primary method of dating geologic phenomena, because they know that radiometric dating gives wildly variable results. The layers are dated by the flora and fauna buried in them. The flora and fauna are dated by the layers they are buried in. Does it sound like there is any circular reasoning going on here? This perplexing situation is supported by the naturalistic assumptions that are not radically different from those made by Hutton, Playfair, Lyell, etc.

The public and media people seem to think that radiometric dating provides a foolproof way to accurately date rocks. What they don't understand is that there are many assumptions that must be made in order to arrive at a radiometric date. Most of the assumptions are extremely unwarranted. How can anyone know what the original amount of material was or if the decay rate has been constant, or if there has been any leakage or infill, etc. In fact, many of the uniformitarian assumptions are in direct conflict with

---

[107] Ibid, p. 459

creationist models. For instance, there was probably 100 times more carbon on the earth prior to the flood than there is now. That would have had a huge effect on carbon dating. Creationists also believe the decay rate was much slower prior to the flood, which would greatly distort any supposed age that is obtained by radiometric dating in the present age.

We do know this: anytime a radiometric date is compared with a known historical date, the radiometric date is usually around 100,000 times higher than the known historical date. For instance, rocks formed in the eruption of Mt. St. Helens that were known to be 10 years old, were radiometrically dated and given a range of 27,000 years to three million years, which brings up another question about the accuracy of radiometric dating: If it is so precise, how is it that the highest figure they project is 100 times what the lowest figure is?

There are many other methods of dating the earth. 90% of them give an age much too young for evolution. Of the remaining 10%, they allow for an old age, but could just as easily allow for a young one. There are no known dating methods that exclude a young earth.

The Dissenters

When I first began studying the life and findings of James Hutton, it seemed to me that his geology was a wedge to foist his view of reality (a world devoid of Christianity) upon society. I think he was trying to convince himself, as well as others, of the truth of his ideas. I anticipated there would be evidence that many of his contemporaries disagreed with his science, and that others objected to the spiritual damage his theory could cause. I also thought there was a possibility that some would see through to his real motives, but would have the politeness to veil their words. So imagine my surprise to find that one of his contemporaries, a well known geologist of that time, and a man that Hutton admittedly had much respect for, viewed Hutton in exactly the same way I did and was quite forthright in stating it. That was over 200 years ago.

Jean Andre Deluc (1727-1817) was born in Geneva and lived there until 1773, when he moved to England. He was a geologist, among other things. The eminent Georges Cuvier ranked Deluc as the foremost geologist of his time. He became a member of the Royal Society of England in 1774, one year after arriving there. For the last 44 years of his life, this French-speaker was the reader for the queen. He must have been quite fluent in English too. He was one of five geologists that Playfair indicated that Hutton relied on in forming his theory of the earth. Feelings were not mutual; however, as Deluc was greatly disturbed by Hutton's theory, so much so that a year after publication of Hutton's *Theory of the Earth*, Deluc came out with a three part, 40 page, critical review that appeared in *The British Critic* in the October, November and December editions in 1796. It is not unusual for one scientist to disagree with another, but it is rare for one to question the integrity of another publicly, as Deluc does repeatedly in his review of Hutton's *Theory of the Earth*. In his most direct assault against Hutton he asked,

> Where do_we see a succession of worlds, as a part of the constitution of the earth? Only in the imagination of this author, who tries to conceal, under the name of the wisdom of nature, what he has himself devised against the Mosaic account of the earth. [108]

In discussing Hutton, he uses phrases such as, "He pretends to have found," "He pretends to not notice," "in order to bend them to his wisdom, Dr. Hutton knows these facts [but ignores them]," "Hutton silently passes over the chasms in his theory," etc. Deluc believed that Hutton was using the appearance of science to advance his cause against the generally accepted religion of that time.

Deluc expressed his opinion about the motives that scientists have for their work that would probably apply today more often than many would like to admit. He emphatically stated:

> Visionary theories of the earth are never without their reference to matters of a higher import: and our readers will, we doubt not, think that attention well bestowed, which terminates in proving that the doctrines delivered, on the highest authority [the Bible], are also those which best correspond with facts and observations. [109]

Obviously, his implication is that Hutton also had a higher purpose for his geology, but it was one designed to come against the Bible, not support it.

> They [some well known naturalists of that day] have studied also the effects produced by the sediments of

---

[108] Deluc, Jean Andre; review of Theory of the Earth in The British Critic for October, November and December, 1796, p. 474
[109] Ibid, p. 352

rivers in the sea, and by the sea itself, on its bed and on differently situated coasts; and from the comparison of the effects which have already been performed by these various causes, with what they have operated in known times, they have derived this general conclusion, as certain in itself as it is different from that of our author [Hutton]; that our continents have not existed a longer time than is determined by the Mosaic chronology since the Deluge....We are now arrived at the end of a laborious task, which nothing but its importance could have determined us to undertake. The nature of the work, of which we take leave, is now sufficiently determined; and it has given us the opportunity of stating some fundamental points in Geology; a science of which it is become necessary to have a just idea, in order to avoid falling into the paths of those, who, fancying they have discovered the secrets of nature, without having studied it with the attention requisite for such a subject, *would make us forget that sacred history*, which, at the same time that it gives us the first true information on the origin of the universe and the history of the earth, teaches the purpose of these Revelations from the author of nature; that of prescribing to men precise duties, and giving a certain, but conditional, foundation to their future hope." [110] [Italics mine]

In reading the above passage we should note that Jean Deluc was so concerned that Hutton was going to lead people astray with his aberrant theory that he spent a great deal of his own time at no profit to himself in order to set the record straight for anyone who might be so affected.

Creationists often complain that modern evolutionists, upon finding data that conflicts with their theory, instead of adjusting the theory, adjust the data. James Hutton, 200 years ago, was no different. Deluc notes that granite does not fit with Hutton's general rule that the mass of the continents is that of former continents wasted away and rebuilt in stratified layers. He enlightens us with this observation:

It is true that in his first publication, he appears, from the following passage, to have some difficulty with respect to the class of granite, and to have been desirous not to

---

[110] *Ibid, p. 606*

notice it, though it is the class which other geologists have considered as throwing the greatest light on the origin of all the strata of our continents.

[He quotes Hutton's book, *Theory of the Earth* (vol. I. p. 27).] "There is a part of the solid earth which we may at present neglect, not as being persuaded that this part may not also be found to come under the general rules of formation with the rest, but as considering this part to be of no consequence in forming a general rule, which shall comprehend the whole, without doing it absolutely. This excluded part consists of certain mountains and masses of granite."

Deluc speaking again:

But since that time, Dr. Hutton has been informed, that these *certain mountains* are very numerous, including even the greatest mountains of the globe, and that insulated masses of granite are found scattered in many countries over the surface of the ground, from which probably he has been convinced, that this great part of our mineral substances could not be brought *under* his *general rule;* but instead of suspecting that *rule,* he has thought of discarding granite, and with it necessarily all the other substances found intermixed with it in the great mountains of its kind, from the rank of *strata.* [111]

Hutton's third proposition in his *Theory of the Earth* states,

The materials of decaying continents, being successively, by the action of rain-water, delivered on their shores, are there taken by waves, tides, and currents, and spread over the whole bed of the sea.

Deluc commented upon that statement by Hutton:

After the first publication of Dr. H's theory, this proposition, which is contrary to the received opinion, and was laid down by him without a proof, was strongly opposed; this he passes unnoticed, and only repeats his assertions, which are as follow.

[From Hutton (vol. I. p.13.)] "In no subject, perhaps, is there less defect of evidence, although philosophers, led

[111] Ibid, p. 342

by prejudice, or misguided by false theory, may have
neglected to employ that light by which they should have
seen the system of this world...(p. 14.) The moveable
materials delivered into the sea, cannot, for a long time,
rest upon the shores; for, by the agitation of the winds, the
tides, and the currents, every moveable thing is carried
farther and farther along the shelving bottom of the sea,
towards the unfathomable regions of the ocean."

Deluc comments:

That every moveable thing that lies, not only on the
shores, but on the bed of the sea, at a certain distance from
the coasts, is moved by the agitation of water, is certain:
but in that motion, which is the *direction* that prevails on
the whole? — This question has long been decided among
observers; there is no doubt that the most common
direction is *towards the shore*, and this acknowledged fact
has even served as a foundation for several systems
contrary to that of our author [Italics Deluc's]. [112]

In this case, Hutton expects his readers to assume the truth of his
assertion that materials flow from the shore to the depths of the
ocean without providing any evidence, and his assertion is in
contradiction to all other geologists of that time. Deluc had good
reason to suspect Hutton's motives. Hutton knew that his
proposition was counter to other theories, but he neglected to tell his
readers and tried to get them to assume that he knew what he was
talking about without providing any evidence.

Hutton, on page 165 of his book, states the following:

Philosophers observing an apparent disorder and
confusion in the solid part of this globe, have been led to
conclude—that there had happened some destructive
change, and that the original structure of the earth had
been broken and disturbed by some violent operation,
whether natural, or from a supernatural cause. Now, all
these appearances, from which conclusions of this kind
had been formed, find the most perfect explanation in the
theory which we have been endeavouring to establish; for
they are the facts from whence we have reasoned, in
discovering the nature and constitution of this earth;

[112] Ibid, pp. 350 and 351

therefore there is no occasion for having any recourse to any unnatural supposition of evil [the evil of man that caused the Genesis flood], to any destructive accidents in nature [the Genesis flood], or to any agency of any preternatural cause [God], in explaining that which now appears." [113]

From the above we see that Hutton denies the biblical account in total and offers no support for his position. He only asks that we trust him as a final authority in these matters and as we've seen previously, he doesn't have the highest credentials that he should be asking that of us.

Deluc again quotes Hutton (page 272 of *Theory of the Earth*)

"Mr. Deluc, in his Theory of the Earth [apparently, Deluc had a publication under the same name as Hutton's], has given us the history of a disaster which befell this well-contrived world; a disaster which caused the general deluge, and which, without a miracle, must have undone a system of living beings that are so well adapted to the present state of things. But, surely, general deluges form no part of the theory of the earth; for, the purpose of this earth is evidently to maintain vegetable and animal life, and not to destroy it— (p. 285.) This is the view of nature that I would wish philosophers to take; but, there are certain prejudices of education, of prepossessions of opinion among men to overcome, before they can be brought to see those fundamental propositions — the wasting of the land, and the necessity of its renovation by the co-operation of the mineral systems." [114]

Of course, being a deist, Hutton believes that God (or the first cause, as he sees it) is just a big Santa Claus that never finds anyone not being good or doesn't care if they are good. He rewards all the same and would never punish the world with a universal flood.

Anyone who has ever read the Bible knows that, yes, the earth was created good, but there was a little thing called "the Fall," that he makes no mention of, for obvious reasons. It totally destroys his argument. It also is not something that is a part of the deist cosmology.

---

[113] Ibid, p. 475
[114] Ibid, p. 476

Deluc goes on,

> we shall now begin to see , why the author, in one of the former passages, pretends, that in this matter [the worldwide flood]there is no question with regard to the memory of man, or any human records which continue the memory of men from age to age; for the above proposition is not only contrary to the Mosaic history; it is also contrary to the records of all nations, which have continued the memory of an event, wherein the preservation of vegetable and animal life from total destruction by water, was operated by a miracle. [115]

What Deluc is saying is that Hutton ignores the fact that he is contradicting written history, not only of the Bible, but of many other cultures which have a historical record of the flood. Those are pretty major things to overlook, and they throw a negative light on Hutton. Deluc goes on:

> The disorder and confusion observed in the solid parts of this globe, have been alleged by some naturalists as a proof of that great event; but Dr. H. considers that conclusion as an absurdity, proceeding from a *prejudice of education* [Christianity]. He acknowledges however that disordered state of the mass of our continents, for he tells us that it is the fact from which he has reasoned in concluding, that there has been a succession of worlds on this globe: [116]

If there is anything that can be gleaned from all of Deluc's observations, it is that he makes it clear how arrogant Hutton was and how little he cared about entertaining the thoughts of those who disagreed with him. His term *prejudice of education* is nothing more than a term used to describe those who believe in the truth of the Bible.

In his concluding thoughts, Deluc stated:

> Such are the thoughts which this author [Hutton] ventures to oppose to the Mosaic account of the Deluge, for the sake of explaining the disorder observed in the solid mass of our continents, without acknowledging that event: such

[115] Ibid, p. 478
[116] Ibid, p. 478

the view of nature that he would wish philosophers to take, instead of those which he considers as *prejudices of education*, not with us only, but with all mankind. The reader who has not been acquainted with the many attempts made in this century, to bring the evidence of the earth against that sacred account, may judge here, from the last of these systems, what the former must have been.[117]

In the century leading up to the time when Deluc wrote this (1796), there had been many who had come up with various contrivances to destroy the flood and the Biblical history that went with it. Hutton was only the last, up to that point, but certainly the most clever.

Stephen Baxter, in his book about Hutton, makes the following comment about what Deluc said about Hutton:

There was no evidence for a succession of worlds except in Hutton's imagination; Hutton's "theory" wasn't an argument about nature but an invention *specifically intended* to attack Moses' holy account."[118]

In 1973, Dennis R. Dean published an article in the Annals of Science, titled "James Hutton and his Public," which offers us some insights. On this occasion he was discussing John Williams, another geologist contemporary with Hutton. Dean writes about Williams' review of Hutton's Royal Society paper, *Theory of the Earth*, written in 1789:

Each of these four propositions [from Hutton's *Theory of the Earth*] is then refuted at length, the most strident objection being the habitual one that Hutton "warps and strains every thing to support an unaccountable system, viz. the eternity of the world; which strange notion is the farthest of all from being defensible," because we can see God everywhere in His works. For Williams, "The wild and unnatural notion of the eternity of the world leads first to skepticism, and at last to downright infidelity and atheism," against which he fulminates, as one might in the

---

[117] Ibid, p. 480

[118] Baxter, Stephen; Ages in Chaos, James Hutton and the Discovery of Deep Time, 2003 p. 181

perilous milieu of 1789, the year of the French Revolution.
[119]

Williams could see the end result of Hutton's theory in 1789 leading to atheism and infidelity. Hutton was also well aware of those consequences and skepticism and infidelity are exactly what he was trying to achieve. It is too bad the churchmen of the time didn't understand things as well as this geologist did.

Dean's observations on the relationship of Hutton and Erasmus Darwin are also interesting:

> Hutton received both publicity and a measure of support during the 1790s from Erasmus Darwin, who was not only Charles Darwin's grandfather and an evolutionist himself but also the most popular English poet of that decade. His heavily foot-noted poem *The Botanic Garden* (1789 – 1791) is not merely a versification of Linnaean botany but a geological treatise in its own right and a compendium of contemporary science. That such a poem gained acceptance (it had several editions) indicates how avid readers were for popularized science at that time. Most of Darwin's extensive notes to the poem are scientific and were probably written in 1788; Hutton's paper of that year is mentioned in them no fewer than twelve times." [120]

Based on Darwin and Hutton's close ties, and the fact that many Huttonisms show up in Darwin's writings, it seems likely that Erasmus Darwin got his transmutation of species from Hutton. After all, Hutton mentions transmutation in his writings more than once. So the link between Charles Darwin and James Hutton actually has two legs, one through Charles Lyell and one through his grandfather, Erasmus Darwin.

Dean's observations of the times are worthy of a look.

> In 1795 Gallic [French] thought, science and letters were unutterably revulsive to the majority of Englishmen, who had just lived alongside the Reign of Terror [in France] and were expecting an invasion. Yet Hutton's *Theory* guilelessly quotes page after page of French, especially in the second volume, and its geology resembles Buffon's

---

[119] Dean, Dennis R.; James Hutton and his public,1785 – 1802, Annals of Science, Vol. 30, Issue 1, March 1973, p. 94
[120] Ibid, pp. 95, 96

perhaps more than it does anyone else's. Like the French, Scottish intellectuals in general were often accused of religious infidelity, largely because of David Hume; and physicians had always been subject to that stigma, being considered materialists. [121]

Well, let's see: Hutton was quoting the French endlessly, had lived in France and emulated a great French naturalist (Buffon), he was Scottish, he was a friend of David Hume's, and he had a medical degree. Would there be any reason to think that he might be a materialist?

We will end Dean's input with one more quote.

Ultimately, of course, religion is the central issue. It is pointless to lament this aspect of the Huttonian controversy because without it the controversy would not have been Huttonian. Like other eighteenth century scientists, Hutton was a deist, which meant in this case that religion and geology were mutually supportive. He would not have agreed that the natural world is amoral or that scientific theories do not have religious consequences. Whether or not Hutton actually believed in an eternal earth remains debatable, but as his critics point out he is under some logical necessity to do so and it is interesting that his close friend Erasmus Darwin specifically attributes this belief to him. [122]

So, here we have another person who has studied the life of Hutton and has made the statement in a secular scientific journal that Hutton's geology is important to his religion [deism] and Hutton's religion wants nothing to do with divine revelation, especially a revelation founded on the first 11 chapters of Genesis.

Hutton had by then laid the foundation for a secular cosmology. Deism is just a big step toward a totally godless worldview. We have gone from the personal God of the Bible at the time of John Knox, who answers prayer and is personally involved with His creation to the impotent god of deism, who cannot be known and very little can be known about him because he isn't allowed to speak to us through his word.

---

[121] Ibid, p. 104
[122] Ibid, p. 105

The next step is to not recognize God at all. Charles Lyell is an intermediate step that will get us there and we will learn about him in the next chapter.

CHAPTER 4
CHARLES LYELL

As previously noted, Charles Lyell was born in 1797, the same year that James Hutton died. He was the first child of ten born to Charles Lyell, Sr. and his wife. The senior Lyell was a man of means and accomplishment. He was a well-known botanist with a strong interest in geology and entomology (the study of insects). In later life, he showed his talents as a writer, publishing a work on Dante, among other things. He inherited a large estate at Kinnordy in Forfarshire (modern day Angus) in the north of Scotland. He also leased for 28 years an estate in Hants (modern day Hampshire) in Southern England. Despite his wealth and worldly success, he was deeply involved in the lives of his children and was largely responsible for the direction that his oldest son's life took.

Charles, Sr. bought Robert Bakewell's *Introduction to Geology* as soon as it came out in 1813. He was no sooner done reading it than Charles, Jr. read it at the age of fifteen. Bakewell was fully indoctrinated in old-earth views, and that was reflected in the book. After reading it, Charles, Jr. and probably Charles, Sr. were fully converted to the long ages of James Hutton, if they weren't already.

It seems the elder Lyell was a believer in the Huttonian system from Charles' earliest years, and he did much to help the younger Lyell advance Hutton's geology in his research and writings. From the earliest writings of the younger Lyell in his teenage years, we see that he is committed to the long-age view of geology, and in his numerous letters to his father he discusses Huttonian geology at length.

He had two brothers and seven sisters. The brothers seemed to have gone their own way upon reaching adulthood, but several of his sisters remained quite close to Charles long into his life, and helped considerably in his geology work.

He started college at Oxford in 1815 when he was 17. He was proficient in the classics, which were stressed in those days. His father seemed to have desired for Charles to know them well.

Because Bakewell's book had piqued his interest in geology, he took William Buckland's course in geology at Oxford. Buckland (1784-1856) started out his career as a geologist trying to harmonize Genesis and the world-wide flood with geology, but the older he got, the more he deserted Genesis. Nevertheless, he had the only game in town, as there was not a course in geology offered anywhere else in Britain.

Young Charles Lyell

It is instructive to note that Buckland was a big proponent of the gap theory of biblical interpretation of the book of Genesis. The gap theory began to be used as early as the 16th century, but experienced a very rapid rise in popularity at the end of the 18th century and into the 19th as more cosmologists began broaching ideas of very long ages for the universe. Theologians felt the need to respond to the seemingly formidable scientific challenge of long ages, and so proposed a gap between Genesis 1:1 and 1:2.

The gap theory postulates that God made the earth millions or even billions of years ago and that the first verse of Genesis describes that event. Then, by the time the second verse starts, it is describing events that occurred only six thousand or so years ago. As illogical as it may sound, the billions of years are covered in one sentence, while the comparatively short period of 6,000 years since, take 66 books of the Bible to cover. The supposed advantage to this interpretation is that one can include all of the geologic ages in that period between the first and second verses of Genesis. But there is a problem with that interpretation. There is no indication that the language is metaphorical. Of course, in the end, it creates more problems than it solves, but the holders of that view seemed willing to turn a blind eye.

Close-up of Isle of Staffa. The softer sandstone can be seen eroding faster than the harder columnar basalt above it.

The perceptive student viewing the gap theory would see that the only reason it existed was because a response was needed to defend the Bible against the attacks of the long age philosophers.

Although I do not know of any document that specifically states that Charles Lyell was a gap theorist, considering the fact that Buckland's course was one of his first exposures to geology, and taking into account his stated positions regarding evolution and the progressive development of the earth, it seems likely that he did buy into that concept.

There were many sound clergymen who did not cave in to the pressure to compromise the scriptures. Many of these men did fine scientific work as well. We are not going to spend much time here discussing them because our inquiry concerns what went wrong, not what went right. Not enough people listened to these scriptural geologists. If more people had listened to them maybe history would have taken a different turn. There is an outstanding book by Terry Mortenson called *The Great Turning Point* that discusses those men and their efforts to defend the truth of the Bible and science as well.

Lyell graduated from Oxford, then studied law and became a lawyer. But, even while he was practicing law, his interests were really in geology, as evidenced by the letters he wrote. In 1821, he introduced himself to Gideon Mantell, who was known for his work with dinosaur fossils, particularly the Iguanodon. Mantell remained a close friend until his death in 1852.

Lyell was extensively involved in geological fieldwork. His first adventure of that kind was at the age of 19 when he went to Staffa, a small island sitting just off the west coast of northern Scotland. Staffa is a fascinating place. It is composed of a conglomerate basalt layer sitting on columnar basalt, which sits on sandstone, which sits on breccia (consolidated materials from various sources). Clear lines of demarcation can be seen separating all of the layers. It is about as good an example of catastrophic processes as can be found anywhere. Lyell didn't see it that way, however. He wrote a poem to his father ascribing the creation of Staffa to Mother Nature.

This is the Isle of Staffa, just off the west coast of northern Scotland. It was Charles Lyell's first exposure to field work, when he was 19. It is a very interesting island for a geologist because of the very clear delineation of the different strata and their exposure to the eye. The top is igneous conglomerate, sitting on columnar basalt, which sits on sandstone, which sits on chalk.

The following year he went with his father, mother and two oldest sisters to visit France, Switzerland and Italy. We know they were gone at least three months, and maybe longer. His journal describing the last part of the trip was lost.

In 1820, he made another long trip with his father to the continent going as far as Rome. On all these trips he had his eyes on the geology of the various places they went. In 1822, he visited Romney Marsh in Kent to observe a tract of land that had been recently retrieved from the ocean. He also made a geological excursion to the Isle of Wight. He wrote many letters to his father on all his trips explaining the geological phenomena he saw; it seems his father must have had an active interest in geology. He had a very close relationship with his father, and often it seems that he related to him the way someone would relate to a business partner rather than a father, although he always ended his letters with, "Your affectionate son."

Lyell the Geologist

In 1819, at the age of 21, Lyell became a fellow of the Geological Society of London and of the Linnaean Society. In 1823, he was elected secretary of the Geological Society, so we can see that he was rapidly getting more involved in geology.

In 1823, he traveled to France, accompanied by letters of introduction from some of the great natural philosophers of Britain, intended for the great natural philosophers of France. Being the son of the senior Lyell also seemed to give him a head start on creating rapport with the French. They were aware of his father's work in botany. He met the illustrious Baron Georges Cuvier and was hospitably received, so much so that he began to attend Cuvier's weekly parties. Being in the company of Frenchmen, his French improved dramatically. It seems he was almost as comfortable speaking French as English. While in France, he also did some studying of the geology there. He went out on at least two occasions with Monsieur Constant Prevost, who was one of the more noted French natural philosophers.

Later, he made other excursions to the Alps, Auvergne (in France), Italy (including Sicily), the Pyrenees, Germany, Denmark, Sweden, Holland, and various places in Britain, including the one to the north of Scotland when he stopped on the way back to see Siccar Point with Sir James Hall in 1824. Many of these trips must have been completely financed by his father, who often paid for laborers and sometimes for expert professional assistance.

By the late 1820s, Lyell decided it was time to publish a book, and in 1830 came out with the first volume of *Principles of Geology.* By 1833, he had published all three volumes. Though he did publish other books, this was his seminal work. He was working on the 11th edition at the time of his death in 1875. It was the first edition that Darwin had on board the *Beagle* when he sailed in 1831.

The two main influences on Charles Lyell's thinking were his father and the French natural philosophers. He spent a great deal of his younger years in France. The worldview of the French in the early 19th century was drastically different from that of the English. France never did accept the reformation. They turned hostile toward the Catholic Church, but unlike the reformed countries that turned to Protestantism, the French just rebelled against all religion and murdered those they didn't like. They did not turn to another religion. Atheism and agnosticism took the place of religion. Hence, the French Revolution, that was one of the most violent popular uprisings of modern times.

The English, with less bloodshed, established a form of Protestantism and transformed a monarchy into a representative government. Of course, the English did not do enough to separate the powers of the Church of England and those of the government. That created the situation that led to the persecution of those outside the Church and people fleeing to America by the millions.

It was possible for a churchman to have the government confiscate property from those not paying their tithe, or the government could have people excommunicated from the church for being behind on taxes or for not supporting the government in the right way. This created resentment against the church by many, not only of the lower classes, but also by some of the landed elites who sought change in the government, the church, or both.

In all of the writings of Charles Lyell, I could not find one comment favorable to the church or Christianity in general. Yet, there are many comments casting aspersions on the same. He, and probably his father, was a part of that populace that abhorred the collusion between the Church of England and the government. The situation in England was mirrored in Scotland by the relationship between the Presbyterian Church and the government there, although it was not as repressive. Years before, the situation caused the following comment by James Hutton when writing to his friend, James Watt, explaining why it had become difficult to find a job for Watt, who would be in need of employment if his steam engine idea failed:

> You have not been out of mind tho out of sight this winter your friends are trying to do something for you what success will attend their endeavours time only will shew—every application for publick employment is considered as a Job and to be carried into execution requires nothing but a passage thro the proper channels; it is then a well digested plan; the honestest endeavour must to succeed put on the face of roguery, but what signifies the dress of a rogue unless you have the address of a wise man; come & lick some great mans arse and be damn'd to you.... [123]

Lyell was an avid reader, and seemed to be well acquainted with David Hume's writings, as Hume is mentioned quite a few times in his personal correspondence with others. He did not just talk geology while in France. He conversed with Frenchmen across the

---

[123] The Correspondence Between James Hutton (1726 – 1797) and James Watt (1736 – 1819) with Two Letters from Hutton to George Clerk-Maxwell (1715 – 1784): Part II, p. 365

spectrum of society, from noblemen to commoners. He was beginning to acquire the French mind. It was a skeptical, godless outlook. Certainly, there were exceptions, but Lyell wasn't interested in the exceptions.

With the success of *Principles of Geology*, he was finally able to support himself. He was rapidly becoming the most well-known geologist in the world. He was offered professorships, but with the exception of a short professorship of a few months at King's College in London, he turned them down, because he felt it would restrict his time and also limit the audience that he would have for his ideas. He was probably right. He could write an article for the *Quarterly Review* or some other publication and get his message to a much larger audience than what he would have in his lecturing classroom.

While Charles Darwin was reading Lyell's book on the *Beagle*, he wrote to Lyell about his observations of the phenomena he encountered on the voyage. When Darwin was in South America, he received volume II of Lyell's *Principles* from Lyell. Within days of disembarking the ship in England in 1836, Lyell greeted him and the two became fast friends. Lyell saw his geology being used in Darwin's biology, and that must have pleased him immensely.

Lyell travelled to North America in 1841, and again in 1845. He was received enthusiastically by many Americans. After all, he was the most eminent scientist in the world by that time. While there, he was able to study the geology. He also met most of the top geologists in North America.

Lyell's Methods

When it was found that Alfred Russel Wallace and Charles Darwin had basically the same idea at the same time with regard to transmutation of species, Lyell was instrumental in convincing them to jointly publish a paper on the subject in 1858.

He, along with Joseph Hooker, who was curator of Kew Gardens, were the most influential a year later in convincing Darwin to publish his book, *On the Origin of Species, or Preservation of the Favoured Races in the Struggle for Life.*

Lyell got in on the issue of human origins with his publication of *The Antiquity of Man* in 1863. While some have said that Lyell did not accept evolution, it would be more accurate to say he did not push the concept in the same manner that some of the X Clubbers did. He always believed that new species arise and existing species go extinct in a continuing process, he just wasn't sure how that had happened and he wasn't sure if Darwin had it right. But, he did become more open to the idea of evolution accomplished through natural selection after Darwin published his book.

He remained active very close to the time of his death in 1875. He was quite interested in the course the world would take in turning his ideas into something even more stunning with the growing acceptance of evolution. As Thomas Huxley, John Tyndall, Herbert Spencer and others were aggressively attacking Christianity by promoting evolution as the new answer to the question of origins Charles Lyell was supporting them all the way. It wasn't his style, however, to be overtly aggressive. Let's also be clear that Huxley, Tyndall and Spencer were not in any way open to including evolution into anyone's theology. To them, it was all or nothing, evolution or religion.

In an 1830 letter to Poulett Scrope, Charles Lyell tips his hand on his methods:

> If we don't irritate, which I fear that we may (though mere history), we shall carry all with us. If you don't triumph over them, but compliment the liberality and candour of the present age, the bishops and the enlightened saints will join us in despising both the ancient and modern physico-theologians. It is just the time to strike, so rejoice that, sinner as you are, the Q. R. [Quarterly Review] is open to you. If I have said more than some will like, yet I give you my word that full *half* of my history and comments was cut out, and even many facts; because either I, or Stokes, or Broderip, felt that it was anticipating twenty or thirty years of the march of honest feeling to declare it undisguisedly [he had to disguise his attack]. Nor did I dare come down to modern offenders. They themselves will be ashamed of seeing how they will look by-and-by in the page of history, if they ever get into it, which I doubt. You see that what between Steno, Hooke, Woodward, De Luc, and others, the modern deluge systems are all borrowed [from the Bible]. Point out to the general reader that my floods, earthquakes, &c., are all very modern, also the waste of cliffs [that came in the previous 40 years from James Hutton]; and that I request that people will multiply, by whatever time they think man has been on the earth, the sum of this modern observed change [millions of years], and not form an opinion from what history has recorded [the Bible]. Fifty years from this, they will furnish facts for a better volume

than mine. The changes in organic life, which I intend to be more generally entertaining than the inorganic [geology], and more new, must be deferred to vol. II. I will attend to your other requests immediately.

Very truly yours,
Charles Lyell.

P.S. – I have been very careful in my work in referring, where I have borrowed, to authors, and am not conscious of having ever done so without citing in a note. I doubt whether I have embodied sentences from any author so much as from you, and you will see that that is in great moderation.

I conceived the idea five or six years ago, that if ever the Mosaic geology could be set down without giving offence, it would be in an historical sketch, and you must abstract mine, in order to have as little to say as possible yourself. Let them feel it, and point the moral. [124]
[Bracketed insertions mine]

Scrope, Lyell's personal friend, was writing the review of his first book, *Principles of Geology* for The Quarterly Review, and Lyell was giving him advice on what he wanted to see in the review! Sounds like neither objectivity nor honesty were his highest priority! Note especially the last paragraph. If we were to put that into modern English: "In order to destroy Genesis 1-11, and thereby all of the Bible, you must not attack it directly, but just give a factual account that contradicts it and say as little as possible yourself. When they think over the implications of what you've said they will see that the Bible is not a reliable document, but they will not blame you for that fact." Never mind that many of the "facts" in the "factual account" are false. This was the whole modus operandi of Charles Lyell, given here in one paragraph. A very crafty man indeed! Note also in the last paragraph before his salutation he is very enthusiastic about biological changes. Evolution was not yet a common term, but it is obvious that Lyell would be a supporter of some type of mechanism to accomplish just that.

---

[124] Life, Letters and Journals of Sir Charles Lyell, Bart, p. 271

Lyell's Beliefs

What did Charles Lyell really believe? From his childhood we find the following admission about attending church:

> Of all the dreaded penances which we had to undergo we thought going to church, sitting whole hours doing nothing, incomparably the worst; far more intolerable than lessons, in which I always had some mixture of pleasure. [125]

While the above could be attributed to childhood intransigence we will find that Lyell never took Christianity seriously throughout his life.

When he was 30, he was in the French province of Auvergne. In a letter to his father he talks about his experiences:

> He [Count Le Serres] organized a geological society here, and they chose Count Montlosier as president; but the Jesuits took alarm, and, declaring that Montlosier had written a book against Genesis, got the Prefect and Mayor and Government to oppose, and at last put the thing down; at least it merged in the regular scientific *Etablissement de la Ville*, and Montlosier is just coming out with a book against the Jesuits, a more popular subject in France at present than geology. We are to visit him at his chateau near Mont Dore. We like the people and the country.[126]

His next letter to his father relates that he has just spent "three delightful days at Count de Montlosier's." Is it an accident that Charles Lyell, who did more to tear down Genesis than any other man up to that time, has just had a rollicking time with a man who was reprimanded for doing the same thing?

From Italy, Lyell wrote to Roderick Murchison, a fellow British geologist, with whom Lyell did some joint French geologizing early in his career:

> There is in the Campagna di Roma a beautiful chain of alluvial phenomena, which, but for Moses and his penal

---

[125] Life, Letters and Journals of Sir Charles Lyell, Bart, p. 6
[126] Life, Letters and Journals of Sir Charles Lyell, Bart, p. 187, 188

deluge, would have thrown more light than any part of Europe on the modern ages of the earth's history.... [127]

The implication is obvious that he didn't much care for Moses and his penal deluge. It was the penal part that bothered the deists the most.

He wrote to Poulett Scrope about Scrope's review of his first book:

> Such a broad-side will do far more than my book to sink the diluvialists, and in short all the theological sophists. [128]

Here, he not only puts down the diluvialists but theologians as well, showing that he is very aware of the theological implications of his war on Genesis.

In his journal to his fiancée, Mary Horner, he wrote:

> Did I tell you that a Belfast Professor of Divinity, Edgar, has been denouncing an unfortunate Dr. Drummond, who gave lectures on geology in the Royal College there, for having declared that "the changes proved with '*tolerable certainty*' by geology must have occupied time to which our historical eras were as nothing;" and then the Professor wrote to me, as Professor of King's College, to know if the lecturer or he was right, expressing great alarm for Christianity if such doctrines were true. [129]

Lyell does not say anything about being alarmed himself.

On a trip to Sweden Lyell exhibited his flippant attitude toward religion in the following tale in his journal to his future wife:

> I visited on the way home Gamma Upsala (Old U.), where there is a church, in which Marklin says the Catholic worship was for some time performed in one part of the ancient temple, while the heathens sacrificed human victims to Thor and Odin in the other. Near the church are three immense tumuli, in which those two idols, and Frigga, Odin's wife, were buried. It is the custom to drink a glass of mead (honey and wine, or spirit from barley, I believe) on the top of Thor's tomb, and as the King had

---

[127] Life, Letters and Journals of Sir Charles Lyell, Bart, p. 240
[128] Life, Letters and Journals of Sir Charles Lyell, Bart, p. 310
[129] Life, Letters and Journals of Sir Charles Lyell, Bart, p. 372

lately done so, said the peasant who drove us, he supposed I should, which accordingly we did. [130]

In his 75th year, he wrote the following to a Miss F. P. Cobbe:

> Your articles on a "Future State" in the "Theological Review" have interested me much, but they confirm my opinion that we are so much out of our depth when we attempt to treat of this subject, that we gain little but doubt in such speculation. [131]

Strange, that if he were a Christian that he would have such doubt about the existence of heaven. He must have either not had much confidence in what the Bible has to say about it or maybe he hadn't even read what the Bible says about it.

Lyell — An Evolutionist?

What did Lyell believe about evolution? We must remember in any discussion about Charles Lyell that he was the ultimate politician. He was like the guy who can smile and insult you to your face, but you don't realize till later when he is no longer there, that he wasn't joking, he really meant every word he said to you. Lyell states in a letter to his friend, J.W. Herschel, about evolution:

> P.S. In regard to the origination of new species, I am very glad to find that you think it probable that it may be carried on through the intervention of intermediate causes. I left this rather to be inferred, not thinking it worth while to offend a certain class of persons by embodying in words what would only be a speculation. [132]

In his comments to Charles Darwin, upon reading "Origin" for the first time:

> My dear Darwin,
> — I have just finished reading your volume, and right glad I am that I did my best with Hooker to persuade you

---

[130] Life, Letters and Journals of Sir Charles Lyell, Bart, pp. 432, 433
[131] Life, Letters and Journals of Sir Charles Lyell, Vol. II, p. 452
[132] Life, Letters and Journals of Sir Charles Lyell, Bart, p. 467

to publish it without waiting for a time which probably could never have arrived, though you lived to the age of a hundred, when you had prepared all your facts on which you ground so many grand speculations.

It is a splendid case of close reasoning and long sustained argument throughout so many pages, the condensation immense, too great perhaps for the uninitiated, but an effective and important preliminary statement, which will admit, even before your detailed proofs appear, of some occasional useful exemplifications, such as your pigeons and cirripedes, of which you make excellent use.

I mean that when, as I fully expect, a new edition is soon called for, you may here and there insert an actual case, to relieve the vast number of abstract propositions. So far as I am concerned, I am so well prepared to take your statements of facts for granted, that I do not think the *pieces justificatives* when published will make much difference, and I have long seen most clearly that if any concession is made, all that you claim in your concluding pages will follow. [133]

The hilarious part about the above quote is that Lyell seems to be using sarcasm about Darwin "here and there inserting an actual case." Unfortunately, I believe he is serious, all the while knowing that Darwin doesn't have any actual cases. Darwin's old college professor friend, Adam Sedgwick, had a view that closely matched Lyell's negativity:

I have read your book with more pain than pleasure. Parts of it I admired greatly, parts I laughed at till my sides were almost sore; other parts I read with absolute sorrow, because I think them utterly false and grievously mischievous. [134]

Jean Baptiste Lamarck (1744-1829) was a French natural philosopher who believed that creatures could change the physical characteristics of their offspring by their actions in the present. In other words, if an animal had to frequently stretch its neck to get

---

[133] Life, Letters and Journals of Sir Charles Lyell, Vol. II, p. 325
[134] Ed. Darwin, F., Life and Letters of Charles Darwin, Vol.2, D. Appleton and Company, New York and London, p. 43, 1911

food its offspring would then have longer necks. Lyell discusses Lamarck in writing to Gideon Mantell:

> I devoured Lamarck *en voyage*, as you did Sismondi, and with equal pleasure. His theories delighted me more than any novel I ever read, and much in the same way, for they address themselves to the imagination, at least of geologists <u>who know the mighty inferences</u> which would be deducible were they established by observations. But though I admire even his flights, and <u>feel none of the *odium theologicum*</u> which some modern writers in this country have visited him with, I confess I read him rather as I hear an advocate on the wrong side, to know what can be made of the case in good hands. I am glad he has been courageous enough and logical enough to admit that his argument, if pushed as far as it must go, if worth anything, would prove that men may have come from the Ourang-Outang. But after all, what changes species may really undergo! How impossible will it be to distinguish and lay down a line, beyond which some of the so-called extinct species have never passed into recent ones. That the earth is quite as old as he supposes, has long been my creed, and I will try before six months are over to convert the readers of the Quarterly to that heterodox opinion. [135] [Underline mine]

In a letter to his father he talks about his meeting with the famous botanist, Augustin Pyramus de Candolle in Geneva:

> I am now convinced that geology is destined to throw upon this curious branch of inquiry [the classification of plants and animals], and to receive from it in return, much light, and by their mutual aid we shall very soon solve the grand problem, whether the various living organic species came into being gradually and singly in insulated spots, or centres of creation, or in various places at once [Biblical creation], and all at the same time. The latter cannot, I am already persuaded, be maintained. [136]

In a letter to Scrope, he aligns himself with Hutton, who often said he did not seek to explain the beginning of the cosmos:

---

[135] Life, Letters and Journals of Sir Charles Lyell, p. 168
[136] Life, Letters and Journals of Sir Charles Lyell, pp. 245, 246

> It is not the beginning I look for, but proofs of a *progressive* state of existence in the globe, the probability of which is *proved* by the analogy of changes in organic life. [137]

This is about as strong a statement as one could expect to get to indicate his belief in evolution. In another letter to Scrope in 1830, we get our first instance of Lyell dating strata by the fossils that are in them:

> The review of his notions [the views of Elie de Beaumont, one of his detractors] will come properly in my next volume, for it is by fossil zoology alone that all dates of the relative upheaving of mountain chains must be decided, or guessed at. [138]

This letter was written in June of 1830 when he was only 32 years old. The admission of guessing at the age of the strata was a rare youthful faux pas that he did not make in his more mature years. This is the old circular reasoning whereby the ages of the fossils are assumed and the layers are dated by the fossils that are in them. Likewise, the layers are used to date the fossils.

In a letter to his sister, Caroline, he makes a statement that should have told him there was something wrong with his system, but Lyell proves that when you've got your eyes focused on proving your own point about something, you are totally blind to any other interpretation:

> This morning all my Etna shells were examined; out of sixty-three only three species not known to inhabit the Mediterranean, yet the whole volcano nearly is subsequent to them, they lived on a moderate computation 100,000 years ago, and after so many generations are quite unchanged in form. It must therefore have required a good time for Ourang-Outang to become men on Lamarckian principles. [139]

---

[137] Life, Letters and Journals of Sir Charles Lyell, p. 270
[138] Life, Letters and Journals of Sir Charles Lyell, p. 272
[139] Life, Letters and Journals of Sir Charles Lyell, p. 308

Wouldn't the logical conclusion be that if they haven't changed, maybe they weren't formed 100,000 years ago? In a letter to his sister, Marianne, he states:

> I shall only go to the end of the tertiary period. It will include the history of the globe as far back as the time when the first of the existing species came in. If I have succeeded so well with inanimate matter, surely I shall make a lively thing when I have chiefly to talk of living beings! [140]

All of the above quotes about evolution come from before 1831 when Lyell was in his twenties and early thirties, before he had ever met Charles Darwin. His later disagreement with Darwin was only about the mechanism of evolution, and whether he was willing to state publicly that he supported Darwin's concept of natural selection. He believed that some species became extinct and others came into being by some unknown, but natural, process. Being the ultimate politician, he knew what public scorn would come to a person who includes man in it.

In a letter to John Herschel he shows his deist streak, but incorporates evolution comfortably with it:

> When I first came to the notion, which I never saw expressed elsewhere, though I had no doubt it had all been thought out before, of a succession of extinction of species, and creation of new ones, going on perpetually now, and through an indefinite period of the past, and to continue for ages to come, all in accommodation to the changes which must continue in the inanimate and habitable earth, the idea struck me as the grandest which I had ever conceived, so far as regards the attributes of the Presiding Mind [first cause]. [141]

In an 1866 letter to Darwin, reminiscing about his complicity in getting *Origin of Species* published, he says:

> We certainly ran no small risk of the work never seeing the light, until Wallace and others would have anticipated it in some measure. But it was only by the whole body of

---

[140] Life, Letters and Journals of Sir Charles Lyell, p. 314
[141] Life, Letters and Journals of Sir Charles Lyell, p. 468

doctrine being brought together, systematized, and launched at once upon the public, that so great an effect could have been wrought in the public mind. [142]

It brings to mind the mantra of Joseph Goebbels, Hitler's propaganda minister: "If you tell a lie big enough and keep repeating it, people will eventually come to believe it." In Lyell's case, he and his friends also struck quickly. I'm not sure which of these two lies has caused more damage, Hitler's or Lyell's.

Was Lyell an Objective Scientist?

As we've stated previously, Charles Lyell was a great "politician." Given the standing of politicians in today's world, that would seem to imply that he may not have been the most honest man around. There is an interesting story about his excursion to Niagara Falls that sheds some light on this. In 1841, visiting Niagara Falls, on his first trip to North America, he was told that the falls were receding more than three feet per year. The gorge that had been cut by the river was 35,000 feet long. A little math tells one that, at that rate, it would have taken less than 12,000 years to have cut the complete gorge. Of course, that is assuming the rate has always been the same as it is today. Let's remember that Lyell's biggest argument about geology is that no processes have operated in the past that are not in operation today. But simple observation would have told him that the gorge is narrower farther downstream. The protective limestone is thinner there as well, so erosion rates would necessarily have been faster in the past. The observation should have been that the falls have been in existence much less than 12,000 years. The limiting factors mentioned above could have easily reduced the actual age to 4,000 years or less.

But Lyell, upon returning to Britain, instead of shortening the erosion rates to match the data, actually increased the erosion time to 35,000 years in his reports of the excursion, or one foot per year with no adjustment for other factors! Even at the rate he was given while there, he should have assigned a rate of no less than three feet a year, which would have made the gorge 12,000 years old. Why would Lyell have done such a thing? I don't think it is being too hard on him to say that he needed more years than what observation would give him to support his life-long attack on the authority of the Bible.

---

[142] Life, Letters and Journals of Sir Charles Lyell, Vol. II, pp. 408, 409

He was a very intelligent man. He knew what the answer should have been, but he lied, because that served his purposes better than the truth. He probably chafed at giving it a mere 35,000-year age. That is much less than the millions of years he threw around regarding other geological events. In those days, North America was a very distant land, and Niagara Falls was obscure to those Brits that might have doubted his word, so I'm sure he did not fear being found out anytime soon.

On another occasion, while in France, he was to meet with an aspiring young French geologist. Lyell wanted to obtain specific information from him regarding the locale at which he was then working, but was afraid the young man would be very prying, since by that time Lyell was pretty highly regarded in France. He didn't care to share all his secrets with the man, so he told his father that if he sensed the young man was going to be too prying, he would pretend to not be able speak French well enough to continue the conversation with him.

There were many occasions where Lyell was confronted with evidence that should have really put doubt into his mind regarding his assumption of present causes being able to explain the past. His unwillingness to allow that he could have been wrong is often times confounding. When he was 25, he wrote the following explanation of what his new book was going to entail in a letter to Gideon Mantell:

> I am going to write in confirmation of ancient causes having been the same as modern, and to show that those plants and animals which we know are becoming preserved now, are the same as were formerly. E.g., scarcely any insects now, no lichens, no mosses, &c., ever get to places where they can become imbedded in strata. But quadrupeds do in lakes, reptiles in estuaries, corals in reefs, fish in sea, plants wherever there is water, salt or fresh, &c. &c. Now have you ever in Lewes levels found a bird's skeleton or any cetacean? If not, why in Tilgate and the Weald beds? In our Scotch marl, though water birds abound in those lakes, we meet with no birds in the marl; and they must be at least as rare as in old freshwater formations, for they are much worked and examined. You see the drift of my argument—*ergo*, mammalia existed when the oolite and coal, &c., were formed. Broderip says, that in spite of all the dogs and cats which float down the Thames, none of their remains have been found in recent excavations in the Thames deposits. Send me your

> thoughts on the subject. If I am asked why in coal there are
> no quadrupeds? I answer, why are there none, nor any
> cetacean, nor any birds, nor any reptiles in the plastic clay,
> or lignite formation, a very analogous deposit, and as
> universal in Europe? Think of these matters, and believe
> me yours most truly [143]

Apparently, after Lyell asked this question of Mantell, he never pondered it again, because we don't find him giving the obvious answer to his question of why we don't find creatures being fossilized today. It is because there are no processes today capable of it, such as a worldwide flood that buried things very quickly. That wasn't the answer Lyell wanted to hear, so he just ignored the question.

On August 25, 1830, he wrote a letter to his mother from the Pyrenees, where he was doing a geologic study. He was describing the work he was doing, and he found something, which to an unbiased observer, would be obvious evidence of a worldwide flood. But to Lyell, with his blinders firmly in place, that option was never acknowledged. To wit:

> In other chains the loftiest and central parts consist of
> rocks which do not enclose any remains of shells and
> corals, and you must go to the flanks or to the low
> grounds at their base in order to collect such objects. Here,
> on the contrary, you find at an elevation of between nine
> and eleven thousand feet, a profusion of sandstones and
> limestones, in the very middle of the Pyrenees, full of
> plants, shells, and zoophytes, many in so perfect a state,
> and in such thick beds, that you cannot doubt for a
> moment that you see the bottom of an old sea, now
> covered by glaciers, or so high that it supports no
> vegetation. [144]

Yes, you could make that observation if you're determined to not admit of a world-wide flood, but, maybe the sea was only at that elevation for a short time and maybe the Pyrenees were lower then. These are all observations Lyell could have made if he were interested in knowing the truth in that situation, but he was only interested in advancing his cause: obliterating Genesis.

---

[143] Life, Letters and Journals of Sir Charles Lyell, p. 169
[144] Life, Letters and Journals of Sir Charles Lyell, p. 293

In 1833, he was again writing to Gideon Mantell, this time about William Buckland's geologic study at Liege:

> ...having not one congenial soul at Liege, and none who take any interest in his discoveries save the priests—and what kind *they* take you may guess more especially as he has found human remains in breccias, embedded with the extinct species, under circumstances far more difficult to get over than any I have previously heard of. [145]

This should have caused him to back up and reassess his views of the past. Human remains buried with extinct species? He must have gotten over it; however, as there doesn't seem to be any change in his attitude.

In 1835 he wrote to Viscount Cole from Germany:

An example of a polystrate fossil, a tree fossilized as it extends through many layers of sediment. Evolutionists, including Charles Lyell, have no explanation for this phenomena. How could the tree be only a few hundred or even thousands of years old and extend through layers that are supposed to be millions of years old?

> I have just come down from a chalet at the southern foot of the Stellihorn in the Urbach Thal, where at the height of nine thousand feet I found ammonites, and got some more from a chamois hunter at whose chalet I slept. [146]

Writing to Charles Darwin in August of 1837, Lyell makes an astonishing admission:

> This gneiss, so ancient that it had been crystallised and then thrown into vertical and curved stratification even before the triloites flourished, this most ancient rock is so beautifully soldered onto the granite, so nicely threaded by veins large and small, or in other cases so shades into

---

[145] Life, Letters and Journals of Sir Charles Lyell, p. 402
[146] Life, Letters and Journals of Sir Charles Lyell, p. 454

the granite, that had you not known the immense difference of age, you would be half staggered with the suspicion that all was made at one batch! [147]

Polystrate tree, Joggins, Nova Scotia

He is telling us that the two rock forms gradually change from one to the other. How he could convince himself that it wasn't made at one batch is difficult to understand. This is about as good an example as there could be of someone seeing the evidence, but it having no effect because it isn't what the observer wants to see. In reality, it was probably impossible for Lyell to accept the evidence because his spirit was in rebellion against God. Accepting the evidence would take him to places he did not want to go. Keep in mind that this young man was still only 39 years of age, and some of the previous quotes were made when he was in his twenties! *Principles of Geology* was written when he was between 32 and 35.

In 1842, Lyell wrote the following to his sister, Marianne, about his experiences in North America:

> We have just returned from an expedition of three days to the Strait which divides Nova Scotia from New Brunswick, whither I went to see a forest of fossil coal-trees — the most wonderful phenomenon perhaps that I have seen, so upright do the trees stand, or so perpendicular to the strata, in the ever-wasting cliffs, every year a new crop being brought into view, as the violent tides of the Bay of Fundy, and the intense frost of the winters here, combine to destroy, undermine, and sweep away the old one — trees twenty-five feet high, and some have been seen of forty feet, piercing the beds of sandstone and terminating downwards in the same beds, usually coal. This subterranean forest exceeds in extent

[147] Life, Letters and Journals of Sir Charles Lyell, Vol. II, p. 22

and *quantity of timber* all that have been discovered in Europe put together. [148]

I wonder how Lyell explained these fossilized trees that had grown up through the layers of sediments supposedly representing millions of years? He doesn't say. He just makes a comment about it being wonderful, and then goes on his jolly way ignoring it.

Near the end of his life, in 1874, he wrote to Charles Darwin about some interesting phenomena he was shown in Northern Scotland by a reverend H. Mitchell:

> He showed me his specimens of crustacean footprints, a long series of tracks, with the mark of the body trailing along, accompanying ripple-marks, and beautiful rain-drops. [149]

The only way these delicate features could be preserved would be for them to have been covered rapidly. Did Charles Lyell think his "present processes" could have made those features? If so, he was even more presumptive than I thought he was.

Was Lyell's Geology Valid?

So, what exactly was it that Charles Lyell came up with that proved the vast antiquity of the earth? Was there some fool-proof indicator he noticed that no on else had ever seen before? After scouring thousands of pages of Lyell's writings, including those written for public consumption and his private notes and diaries, it is hard to come up with anything that has any teeth in it. He took the same tack that Hutton took with regard to the strata. The layers were deposited in a consecutive fashion, indicating that the top one is the newest and the bottom one is the oldest, and all the ones in between are dated accordingly. He added the wrinkle that he obtained from the French and from William Smith of Britain of using the faunal and floral fossils to further the idea that there is a considerable time gap between the different layers. After all, as Lyell reasons, if some of the layers have fossil animals in them that are now extinct those layers must be very old. Amazingly, Lyell never discusses any other reasons why the faunal fossils could vary.

---

[148] Life, Letters and Journals of Sir Charles Lyell, Vol. II, pp. 64, 65
[149] Life, Letters and Journals of Sir Charles Lyell, Vol. II, pp. 455, 456

If we were to suppose a worldwide flood, many factors could affect the distribution of fossils. In fact, we could hypothesize endlessly and still not come up with all of the possible factors involved, but some of the more obvious ones; ones that should have influenced Lyell but apparently did not, are as follows: The creatures buried first would be those living in or near the water. Creatures that had little mobility would be buried quickly if they lived in or near the water. Those that had hard parts would produce fossils much more often than those which did not. Some animals have a higher specific gravity than others. Many mammals float after death. Birds would be even lighter than mammals, since they have feathers that

Charles Lyell, the famous geologist

seal air inside, and have hollow bones. A factor in whether a creature would float or sink would be the salinity of the water. There may have been different levels of salinity in different locations. We never hear Lyell talking about how fast the water was moving, or where it came from. There are strata that cover millions of square miles. Those sheets of water would have to be moving very fast in order to cover that much area without losing the sediments they were carrying, and the evidence shows that for the most part, they were uniform. They did not drop heavier sediments as they moved. Fast moving water would also carry heavier fauna and flora.

If we postulate a worldwide flood, we have to consider whether the fauna and flora prior to the flood were evenly distributed over the earth. It would seem a logical assumption that they were not. If that were the case, then we have one more factor regarding why we find a variation of fossils from place to place. Those species that had a large population at the time of burial would leave more fossils if all the other factors were equal.

All these factors and more could have been considered by Lyell, an intelligent man and trained geologist, but in his writings there is no indication that he ever considered any of them. It seems that because his goal was to demonstrate that the earth was very old, the only view that he was willing to consider was that the placement of the fossils indicated the epoch when the animal lived.

The truth is that almost all of Lyell's assumptions about age are based on conchology, the study of clams and other shells from the sea, both living and fossilized. He was not well versed in that field but relied primarily on the expertise of Gerard Paul Deshayes of Paris. Lyell supplied him with shells, and Deshayes catalogued them. It is not clear how Deshayes became such an expert, since he had little more time than Lyell in the field of geology. He was two years older than Lyell, and spent his formative years studying medicine.

Terry Mortenson has researched this subject, and has given a reasoned argument that the identification of shells is a very unreliable way to date rock strata.

> In both the 1812 and the 1831 editions of his *Theory of the Earth*, [Georges] Cuvier rejected the use of shells as a means of reconstructing Earth's history, because differences in fossil species in the strata may have been the result of slight changes in salinity or temperature of the water or some other accidental cause, and because testaceous animals were still too poorly known to confidently claim that some were extinct (Cuvier, 1813; 1834). From 1808 to 1813 Beudant (to whose work the scriptural geologist George Young referred) had experimentally shown that marine shell creatures could adjust to life in fresh water and similarly fresh-water shellfish could become accustomed to life in the sea if the change in salinity was gradual as in the brackish waters of river deltas (Beudant, 1816). The old-earth geologist Macculloch (1824) referred to this and other observations about fish and shell creatures when he cautioned geologists about the use of these fossils to distinguish fresh water geological formations from those of marine origin. Six years later, he said that the use of fossils to identify, correlate and date strata from different locations was "groundless" and "nearly, if not entirely, useless" (Macculoch, 1831, pp. I:422-428, 453). [150]

Lyell refers to freshwater formations and marine formations with great frequency, as if there is some kind of irrefutable method of

---

[150] The Geologic Column, Perspectives within Diluvial Geology, John K. Reed and Michael J. Oard, Editors, Chapter 2, Terry Mortenson, p.19

knowing which is which, when all he really has to go by are the index shells mentioned above, which are said to be totally unreliable by men much more accomplished than he in the field of conchology.

There is no indication that Charles Lyell ever thought about the fact that the ocean is getting saltier at a rate that we can now measure. That being the case, there must have been a time not too long ago, when it would have been easy for marine creatures to exist equally in either the inland waters or the ocean. That time might have been only a few thousand years ago. The worldwide flood undoubtedly changed that relationship on a large scale. But Lyell didn't believe in a worldwide flood, so he never considered a change in the saltiness of the ocean.

Mortenson goes on to quote three other prominent old-earth geologists of the time when Lyell wrote his first and most important work.

> In an article on *mollusca* in the *Edinburgh Encyclopedia* (1830) the old-earth zoologist John Fleming remarked on persistent difficulties in classifying shell creatures into species, genera and even the correct orders. The next year, De la Beche (1831) expressed strong caution in using shells to date strata, because of the considerable errors and confusion in the catalogues of fossil shells.
>
> In the five editions of his *Introduction to Geology* published and revised between 1813 and 1838, the respected old-earth geologist, Robert Bakewell, repeatedly expressed his conviction that many of his fellow geologists relied too much on shells in their interpretations of the rocks: both in identifying distant, non-contiguous formations and in distinguishing fresh-water marine deposits. [151]

It was Bakewell's book that first got Lyell interested in geology, but Bakewell was not influential enough in Lyell's life to influence him in this regard. It should be noted that Bakewell never did gain acceptance in the fraternity of professional geologists because he was not an academic, and did not seem interested in the social aspect of the profession, and yes, there was definitely a necessity to stroke the right egos in the field.

Many of the differences in shells were attributed to them being of different species distributed over time, when the actual differences

---

[151] The Geologic Column, Perspectives within Diluvial Geology, John K. Reed and Michael J. Oard, Editors, Chapter 2, Terry Mortenson, p.19

were sexual, developmental or environmentally caused. Those kinds of errors are seemingly endemic to the process of dating strata by the fossils in them.

Shedding further light on this problem is an article concerning the now extinct moa of New Zealand. According to the author, David Catchpoole, moas became extinct about 600 years ago. There are, however, numerous remains of the birds available to study. It has always been dogmatically stated that there were three species of moas, a small species, a medium-sized one, and an exceedingly large one, some three meters tall. Now, through the efforts of Professor Alan Cooper, information has come to light that indicates they were all of one species! The small ones were the males, who were responsible for incubating the eggs and raising the young. The medium-sized ones and the very large ones, formerly called "giant moas," because it was thought they were a different genera, were females. Professor Cooper, an apparent evolutionist, summarizes the difficulties facing paleontologists when reconstructing the past based on what they are seeing in the animal kingdom in the present.

> So the moas have turned out to be just remarkable in so many ways about basic evolutionary processes, and you think you've got the whole thing sorted out...and you've got to remember they only went extinct 650 years ago and we've got thousands if not tens of thousands of skeletons of these things, and we still couldn't work it out. [152]

In light of the above, what is there to make us think Lyell had any chance of getting it right with clams, when all he had were fossils, and he had no direct knowledge of them himself! Nevertheless, the assignments of age that Lyell gave to the strata are largely still in force today.

In the following statement Lyell makes an admission that through several layers of strata, comprising hundreds of million of years, on the evolutionary scale, animal species have changed several times, but the plants remained relatively stable. That should have been a real problem for his worldview.

> From the Cretaceous through the Tertiary period, all the classes of land plants were represented and four or five almost complete changes of species had occurred, yet

---

there had been no significant advance in plant organization or complexity. [153]

However, Lyell never did let the facts get in the way of the philosophy he was trying to foist upon the world. Early in his career, when he wrote the first volume of *Principles of Geology*, he made the following statement:

> The organic contents of the secondary strata [all sedimentary strata above the basement rocks and below the tertiary layer] in general consist of corals and marine shells. Of the latter, the British strata (from the inferior oolite to the chalk inclusive) have yielded about six hundred species. Vertebrated animals are very abundant, but they are almost entirely confined to fish and reptiles. But some remains of cetacea have also been met with in the oolitic series of England, and the bones of two species of warm-blooded quadrupeds of extinct genera allied to the Opossum. The occurrence of one individual of the higher classes of mammalian, whether marine or terrestrial, in these ancient strata, is as fatal to the theory of successive development [later known as evolution], as if several hundreds had been discovered. [154]

Sedimentary strata formed by Mt. St. Helens Eruption (courtesy of John Morris)

Since he found possums with dinosaurs and clams in the Stonesfield excavation the above reasoning seems sound, but he forgot that rule later in life, when he yielded to his friends, Darwin, Huxley, Wallace et al., who used his geology to justify their transmutation of species. The motivating impetus for Lyell to have inserted that statement about one mammal nullifying the whole index fossil concept came from his early days when he was just

[153] Charles Lyell, *Address delivered at the Anniversary Meeting of the Geological Society of London, on the 21st of February, 1851*, London, Taylor, 60 pp.
[154] Principles of Geology, Vol. I, Ch. 9, p. 6, Charles Lyell

getting his feet wet in the field of geology. He was using it as an argument meant to convince people against progression [extinction of some species and advent of new species occurring over time]. He was concerned about them associating him with Lamarck, who by that time had fallen into disfavor with natural philosophers and the public at large, and thought a statement against progression might allay some of those fears. He needed to make sure his first book would sell well. Lyell later advocated progression, but left it a mystery as to how new species came into being. That would not do for most of his fellow natural philosophers, however, because the obvious assumption, if it were not happening through natural processes, would have to be that the "first cause" was doing it and it was enough that they had to allow for the "first cause" to be the *first* cause only, without having to invoke His continual doctoring with His creation.

Throughout his life there were a number of instances where he came upon anomalies, in which one or more fossils were dramatically out of place according to his timeline, as in the aforementioned finding of a human skeleton embedded with extinct species.

There is a strong opinion by many that Lyell was always a progressionist and that he only pretended not to be one in the beginning in order to appease those who thought he was doing injustice to the biblical account. Knowing how calculating he was, it seems a good bet they were right. In the introduction to the modern printing of *Principles of Geology*, James A. Secord makes the following observation:

> Lyell's concern with respectability permeated the *Principles*. Divisive issues were introduced in measured prose, with quotations from Horace, Ovid, Pindar, Pliny, Virgil, Thucydides, Dante, Milton and Shakespeare. The classical authors were known and accepted by most readers in that day when the classics were a much bigger part of the scholastic curriculum. The popular travel author Captain Basil Hall praised 'the calm, dispassionate, gentlemanlike style in which he handled, not one, but every controversial subject'. [155]

---

[155] Principles of Geology, vol. I, Introduction, p. xxviii, James A. Secord

What Was Lyell's Objective in Geology?

All this brings us back to exactly what it was that Charles Lyell was trying to accomplish when he ended his short life as a lawyer and decided to be a geologist, even though geology wasn't a profession with which one could make a living at that time.

Pyroclastic mud flow at Mt. St. Helens (courtesy of John Morris)

His ideas gave rise to evolution and humanism, which have caused considerable problems for modern Christianity. Charles Lyell was a true deist, although a rather disinterested one. He saw Christianity and the English church as being one and the same. He had an antipathy for the church, as we've already seen, and he was not averse to doing what he could to make the parson's job a little more difficult. He understood well that destroying Genesis would go a long way toward destroying the basis of religion as it was known in that part of the world. In *Principles* he explains the situation in France in the last couple of generations leading up to his own, generations which gave us the French Revolution:

> A class of writers in France had been laboring industriously for many years, to diminish the influence of the clergy, by sapping the foundation of the Christian faith, and their success, and the consequences of the Revolution, had alarmed the most resolute minds, while the imagination of the more timid was continually haunted by dread of innovation, as by the phantom of some fearful dream.
> Voltaire had used the modern discoveries in physics as one of the numerous weapons of attack and ridicule directed by him against the Scriptures. [156]

---

[156] Principles of Geology, Vol. I, Ch. 4, p. 10, Charles Lyell

Let's remember that Lyell had a very high regard for Voltaire and the French, and what he describes the French writers and Voltaire of doing in physics is exactly what Lyell did at a later period in geology. In Lyell's case, it was the church hierarchy he was after, not the faith of individual believers. However, the two proved to be inseparable. Throwing light on his view of the church is the following statement made in a letter to his sister, Marianne, in 1829:

> Longman has paid down 500 *guineas* to Mr. Ure of Dublin for a popular work on Geology, just coming out. It is to prove the Hebrew cosmogony, and that we ought all to be burnt in Smithfield. So much the better. I have got a rod for the fanatics, from a quarter where they expect it not. The last pope did positively dare to convoke a congregation, and *reverse* all that his predecessors had done against Galileo, and there was only a minority of one against; and he instituted lectures on the Mosaic cosmogony to set free astronomy and geology. How these things are so little known in Paris and London, heaven knows. They are golden facts, and I find the state of the question here to shame the Granville-Penn school of England. [157]

Granville Penn was a scriptural geologist, as was Andrew Ure. Unlike most of the other diluvialists, they had not compromised the scriptural text in order to appease the modern views. Lyell, on the other hand, paid no attention to scripture, and made no effort to make his geology conform to

"The Little Grand Canyon" at Mt. St. Helens (courtesy of John Morris)

scripture in any way. In fact, he did everything possible to make it not conform to scripture.

---

[157] Life, Letters and Journals of Sir Charles Lyell, Vol. I, p. 238

According to Lyell, if the pope issues a statement saying it is okay to trash the first eleven chapters of Genesis, then we can just go

ahead and do that with no feelings of guilt, because the pope saying that is just like God saying it. Of course, Britain was not under the auspices of the Roman pope, but Lyell thinks he has some kind of trump card with that edict. He didn't recognize any such thing as a personal relationship with Christ. Institutional religion was all he understood, and his aim was to cut the foundation out from under it. Note

This anomaly is found in the Columbia River Gorge. Is there any way Hutton and Lyell could make this formation look millions of ages old? The dark material is basalt. Wedged into it is the lighter material in the center, which is limestone and filled with a great deal of organic material. Both are sitting on an older (maybe hours older?) layer of basalt. The dark spot in the center of the limestone is a log, partly permineralized and partly still organic.

also, that at the beginning of that statement, he throws himself into that group of people that should be burnt at the stake at Smithfield for opposing the Hebrew cosmology. He is speaking sarcastically, of course, but his own identification as being in that group is sincere.

Adrian Desmond, an excellent science historian, talks about Lyell's lifestyle adjustments in his twenties.

> By the mid-1820s he had become an ardent liberal Whig, advocating electoral reform and <u>disestablishment of the Anglican Church</u>. His experience of the ancient universities, which he thought were in a bad way, was instrumental in his change. [158] [Underline mine]

There were no places in England where church authority was more abused than at Oxford and Cambridge universities, the only universities in that country. Lyell saw that up close and personal in his years at Oxford. In order to get into those universities it was necessary to be a member of the Anglican Church and before one

[158] Principles of Geology, vol. I, Introduction, p. xii, James A. Secord

could graduate they would have to swear allegiance to the *39 articles* of the Church, some of which were truly acceptable to only a few people. Those two universities were run by the Church, and most of the professors were prelates of the Church.

When the Protestant Church broke away from the Church of Rome, it did not totally lose the character of the mother church. It's a little like a person who sees faults in their parents and makes a determination to be different upon reaching adulthood. They may be different in some ways, but some behaviors have become too deeply ingrained and habitual, marking that person as a child of such-and-such an adult. The Roman Church was never much for allowing dissent, or even a divergence of opinion. The Church of England adopted a stance that wasn't noticeably different, and that attitude applied to all of its functions, whether it was education, business, or church administration. They were more concerned with making people obey their blueprint for society than leading the people in the correct worship of God. For many of the church hierarchy, it would seem that God was an afterthought. Their haughty attitude was not something that could be hidden either. The evidence stuck out everywhere.

Thomas Jefferson, who was well acquainted with both England and France, made a very poignant comment regarding the improper relationship of the state and church to the people.

> When the state uses church doctrine as a coercive tool, the result is hypocrisy and meanness. [159]

Quoting David Herbert in *Charles Darwin's Religious Views* we find the following:

> The Cambridge setting would do nothing to develop a deeper devotion to Christ and his Word. Here, Christianity was merely a veneer; one's commitment or lack of it mattered little. Chapel services were compulsory but, in reality, they were meaningless…University life also allowed this teenage aristocrat [Darwin] to join "mainly well-to-do upper-middle class young men who came to school with dogs, guns and horses…attending lectures and their studies only when these were fun." Hunting, riding and, most of all, partying marked this lifestyle.

[159] Ancient American magazine, vol. 14, issue 89, Jan. 2011, Five Hundred Years of Injustice: The Legacy of Fifteenth Century Prejudice, p. 39

Darwin's own dog was named Sappho {after the seventh century BC Greek poet known for her partying lifestyle and who lived on the island of Lesbos]. These were British gentlemen; attending university was one of the entitlements that their social status afforded them.

Charles joined the Gourmet or Glutton Club. Their gala events were "long-drawn-out dinners of an evening. They played cards. They actually sometimes drank too much." One would hardly associate this type of conduct with a person entering the service of Christ. But it should be noted that more than education gained at Cambridge were the social connections that one garnered; these privileged classmates would be the doctors, lawyers, politicians and clergymen of the future.[160]

Charles Lyell's experiences at Oxford must have been very similar, and it doesn't take a great deal of perception to see the hypocrisy of it all. Even though one may disagree with Lyell's methods, it is easy to see why he had a desire to knock the Church of England down to size. However, he had no illusions about the size of the task at hand, so he sought to accomplish his purpose by stealth rather than force.

He had laid the perfect foundation for the next step in the process of tearing society away from the God that had given it so much hope 300 years before with the Reformation. If there were any doubt that Lyell's hypothesis was responsible for setting up the climate for the wholesale embracement of evolution in the second half of the nineteenth century some quotes from the major players in that scene should set the record straight. Darwin wrote in *Origin*:

> He who can read Sir Charles Lyell's grand work on the Principles of Geology, which the future historian will recognize as having produced a revolution in natural science, yet does not admit how incomprehensively vast have been the past periods of time, may at once close this volume.[161]

Darwin wrote in his letters:

---

[160] Charles Darwin's Religious Views, From Creationist to Evolutionist, David Herbert, 2009, pp. 24, 25
[161] On the Origin of Species, or Preservation of the Favored Races in the Struggle for Life, Charles Darwin, J. Burrow (ed.), 1968 pp. 293

> I always feel as if my books came half out of Lyell's brain,
> and that I never acknowledged this sufficiently...for I
> have always thought the great merit of the *Principles* was
> that it altered the whole tone of one's mind.[162]

After Lyell made his obligatory case against transmutation in
Principles, William Whewell, a natural philosopher with a scriptural
bent, wrote a review of *Principles* that commended Lyell for his stand
on that issue. This is part of Michael Bartholomew's discussion of
that review.

> Lyell must have been gratified that the anti-evolutionary
> significance of his discussion had been appreciated. But
> Whewell's response was not typical. The future
> evolutionists read quite a different story from *Principles*.
> Herbert Spencer [the noted atheist X Clubber], for
> example, after reading what Wilson confidently calls
> Lyell's 'devastating criticism' of Lamarck, decided that
> Lyell had *expounded transmutation so plausibly* that the
> exposition, rather than Lyell's subsequent rejection,
> commanded assent. And we have the testimonies of
> Wallace, Hooker, Huxley, Asa Gray, and Darwin himself,
> all saying that *Principles* stimulated evolutionary thought,
> and none of them ever mentions being deflected from his
> work by Lyell's anti-progressionism. [163]

What it all comes down to is that Lyell was a bridge between the
days of Hutton and Erasmus Darwin to the time of the X Clubbers in
the mid-nineteenth century. He had enough of the 18th century in
him to know there was much to fear in opposing the reigning
paradigm of the western world, and that to be successful in that
endeavor he would have to be clever. He had enough of the X
Clubber from the 19th century in him to be encouraging to those who
were trying to bring about the fall of the Judeo-Christian paradigm
that had dominated Europe for close to two millennia. He did his
part by erecting the base for evolution to be built upon.

If anyone doubts the objectivity of this author's analysis, a
comment from one of the twentieth century's brightest lights in

---

[162] Charles Darwin's Religious Views, from Creationist to Evolutionist,
David Herbert, 2009, p. 50, from Life and Letters of Charles Darwin, 1:234
[163] Lyell and Evolution: An Account of Lyell's Response to the Prospect of an
Evolutionary Ancestry for Man, Michael Bartholomew, p. 278

evolution, Stephen J. Gould of Harvard University, someone who would love to be able to make favorable comments about Charles Lyell, should clarify things a bit:

> Charles Lyell was trained as a lawyer, and his book is more a brief for gradualism than an impartial account of evidence.... Lyell denigrated catastrophism as an antiquated, last-ditch effort by miracle-mongers trying to preserve the Mosaic chronology of an earth only a few thousand years old.
>
> I doubt that a more unfair characterization has ever been offered for a reputable scientific worldview[164]

Floating Logs in Spirit Lake near Mt. St. Helens (courtesy of John Morris)

If Stephen J. Gould felt that way, can there be any doubt that that was indeed the case? Gould is saying that the biblical model was a reputable worldview and that Lyell was grossly unfair in tearing it down! I couldn't have said it better myself.

With Lyell's help and encouragement Charles Darwin was the one who composed the book that set the world on its ear, and has not loosened its grip on the mind of man ever since.

---

[164] Ariel A. Roth, Origins, Linking Science and Scripture, 1998, p. 199

CHAPTER 5

CHARLES DARWIN

CHARLES Darwin is generally known as the originator of the theory of evolution, but in reality he was just a conduit. He transferred information from his grandfather and Charles Lyell to the X Clubbers and then to the world via his book, *On the Origin of Species, or Preservation of the Favored Races in the Struggle for Life.* He then pretty much just sat back and watched the whole thing unfold, while playing cheerleader for those who were doing the heavy lifting. He had to be urged to write the book by his friends, and then after it was published he did little to promote it. Many have speculated that the seemingly unknown illness he constantly suffered from was caused by the anxiety of producing such a controversial book that had far-reaching negative consequences all over the world. Those consequences probably did little to endear him to his in-laws.

We will get into the personal life of Charles Darwin to study these issues in more detail, but first, it is necessary to look back at the life of his paternal grandfather, Erasmus Darwin, in order to understand how Charles came to believe the way he did.

Erasmus Darwin was born in 1731 in Elston Hall near present day Newark, in Nottingham, the seventh and last child of Robert Darwin (1682-1754), a lawyer, and his wife Elizabeth Hill (1702-1797). Erasmus attended grammar school in Chesterfield and matriculated to St. John's College, Cambridge. He then went to medical school at the University of Edinburgh.

He set up a successful medical practice in the town of Litchfield, about 20 miles southwest of Derby and 10 miles north of Birmingham. He was very successful as a medical doctor; so much so that he was asked to be the doctor for the Royal Family of England, but turned it down. It would seem that he might have had problems working for people that he had so many political differences with, especially when they were largely responsible for those issues. He was opposed to slavery, supported the American and French revolutions and was a supporter of democracy everywhere, including Britain. Britain received a large stimulus to its economy from the slaves in America. Cotton and other products such as tobacco and liquor were sent as raw materials to Britain to be processed for retail trade. Those raw materials would have been much more expensive if not for the free labor of the slaves. One who supported the abolition of slavery could be accused of wanting to deny prosperity to the British people.

He had 12 children by two different wives, and two or three illegitimate children. His first wife died in 1770 after bearing him five children, four boys and one girl. After that, he had two children by his maid and governess, Mary Parker. It is suspected that he was also the father of a child of a married woman around that time. Then, in about 1781, he met and became enamored with Elizabeth Pole, who was married when he first became interested in her. Her husband then died, making it possible for Darwin to marry her without recriminations. They had seven children.

His oldest child was Charles Darwin; who was the uncle of Charles Darwin, the writer of *Origin*. The older Charles was enrolled at Edinburgh Medical School, apparently an excellent student. During the course of dissecting a cadaver he cut his finger and contracted some kind of pathogen that ended his life within 48 hours. Erasmus made his way to Edinburgh for the funeral of his son and while there stayed at the home of his good friend, James Hutton. It should also be noted that Hutton is known to have spent days at a time at Darwin's residence on his journeys to the south.

Erasmus' fourth child was Robert, named after Erasmus' father. Robert also became a very successful medical doctor, although not as well known as Erasmus. Robert was the father of Charles Darwin, the author of *Origin of Species*. Robert was very adept with his investments and this was greatly to the benefit of his progeny, including his son, Charles.

While Erasmus made a living at medicine, he, like many people of that time, had interests in several different fields and significant accomplishments in many of them. He was an inventor of note, although he did not seem to be motivated to pursue his ideas all the

Erasmus Darwin

way to their production as consumer products. He was an able writer and poet. He was a philosopher of science, and some of his writing covered those subjects, which is what makes him interesting to those of our modern world.

He was involved extensively with the Lunar Society in Birmingham, and was also a member of the Derby Philosophical Society. He founded the Litchfield Botanical Society.

The writing of Erasmus Darwin reveals the clear imprint of his years of friendship with James Hutton. The terms he uses, such as "millions of ages," come directly from Hutton. Darwin wasn't a geologist, but one passage was about as good an explanation of Hutton's theory of the earth as Hutton could have given; better, if you stop and think about Hutton's problems with written communication.

> The late Mr. David Hume, in his posthumous works, places the powers of generation [a term synonymous with evolution, but without the details] much above those of our boasted reason; and adds, that reason can only make a machine, as a clock or a ship, but the power of generation makes the maker of the machine; and probably from having observed, that the greatest part of the earth has been formed out of organic recrements; as the immense beds of limestone, chalk, marble, from the shells of fish; and the extensive provinces of clay, sandstone, ironstone, coals, and decomposed vegetables; all which have been first produced by generation, or by secretions of organic

life; he concludes that the world itself might have been
generated, rather than created; that is, it might have been
gradually produced from very small beginnings,
increasing by the activity of its inherent principles, rather
than by a sudden evolution of the whole by the Almighty
fire.[165]

The above quote also shows us that Mr. Darwin, like James
Hutton, was well aware of the atheist philosopher, David Hume and
may have visited him on his many trips to Edinburgh. Possibly,
Hutton introduced the two men. Quotes such as the one above lend
credence to the idea that Erasmus Darwin got not only his geology
from Hutton, but quite possibly his biology as well. If you will
remember, Hutton had early on mentioned biological evolution as a
part of his theory of the earth. They both gleaned much from the
writings of the Frenchman, Comte De Buffon, as the following quote
of Erasmus Darwin shows.

> Mr. Buffon mentions a breed of dogs without tails, which
> he supposes to have been produced by a custom long
> established of cutting their tails off. [166]

Apparently Jean Baptiste Lamarck also read Buffon, as this quote
describes what became known as Lamarck's main idea with regard
to the generation of new features in the animal world. The following
quote of Erasmus Darwin's was probably inspired by Hutton. We
should remember that Hutton was both a geologist and a chemist.

> Hence the modern discoveries in chemistry and in
> geology, by having traced the causes of the combinations
> of bodies to remoter origins, as well as those in astronomy,
> which dignify the present age, contribute to enlarge and
> amplify our ideas of the power of the Great First Cause. [167]

It seems as if Erasmus Darwin found the time he needed for
evolution to work directly from James Hutton. The combination of
that new found time and his imagination produced the following
quote.

---

[165] Erasmus Darwin, *Zoonomia*, 1794, p. 331
[166] Erasmus Darwin, *Zoonomia*, 1794, p. 326
[167] Erasmus Darwin, *Zoonomia*, 1794, p. 346

> From this account of reproduction it appears, that all animals have a similar origin, viz. from a single living filament; and that the difference of their forms and qualities has arisen only from the different irritabilities and sensibilities, or voluntarities, or associabilities, of this original living filament....[168]

He seems to have a gift for "words" that would fit right in with our modern technocrats! He also put it another way:

> As the habitable parts of the earth have been, and continue to be, perpetually increasing by the production of sea-shells and corallines, and by the recrements of other animals, and vegetables; so from the beginning of the existence of this terraqueous globe, the animals, which inhabit it, have constantly improved, and are still in a state of progressive improvement. [169]

Not only did he come up with evolution, he gave us the mechanism that his grandson used to explain how it happened.

> The final cause of this contest amongst the males seems to be, that the strongest and most active animal should propagate the species, which should thence become improved. [170]

And since his grandson, Charles, studied his writings, we can see where he at first got his deep time. Lyell's *Principles* probably reawakened Charles Darwin's awareness of deep time and how it might apply to his system of evolution, but he was definitely exposed to it through his grandfather's writings. Erasmus Darwin goes on:

> By considering in how minute a portion of time many of the changes of animals above described have been produced; would it be too bold to imagine, that in the great length of time, since the earth began to exist, perhaps *millions of ages* before the commencement of the history of mankind, would it be too bold to imagine, that all warm-blooded animals have arisen from one living filament,

---

[168] Erasmus Darwin, *Zoonomia*, 1794, pp. 324, 325
[169] Erasmus Darwin, *Zoonomia*, 1794, p. 343
[170] Erasmus Darwin, *Zoonomia*, 1794, p. 328

> which THE GREAT FIRST CAUSE endued with animality,
> with the power of acquiring new parts, attended with new
> propensities, directed by irritations, sensations, volitions,
> and associations; and thus possessing the faculty of
> continuing to improve by its own inherent activity, and of
> delivering down those improvements by generation to its
> posterity, world without end! [171] [Italics mine]

He goes on in another section about how changes in creatures caused by their maturing or caused by the artificial selection of man suggest that all creatures have evolved. Charles picked up on the artificial selection idea and used it extensively to try to get his readers to accept natural selection. It is a specious argument, but many undiscerning people were pulled along in accepting it. It is very similar to the idea that if scientists can spend decades and millions of dollars to produce a precursor to life, it will prove that life originally came about by accident with no intelligence involved!

The Life of Charles Darwin

Charles Darwin was born in Shrewsbury, Shropshire, just to the east of the border with Wales, on February 12, 1809, the same day that Abraham Lincoln was born. He was the fifth of six children of Robert Darwin (1766-1848) and Susannah Wedgwood (1765-1817), daughter of Josiah Wedgwood of Wedgwood Pottery fame. Charles married his first cousin, Emma. His mother and his wife's father were siblings.

Robert Darwin's family maintained a veneer of Anglicanism, but they were all over the map as far as what they actually believed. While it seems Robert, in reality, was an atheist, the Wedgwood side largely adopted Unitarianism. In England at that time there was a necessity to at least appear to be Anglican in order to avoid being discriminated against in the public sphere. Charles and his siblings attended a Unitarian grammar school according to his mother's wishes. But she died at the age of 52, when Charles was eight years old. Robert then sent Charles and his brother, Erasmus, off to the Anglican boarding school at Shrewsbury.

At his father's urging, Charles enrolled at Edinburgh University to study medicine. Being that his grandfather and father were highly successful doctors, it was expected that Charles would follow in the

---

[171] Erasmus Darwin, *Zoonomia*, 1794, p. 329

family tradition. Charles, however, had no taste for medicine. He could not bear the gore involved, and the pain that was inflicted during surgery was too much for him. That was just before the time when they started using anesthetics.

His father went to plan B. There were not many vocational options at that time in the professions. You could enter one of three professions: doctor, lawyer or clergyman. It's sad to say it, but clergyman was for those who could not make it as a doctor or lawyer. So, I'm sure at that point Robert Darwin had a heavy heart and Charles must have felt pretty bad about himself. He made the best of the situation, however, and enrolled at Cambridge in the divinity school. While there, his cousin, William Darwin Fox, who also was a student there, got him interested in collecting beetles. Some of Charles' finds were published in the *Illustrations of British Entomology.* He took botany under John Henslow and was quite absorbed by it. Henslow was impressed with Darwin, and spent extra time with him outside the classroom. He encouraged Darwin to spend even more time learning about natural philosophy. Darwin became known on campus as "the man who walks with Henslow."

He was also quite engrossed in William Paley's evidences of intelligent design. On his final exams, Darwin finished tenth out of 178 students. In the summer after graduation he went on a field trip

Young Charles Darwin

to Wales with geology professor Adam Sedgwick. Arriving home, there was a letter from Henslow recommending him for a possible position aboard *H.M.S. Beagle*, which was to map the coast of South America, some islands in the Pacific, and part of the coast of Australia. His job would primarily entail being a second mate to the captain. There were a number of applicants, although it was a non-paid position. All expenses were to be paid by the applicant. Of course, this was no problem for Darwin, since his father would have no trouble funding his projected two-year trip.

The problem was that his father was completely against it. He thought Charles should get on with his life in some more meaningful way.

Robert Darwin was swayed, however, after consultation with his brother-in-law, Josiah Wedgwood. Wedgwood thought it could be a good experience for the young lad. Charles got the position, probably because of the well known men that gave him good referrals, but the trip ended up being a five-year trip, not two.

They weren't long out of port before Darwin started taking notes, collecting specimens and making observations on everything he saw. He also kept a detailed journal. The man designated as the ship's naturalist, Robert McCormick, wasn't nearly as prolific as a naturalist, probably because he was also the ship's surgeon. Before long, Captain Fitzroy noticed the disparity, and made Darwin the ship's naturalist. Darwin sent many specimens home with explanatory notes, and also sent parts of his journal home as he went. Henslow read his letters to the Philosophic Society of Cambridge. These became quite popular, and Darwin must have been surprised when he arrived back home to find that he was a well-known personality in England.

Aboard the ship, when he wasn't busy with the above, he was reading and re-reading Charles Lyell's book, *Principles of Geology*. About 85 percent of the observations made in his journal had to do with geology, not biology. After his return to Britain, he began to speculate in the biological realm, but he seldom referenced his voyage on the *Beagle*. Despite all the material he gathered on the voyage, undoubtedly the most significant thing that came out of it was what it did to Darwin's mind. Combining Lyell's active imagination, exhibited in his book, with Darwin's equally active imagination with all that he saw, it started him on a journey culminating in his world-changing book. Darwin's life was changed forever after the voyage of the *Beagle*.

One thing that probably did stick in Darwin's mind from the trip was Lyell's view that species had been going extinct for millions of years, but new species were replacing them. This was a reinforcement of what he had read in his grandfather's writings. Lyell offered no explanation for how new species might be formed, so Darwin, with the inquisitive mind he had, must have spent some time thinking about that.

In March, 1837, Darwin began his Red Notebook, which was divided into two sections, one labeled "A," which were his ideas on geology, and one labeled "B," which were his evolutionary ideas. Across the top of the first page of section "B" was written "ZOONOMIA," the name of his grandfather, Erasmus' book. He had read it again, which is further evidence that this replacement of species question was really troubling him. He felt that his grandfather's idea on evolution was good, as far as it went, but he needed to flesh it out more in order to be able to convince people of the veracity of evolution. He began interviewing people, including his father, reading anything he could get his hands on that related to the subject, and did a lot of brainstorming. Finally, he read Thomas Malthus' *Essays on the Principle of Population* in September of 1838 and made the declaration, "I had at last got a theory by which to work."[172]

Malthus' basic premise was that in nature, population tends to outstrip the food supply. As the competition for the available food becomes more severe, the strong are more likely to survive that battle. He applied this theory to man as well, leading to a callus attitude toward human suffering, since suffering was just viewed as something that had to happen as a way to keep the population in check. Darwin saw Malthus' ideas as his key to natural selection, and he began to branch out to other sources of competition besides food, such as sexual attraction, etc.

According to Darwin's *Autobiography*: "I began to think much about religion" in the period from 1836 to 1839.[173] He was haunted by Lyell's book aboard the *Beagle*, but he was haunted by Lyell himself after he got back to England, and Lyell was not afraid to let his deism out in private company. Lyell did not believe in the revelation of the Bible, and Darwin began more and more to lose any semblance of belief in God's Word. Darwin increasingly removed himself from the presence of those who might have drawn him closer to a Christian worldview, but instead, attracted others of a deist or atheist leaning.

Darwin started compiling notes on the transmutation of species question from the late 1830s onward. Darwin, of course, had no job, so he was free to spend vast amounts of time pondering this question and was in no hurry to come up with a complete system.

---

[172] David Herbert, Charles Darwin's Religious Views, From Creationist To Evolutionist, 2009, pp. 56, 57
[173] David Herbert, Charles Darwin's Religious Views, From Creationist To Evolutionist, 2009, p. 59

In 1844, when Darwin read *Vestiges of the Natural History of Creation,* by Robert Chambers, he said it
> was "a grand piece of argument against immutability of species" and read it "with fear and trembling."

Chambers wrote the book anonymously and it wasn't until years later that it was found out that he had written it. This book was a much more comprehensive explanation of the evolutionary system than anything that had been published up to that time.[174] He commented though that, "The writing and arrangement are certainly admirable but his geology strikes me as bad and his zoology far worse." [175]

The book sold well, and it must have impressed Darwin in two ways. It showed that a book on evolution, although not of high caliber, would sell well, and it showed that the person who writes that book will be at the center of a storm of controversy. It was obvious why Chambers did not identify himself. As a matter of fact, Chambers died in 1871, and it wasn't until 1885 that it came out that he had been the author. If Darwin had been reticent about publishing a book on evolution before he read *Vestiges,* he had certainly been given pause after that.

Although Darwin was a recluse, who didn't even attend the funerals of his father or his beloved 10-year-old daughter, he did get out some in his younger years, and he maintained his relationship with Lyell. Because of that, he began to meet other people who would influence him in ways that would direct him to write the book that would change the world.

Joseph Dalton Hooker (1817-1911), whose father, William Hooker, was director of Kew Botanical Gardens, became a close friend of Darwin's in 1843. Darwin, knowing Hooker was well versed in botany, asked Hooker to classify the plants he had collected in his voyage on the *Beagle.* They had been acquainted with each other before that, but the connection in biology seemed to cement their friendship. Hooker's mother, Maria Turner, was the daughter of Dawson Turner. The Turner family and the Lyell family had been close for many years. Joseph Hooker married Frances Henslow, the daughter of Darwin's old college professor, John Henslow.

---

174 David Herbert, Charles Darwin's Religious Views, From Creationist To Evolutionist, 2009, p. 87
175 David Herbert, Charles Darwin's Religious Views, From Creationist To Evolutionist, 2009, p. 89

Hooker was a deist. As Darwin explained his ideas on transmutation, Hooker was receptive. He was at times critical of different aspects of the system, but overall, was encouraging to Darwin. In 1858 Darwin wrote that Hooker was "the one living soul from whom I have constantly received sympathy."

Hooker was the one primarily responsible for orchestrating the co-authored paper of Darwin and Alfred Russel Wallace in 1858, and it was Hooker and Lyell who later that year urged Darwin to get his book done and published.

While life went on for Darwin, as he ruminated on his slowly developing system of evolution he was about to have some experiences in the late 1840s and early 1850s that would change things. In 1848, his father, with whom he had a close relationship, died. He had been very dependent upon his father for emotional and financial support.

According to Darwin's notes, he read Francis William Newman's book, *Phases of Faith* (1850), a spiritual autobiography that paralleled Darwin's in some ways. As a young man, Newman had studied for the clergy in the Anglican Church, was trained at Oxford, and went abroad as a missionary to India. Everywhere he looked in the Anglican Church, he saw hollowness. People were carrying out functions only because of the pay involved and for the prestige it might obtain them. After much soul-searching, Newman came to the conclusion that much of Christian doctrine was a sham, and most importantly, that Christ was only a man.[176] According to David Herbert,

> Newman had been powerfully affected by the new thinking on natural history. Geologists assured us, that death went on in the animal creation many ages before the existence of man…to refer the death of animals to the sin of Adam and Eve was evidently impossible. [177]

As anticipated by Lyell, if you just lay the "facts" out there for the reader to see, they will come to their own conclusions that the Bible is not a reliable document, and if there was death and destruction long before man sinned, then sin is not the cause of death. The

---

[176] David Herbert, Charles Darwin's Religious Views, From Creationist To Evolutionist, 2009, pp. 93-95

[177] David Herbert, Charles Darwin's Religious Views, From Creationist To Evolutionist, 2009, p. 95

destruction started by Hutton and Lyell and others like them was already beginning to take a toll on society before Darwin ever published his book, and was, in fact, a prime motivating factor for him to publish the book. He wanted to continue the assault on the validity of the Word of God.

In 1850, Darwin met Thomas Henry Huxley (1825-1895). When it came to demeanor, Huxley was the opposite of Darwin. Darwin was a recluse. Huxley was comfortable on the big stage and could captivate an audience. He enjoyed public confrontations and excelled at winning those confrontations. Huxley liked Darwin's evolution idea, even if he didn't agree with all of it. He saw the potential to use it to strike down the church and elevate his brand of science.

In 1851 Charles Darwin's beloved 10-year-old daughter, Annie, died from a childhood disease. The notes in his diary make it clear that Darwin, by that time, had become convinced that a loving God that cares for each of His created beings in a manner described in the Bible was a myth. Herbert writes in *Charles Darwin's Religious Views*:

> Seven days after his daughter's death, in the seclusion of Down House, Charles penned a memorial to his beloved child. He portrayed Annie "as a type-specimen of all the highest and best in human nature. Physically, intellectually and morally, she was perfect.... Annie did not deserve to die; she did not even deserve to be punished — in this world, let alone the next." [178]

At that point Darwin was like someone trying to swim against a strong current that gets swept away to a place they do not want to go. He was responsible for what he was becoming, but once it reached a certain point, his friends were going to make sure his ideas would get published despite what Darwin might have wanted, and they had every intention of using those ideas to secularize the world.

In addition to Lyell, Hooker and Huxley, there were a number of others involved. Herbert Spencer was the atheist writer, who was like an attack dog against the church. Lyell, Hooker and Huxley handled him very carefully, not wanting to create enemies where there didn't need to be any. John Tyndall, one of Huxley's best friends, the Irish physicist from Belfast, probably spoke about

---

[178] David Herbert, Charles Darwin's Religious Views, From Creationist To Evolutionist, 2009, p. 96

evolution and against the church more than any other man except Huxley, and he helped Huxley organize what later became known as the *X Club*. Adrian Desmond describes that environment in his book, *Huxley, From Devil's Disciple to Evolution's High Priest*.

> For 15 years, since they had swept into the town halls, Dissenters [those who opposed the status quo in Britain, with the church and the politicians colluding to control most segments of society] had been prying the professional institutions out of Anglican hands. They resented the Church's privileges, its Oxbridge exclusivity, its divine justification of the status quo and its damnation for all who disagreed.
>
> By 1850 the Dissenters and rationalists had moved in from the fringes to become London's avant garde – and Huxley would meet them all, men such as George Henry Lewes (author of *Ranthorpe*) and Herbert Spencer. "Secularism" was their watchword, coined by the former firebrand George Holyoake [the last person sent to prison for blasphemy in 1842] who was now settling into cigar-smoking respectability with the literary radicals on Lewes' weekly, *The Leader*. Dissolvent literature was their rage, books that eroded the clerical cement in the Anglican edifice. They pitted the Dissenting vision of a reforming society against the bishops' rigid hierarchies. Everywhere Huxley felt the meliorist ethic – improvement on earth rather than redemption in heaven. These were the real Pendennises [people who had improved their social class above their early station in life], breaking the old shackles. They wanted scientific standards for judging truth, standards in their hands, legitimating their own claim to intellectual authority. The "crisis of faith" was a collision of creeds, a product of the rents and changes in an industrializing society. "The result is everywhere the same," Huxley said. "Every thinking man I have met with is at heart in a state of doubt, on all the great points of religious belief. And the unthinking men...are in as complete a state of practical unbelief." It was agonizingly congenial. [179]

Holyoake's arrest and six-month imprisonment was actually a sign of the changing times. There was a public uproar over his arrest,

---

[179] Adrian Desmond, Huxley, From Devil's Disciple to Evolution's High Priest, 1997, p. 160

and some of the press was on his side. The public pressure caused the judge to release him early. There had been no such mercy for Thomas Aikenhead in 1696. Holyoake continued to advocate for secularism after his brief prison term and was never arrested again. That must have emboldened many others who might have previously kept their peace.

After *Origin* was published in November of 1859, Darwin laid low at his down residence. He bought a pool table for the room next to his study to get his mind off the controversy he knew his book was causing. Huxley, Tyndall, Spencer and others were now doing the proselytizing for his ideas. He read the reviews in the press and communicated with them by letter and an occasional visit by one of them to Down House.

He had specifically avoided the subject of the origin of man and Genesis in the book. He knew the book would be volatile enough without bringing those two subjects out into the open as well. He expressed great satisfaction at Huxley's and Tyndall's success at advocating for evolution against the established hierarchy in the church and in science.

Finally, in 1871 he published his book, *Decent of Man*, in which he addressed the belief that man is descended from an ape. Everyone knew that was the implied meaning conveyed in *Origin*, so he must have figured it was safe by then to make it explicit. He still did not make direct statements contradicting the Bible, however. From the X Clubbers' viewpoint, that approach was necessary, because as long as it did not directly attack the Bible liberal clergymen could support their position without losing face, or at least that was the thinking. Perceptive people saw through their guise, of course, but they weren't worried about a few dissenters. It was the masses they were concerned about, and some of the intellectuals who were only too happy to overlook a few inconsistencies. Because the church-going populace was used to being told what to believe and not believe, and the proper way to behave, they were easily led by the intellectuals and the liberal clergy.

In today's world, we've become blasé about great technological advances. Not so in the late 19th century. The telegraph was a wonder to behold for those people, sending messages across the Atlantic in seconds. Only a few years previously, the letter went by ship and took weeks or months. Speaking of the Atlantic, it could be crossed in ten days by steamship, whereas by sail it took two to four months. Steam locomotives whisked people about at previously unthinkable speeds. Photography made it possible for pictures to be made in a few minutes that in many cases far surpassed what a painter could produce. The changes taking place in that society were more impressive than what we see today because of what the condition of things had previously been.

Anyone who could call himself a scientist was respected and listened to with great interest, due to the track record of science at that time. That was a major factor in Thomas Huxley's ability to get public funding for science at a level that was never approached before. The pushers of evolution called themselves scientists and others did as well, although not one scrap of scientific evidence was presented in *Origin*. It consisted solely of speculation and storytelling. Because they were called scientists, they were listened to as though they had the sole authority to determine truth in the science of origins.

Adrian Desmond wrote about another credibility-boosting event that took place in 1850:

> The Church needed strong progressives, the liberal *Telegraph* said, rather than these "old style Tories" [people who supported the status quo] who have not budged "one iota beyond their ancient notions." Church liberals hated Wilberforce's hard line, as he condemned their softpedalling on miracles. He castigated the "seven against Christ," the liberal Anglican contributors to the innocent-sounding *Essays and Reviews,* whose critique of the Genesis Myth and biblical literalism inflamed more passions in a year than Darwin managed in a lifetime. [180]

The stage was certainly being set for the acceptance of this most unscientific of views, evolution. Desmond elaborates about the formation of the *X Club*:

> In November 1864, after years of abortive efforts, Huxley finally created an invisible club. He brought together a robust group, all of a mind on Darwinism and Colensoism [supporters of Bishop Colenso's watered down interpretation of the scriptures]. He needed to pull his cadre together. Work was a centrifugal force pinning them to their posts....

---

[180] Adrian Desmond, Huxley, From Devil's Disciple to Evolution's High Priest, 1997, p. 278

Huxley called a meeting at St. George's Hotel, close to the Royal Institution, on 3 November. The greatest constellation of New Reformers came together. Hooker was lured in, and the omnipresent Tyndall (he and Hal [Huxley's most intimate nickname] had become "a sort of firm" in the public mind). There was Hirst (about to take the physics chair at University College), Busk and Lubbock, and Spencer too. The group was completed by Edward Frankland (Tyndall and Hirst's fellow student at Marburg, and the new chemistry professor at the Royal Institution). These men had grown up on the perimeter, in London's medical schools, German universities or around the midlands Chapel; Lubbock being the oddity as an old Etonian. None was Oxbridge educated; but this *was* an elite. They were the new intellectual clerisy, slim and fit after an evolutionary sauna. Not all the members were academics – Spencer lived by the pen, Lubbock by the ledger. And to the eight the mathematician and Queen's Printer William Spottiswoode was later added. In clubbable London this was the most elite club of all, with nine members and a closed entry book.

"Amongst ourselves there is a perfect outspokenness," Hirst said. And they showed it. Militancy was increasing on all sides, and they met as the conservative outrage grew at *Essays and Reviews'* non-miraculous Christianity. [*Essays and Reviews* was a book that was published in 1860. It had seven sections, each authored by a different liberal theologian. The themes seemed to support naturalism and rejection of the miracles of the Bible]Two of the *Essays'* authors had been convicted of heresy. When the judgment was overturned on appeal, "dismissing hell with costs," there was uproar in the parishes. Wilberforce drew up a petition declaring that "the whole Canonical Scriptures" was the literal "Word of God," and almost half the nation's clergy signed. He presented it to the Church Convocation, which formally condemned the book.

A group of evangelical chemists, led by Capel Berger, the Plymouth Brethren paint manufacturer, took their own petition to the BAAS [British Association for the Advancement of Science], demanding that the Association "maintain a harmonious alliance between Physical Science and Revealed Religion." They were sick of Huxley's "dangerous clique" baiting parson's with the glee "a small boy feels when he is tying a tin kettle to a dog's tail."

Wilberforce's Convocation and Berger's petition put the fire into Huxley's night conclave in November. All present shared a "devotion to science, pure and free, untrammeled by religious dogma." And that explains some noticeable absences. The older Unitarians Lyell and Carpenter were out [Lyell wasn't willing to be as combative as they wanted him to be, and unlike most of the X Clubbers, did believe in a First Cause].

No other nine-member Club could have written "a scientific Encyclopaedia." No other nine members could have staffed a German Technical University. But that was not the most significant point. This was no longer an outsider cadre trying to break in, but an insider caucus spreading out. For all its scientific exclusivity, the club had direct access to the city, Parliament, medicine, industry and the liberal Church – to the cultural heart of the country. Huxley's irregulars had become a National Force....

As the masters of cultural politics, they would snatch Science from noble patrons' hands and put it on a par with medicine and the Church. They would dine at 6 pm. on the first Thursday of each month, and then take a post-prandial stroll to the Royal Society, which met at 8.30, where their plans for altering Council procedures would soon tip the balance of power.[181]

After Charles Darwin released *Decent of Man* in 1871, except for personal correspondence, letters to the editor and such, he was through with his publications on the evolution issue. He observed the tussle from afar and discussed it with the X Clubbers, who vociferously argued his cause throughout the 19th century. Others took up the armaments of war in the 20th century, and the battle is still going on today, although, in terms of numbers, the evolutionists seem to be winning the war.

What motivated Charles Darwin?

The writings of Charles Darwin, whether public or private, do not reflect the same kind of sarcasm and hostility toward the church and Christianity in general that we've seen in the writings of Charles Lyell, James Hutton, and other like minded people prior to our discussion of Darwin. He presents a unique picture compared with the other men we've discussed and will be discussing. Remember, he

---

[181] Adrian Desmond, Huxley, From Devil's Disciple to Evolution's High Priest, 1997, pp. 327-329

had trained for the clergy. Not that he had been dedicated to be a clergyman, but at least he was seemingly willing, which would indicate that, at worst, his feelings toward the church were not hostile.

One might wonder why his father, an atheist, would want him to train for the clergy, and he indeed did push Charles in that direction. To understand that we must remember that most atheists throughout history, unlike some of the modern ones who are quite aggressive in pushing their views, have been very quiet and even secretive about what they believe. They honestly did not believe there was a deity in control of all things, but they did not wish to alienate themselves and their families from others, and they may have felt that if someone they love could find satisfaction in believing in god, then, more power to them. Besides, in those days, if you wanted to be a well-respected professional, and you didn't want to be a medical doctor or lawyer, the clergy was one of the few other options available, and the pay was descent, though not what the law or medical professions paid.

But, Charles Darwin was not destined for the clergy, and all of the circumstances he found himself in after Cambridge conspired to shunt him off toward that course he ended up taking. He had been exposed to evolution and deep time through his grandfather. His father certainly did not strengthen any leanings Charles might have had toward Christianity, and his mother, who could have had some influence in that matter, died when he was eight years old.

Charles Darwin in the twilight years

Upon Darwin's graduation from Cambridge, Adam Sedgwick, who was a professor there, whisked him off to Wales to look for fossils and geological formations. Upon returning home, a letter was waiting from John Henslow, his botany professor at Cambridge, telling him about the opportunity on the *Beagle*. Before the summer was over he was on a five-year voyage of exploration around the world, having been handed a copy of Lyell's newly released *Principles of Geology*, compliments of Henslow and given to him by the Captain, Robert Fitzroy. Included was a note from Henslow, a Christian and a diluvialist, telling Darwin to enjoy the book but don't take the dates too seriously. You have to wonder about Henslow's judgment!

When he got back to England, Lyell was desirous of being his friend, and Lyell's deism erased any remaining spark of desire for Christianity Darwin might have had. Then, he had years of idle time to let his imagination run wild about how his grandfather's ideas and those of Lyell could have happened through natural processes. As he indicated in his diary, the three-year period immediately after the voyage was a time of religious turmoil. It was at that time that he decided to stop his quest to understand Christianity. He had to make that decision in order to be able with full vigor to pursue the details of evolution, because he was fully aware that what he was doing was diametrically opposed to Christian beliefs. He could never have dreamed that 150 years later liberal theologians would still be trying to assimilate evolution into the church's doctrine!

He never did oppose Christianity the way the X Clubbers, Lyell and Hutton did. He was simply apathetic toward Christianity. He wrote and received many letters from Asa Gray, the Harvard professor of botany, and he was willing to share things with him that he did not share with others. In 1860, after publication of *Origin,* he wrote:

> My dear Gray,
> I thank you for two letters…. Yesterday I read with care the third Article [that Gray wrote]; & it seems to me, as before *admirable.* But I grieve to say that I cannot honestly go as far as you do about Design. I am conscious that I am in an utterly hopeless muddle. I cannot think that the world, as I see it, is the result of chance; & yet I cannot look at each thing as a result of Design. [182]

Later he wrote:

> If I was to say that I believed this [humankind designed], I should believe it in the same incredible manner as the orthodox believe the Trinity in Unity, — You say that you are in a haze; I am in thick mud; — the orthodox would say

---

[182] David Herbert, Charles Darwin's Religious Views, From Creationist To Evolutionist, 2009, p. 120

in fetid abominable mud. ...yet I cannot keep out of the question. [183]

In 1876, six years before his death, he wrote the following to a Dutch student:

> I may say that the impossibility of conceiving that this grand and wondrous universe, with our conscious selves, arose through chance, seems to me the chief argument for the existence of God; but whether this is an argument of real value, I have never been able to decide. [184]

We've already seen how one event after another pushed him farther and farther away from God. Darwin had been urged by his friends to turn his voluminous notes into the book, *Origin*. But Charles Darwin never could make up his mind about what he believed about most things, and his own system of evolution was one of those.

Did Darwin deny his own theory?

In an encapsulated version of natural selection, he presents the unifying concept that sold his idea to the world. Darwin wrote the following in the first edition of *Origin* in 1860:

> I have now recapitulated the facts and considerations which have thoroughly convinced me that species have been modified during a long course of descent by the preservation or the natural selection of many successive slight favourable variations. [185]

This is essentially the process called natural selection. It is what set his system apart from the ones that went before it. Many people rejected natural selection as a viable vehicle to accomplish evolution. Darwin never used examples of natural selection in his book. To help his readers imagine how it worked, he used examples from artificial

---

[183] David Herbert, Charles Darwin's Religious Views, From Creationist To Evolutionist, 2009, p. 120
[184] David Herbert, Charles Darwin's Religious Views, From Creationist To Evolutionist, 2009, p. 130
[185] Randall Hedtke, Secrets of the Sixth Edition, Darwin Discredits His Own Theory, 2010, p. 39

selection with man as the selector. This was just one of many contrivances he used that helped him persuade people that his theory had merit. Randall Hedtke, in his book on Darwin, makes the following observation:

> Faced with this mental slight-of-hand technique [exchanging artificial selection for natural selection], the less critical reader is apt to accept artificial selection as proof of natural selection and not demand the obvious proof, which Darwin could not deliver; observation of the mechanism in action, in the environment….
>
> As usually happens when analogies are applied, similarities are emphasized while differences are ignored. There are two things wrong with the natural-selection/artificial-selection analogy. First, man does not create new kinds by artificial selection; and second, we observe limited variability. Consequently, the analogy shows, if anything, that change from one kind to another kind would be impossible. It is one of the great ironies of this controversy, and it also demonstrates an ambivalence common among all the founders of the evolutionary hypothesis, that Thomas Henry Huxley, Darwin's "bulldog," should be the one to reject Darwin's analogy and explicitly use artificial selection as a test against natural selection. [186]

What Hedtke is saying is this: because man can, with strict controls in place, and with constant surveillance, alter a species to a certain extent, one is supposed to believe that a species in the wild, with no controlling factors and no surveillance, changed not only within their own kind, but changed into a totally new kind. That is something that has never been observed to happen.Darwin was very intelligent, and he was good at writing in such a way as to excite in the reader the possibility that he *could* be right, and if you were so disposed as to want to believe him you would probably be persuaded, despite the fact that no scientific evidence had been provided. Gertrude Himmelfarb in her book, *Darwin and the Darwinian Revolution*, writes describing the *Origin*:

> It was probably less the weight of the facts than the weight of the argument that was impressive. The reasoning was

---

[186] Randall Hedtke, Secrets of the Sixth Edition, Darwin Discredits His Own Theory, 2010, pp. 83, 84

so subtle and complex as to flatter and disarm all but the most wary intelligence. Only upon close inspection do the faults of the hypothesis emerge. And this close inspection, by the nature of the case, was rarely vouchsafed. The points were so intricately argued that to follow them at all required considerable patience and concentration—an expenditure of effort which was itself conducive to acquiescence. Only those determined in advance to be hostile were likely to maintain a vigilant and hence critical attitude. [187]

Regarding the glaring problem of design in nature, Himmelfarb writes:

Darwin was quick to see the problem, but not so successful in resolving it. His technique here, as elsewhere, was first to assume that by acknowledging the difficulty, he had somehow exorcised it; and second, if this act of confession did not succeed in propitiating his critics, to bring to bear upon the difficulty the weight of authority of just that theory which was being called into question. [188]

What she is saying is that he would quickly acknowledge the problem, but throw out several "possible" solutions, none of which, upon close inspection, had any validity. Most people did not do the close inspections because of the problems cited above; it was just a lot more work than the average reader was willing to do.

Darwin never spoke in absolutes, only in possibilities. How can you prove a possibility wrong? Somehow, it is appropriate that he was that way in his writing, because every aspect of his life was the same way. He didn't know—or, for that matter, believe—anything for sure.

In the first few editions of *Origin*, Darwin defended the accuracy of his observations when his critics attacked. Hedtke explains:

Formerly, as we have seen, he would simply deny or not give credit to any criticisms. For example, his view requires unlimited variability, but we observe limited variability. Darwin simply denied that conflicting fact. Or

---

[187] Randall Hedtke, Secrets of the Sixth Edition, Darwin Discredits His Own Theory, 2010, p. 23

[188] Ariel A. Roth, Origins, Linking Science and Scripture, 1998, p. 97

consider the fossil record—his hypothesis predicts numerous intermediate fossils. He simply makes excuses as to why they are not discovered.[189]

As Darwin got along in years, he grew tired of defending his hypothesis. Then, in 1867, an article appeared in the *North British Review* that was highly critical of natural selection. It was written anonymously, although today we know the author was none other than Darwin's good friend from across the ocean, Asa Gray. That article was referred to in 1869, when Darwin was explaining his previous reasoning processes in a letter to that publication:

> I saw, also, that the preservation in a state of nature of any occasional deviation of structure, such as a monstrosity, would be a rare event; and that, if at first preserved, it would generally be lost by subsequent intercrossing with ordinary individuals. Nevertheless, until reading an able and valuable article in the *North British Review* (1867), I did not appreciate how rarely single variations, whether slight or strongly-marked, would be perpetuated.[190]

I wonder if Gray wrote the article in that publication because he had learned in all of his correspondence with Darwin that Darwin was a regular reader of *The North British Review*. Of course, he knew exactly how to write it in order to have the maximum effect on Darwin. It is a wonder that Darwin did not know that Gray had written it. Darwin thought the writer was a Fleeming Jenkin.

Darwin was aware of the problem of incipient structures. Incipient structures are those new structures, according to evolution, that are there but have no use. For instance, if a fish is born with a fin that is half way toward becoming a leg that structure has no use. Its offspring, if they develop a real leg in that spot may have a use for the structure but this particular individual will always have an incipient (useless) structure in the place where there should be a fin. Of course, a casual glance tells us that, far from this individual being the fittest to survive, it is actually the least fit to survive. So, Darwin was attacked often about incipient structures.

---

[189] Randall Hedtke, Secrets of the Sixth Edition, Darwin Discredits His Own Theory, 2010, p. 33

[190] Randall Hedtke, Secrets of the Sixth Edition, Darwin Discredits His Own Theory, 2010, p. 34

Natural selection was what made Darwin famous, not evolution. Evolution had been around in one form or another since the Greeks of classical times. Darwin's natural selection gave it a scientific-sounding mechanism, making evolution seem like more than just a figment of some philosophical mind. But in the quote above, Darwin appears to be caving in on natural selection. Hedtke provides more detail from the sixth edition with this quote from Darwin:

> The belief that any given structure, which we think, often erroneously, would have been beneficial to a species, would have been gained under all circumstances through natural selection, is opposed to what we can understand of its manner of action. [191]

Adrian Desmond comments regarding a letter written in 1860 from Charles Darwin to Tom Huxley about Charles Lyell's need for numerous new "creations" to bring new species into the world as others die out. It pertains to Darwin's assertion that natural selection is the only method of accomplishing evolution:

> His [Lyell's] lingering need for the "intervention of creative power" to supercharge the process made Darwin cringe: "I cannot see this necessity," he replied. It would make his mechanism superfluous. "Grant a simple archetypal creature, like the ... [lungfish] Lepidosiren, with the five senses & some vestige of mind & I believe Natural Selection will account for production of every Vertebrate animal." [192]

This statement was made early on after the publication of *Origin*, before he had endured the incessant attacks on natural selection. Eventually, Darwin's system gained acceptance, and no one seemed to care if he acknowledged that the undergirding principle might not be valid. It has been said today that all of the main principles in *Origin* have now been refuted by evolutionists themselves, but does anyone care?

---

[191] Randall Hedtke, Secrets of the Sixth Edition, Darwin Discredits His Own Theory, 2010, p. 37
[192] Adrian Desmond, Huxley, From Devil's Disciple to Evolution's High Priest, 1997, p. 258

Is there any other scientific hypothesis where the original basic principles have now been found to be 100% false, but people go right on building their science on that theory?

There is another possible reason Darwin became lax about defending his hypothesis. By 1872, social Darwinism had gained public acceptance to the point that the scientific aspect of it was no longer an issue. Social Darwinism postulates that all norms and functions of society are evolving. It is a convenient concept for people who want to change society to their liking. People like John Dewey were more than willing to sell biological evolution as if it was a locked-down concept because of its utility in spreading their progressive social agenda. If biological evolution is not valid it makes it hard to believe in social evolution. Hedtke writes:

> There is evidence that the main attraction to evolutionary hypothesis for some of the founders was not the "scientificness" of it, but the negative effect it had on organized religion. Evolutionary views were seen as a way to advance their philosophy while diminishing the influence of religion. [193]

Julian Huxley, one of the grandsons of Thomas Huxley, wrote of Darwin:

> He was an atheist [not true, according to Darwin himself], and Darwin's real achievement was to remove the whole idea of God as a creator of organisms from the sphere of rational discussion. [194]

If God is not even allowed to take credit for creating the cosmos, who is going to allow Him to set the rules for living in it?

The German evolutionist, Ernst Haeckel, a Darwin contemporary and admirer, also gave us a telling comment on the relevance of evolution:

> Christianity had been superseded by a worship of humanity in general combined with enthusiasm for the

---

[193] Randall Hedtke, Secrets of the Sixth Edition, Darwin Discredits His Own Theory, 2010, p. 136
[194] Randall Hedtke, Secrets of the Sixth Edition, Darwin Discredits His Own Theory, 2010, p. 136

enlightened minds of classical antiquity and hatred against the ecclesiastical reaction. [195]

Ernst Haeckel was living in the midst of all that change and was one of the main instigators of it. He's telling on himself and all of his friends. I could not put it any more succinctly. Should there be any doubt that humanism came about because of the open door that was created for it by evolution?

A story came to light years after Darwin's death regarding a Christian evangelist known as Lady Hope. She was invited to Charles Darwin's house for a visit in the early autumn of 1881, some six months before he died. He was in bed most of the time then, but still very sharp mentally. She found him reading from the book of Hebrews. He exclaimed that he enjoyed that book very much. When she expressed some consternation that his view of our origins contradicts the Bible, he had the following comment about the days of long ago when he formulated his ideas on evolution:

> I was a young man with unformed ideas. I threw out queries, suggestions, wondering all the time over everything; and to my astonishment the ideas took like wildfire. People made a religion of them.[196]

I don't know whether the story is true. There are strong protagonists both ways. I tend to believe that it is. If one is interested in the full story, Herbert's book covers it well and in depth. Whether or not it is true has nothing to do with our analysis of Darwin's impact on evolution, but I find the above quote extremely pertinent. No statement could more accurately describe my views regarding Charles Darwin after thousands of pages of inquiry and nearly half a century of studying his life. The statement is so appropriate it seems like it could not have been made up. Nor could the result of his book be better described. People did make a religion of evolution, which this book contends was by design. As the evolutionist, Michael Ruse, has stated, that was true of evolution in the beginning and it is still true of evolution today.

---

[195] Randall Hedtke, Secrets of the Sixth Edition, Darwin Discredits His Own Theory, 2010, p. 137
[196] David Herbert, Charles Darwin's Religious Views, From Creationist To Evolutionist, 2009, p. 145

Darwin had no illusions, unlike many others, that his work was real science. In one of those confidential letters to Asa Gray he writes:

> I am quite conscious that my speculations run quite beyond the bounds of true science.[197]

Unlike the other giants of evolution, Charles Darwin was not aggressive in his attacks upon Christianity, though he certainly had conflicts with it. Hutton, Lyell, Huxley and Dewey, along with many of the other lesser lights had a deep antipathy for organized religion that Charles Darwin did not share. He just never made up his mind about what to believe. Because of that, it was easier for him to stop defending his hypothesis when it came under severe attack.

He was a very kind man. He was very generous with the local church that his wife and children attended. He supported a local temperance organization. He initially called the natives of Tierra Del Fuego the lowest beings in the human race and a link between the apes and man. He stated that there was no way that race of people could be civilized. Later, he learned that a missionary friend of his, who had also been a part of the *Beagle* voyage, had gone there, and had some success converting many of them to Christianity. From that time until the end of his life, he was a regular supporter of that mission.

A telling comment was made about Darwin by British political journalist, Dennis Sewell, a believer in evolution. This was his answer when asked if, all things considered, he believed Darwin was a great luminary in the path of human progress:

> What has the theory of evolution done for the practical benefit of humanity? It's helped our understanding of ourselves, yet compared to, say, the discovery of penicillin or the invention of the World Wide Web, I wonder why Darwin occupies this position at the pinnacle of esteem. I can only imagine he has been put there by a vast public relations exercise.[198]

---

[197] Randall Hedtke, Secrets of the Sixth Edition, Darwin Discredits His Own Theory, 2010, p. 138
[198] Time Magazine on-line, http://news.yahoo.com/s/time/20091124/hl_time/08599194248300/print, 11/24/2009

Oh, Mr. Sewell, if you only knew! It's the greatest public relations exercise in modern times, and Thomas Henry Huxley was just the man for the job. What Darwin lacked in aggression and focus, his friend, Thomas Huxley, had in abundance. Just as Lyell rescued Hutton's hypothesis from the garbage bin of history, so Huxley took Darwin's idea and forced it into mainstream society and even into the church.

Many had broached the subject of evolution in the 17th, 18th and 19th centuries, but no one had given a detailed outline of how it might have happened. That job fell to Charles Darwin, but bringing the idea to a point where it would be accepted by mainstream society was too big a job for one man. Darwin was the life of the party, but after that it was Tom Huxley and others who drove the car home.

CHAPTER 6
THOMAS HUXLEY

T HOMAS Huxley (1825-1895), more than any other man, was responsible for the meteoric rise of evolution from an interesting concept involving a few men on the fringes of science to a generally accepted philosophical view that still passes for science today. He was aggressive, intelligent and had the ability to speak before crowds, drawing large numbers of people to hear his talks. He always kept before him his objective and was seldom deterred.

Cyril Bibby had the following comments on Huxley's talents:

> Wallace [Alfred Russel Wallace, the co-discoverer of natural selection] experienced in his presence a feeling of awe and inferiority which neither Darwin nor Lyell produced; both Darwin and Hooker declared that in comparison with Huxley they felt quite infantile in intellect. And it was not a narrow or merely scholastic sort of intellect; it was many-dimensioned and as effective in practical affairs as in abstract reasoning. As a modern American writer has perhaps too colorfully put it, "Huxley had more talents than two lifetimes could have developed. He could think, draw, speak, write, inspire, lead, negotiate, and wage multifarious war against earth

and heaven with the cool professional ease of an acrobat supporting nine people on his shoulders at once."[199]

Randall Hedtke writes:

> It is no wonder that the reclusive Darwin was overjoyed when Huxley found favor with his hypothesis and agreed to publicly defend it. It is no wonder, also, that Huxley should be attracted to evolutionary views as a weapon against established religion, which was anathema to him.[200]

Desmond describes the scene immediately after *Origin* was released:

> All eyes were now fixed on the *Origin*. Darwin was on tenterhooks: "I long to hear what Huxley thinks," he told Hooker on 20 November. The following day he heard. Huxley "is vastly pleased with it," Hooker wrote. He was even thinking of turning over his next Royal Institution talk to the book. Darwin's mood brightened. How "unspeakably grand if Huxley were to lecture on the subject."
>
> A public stand became imperative after the *Athenaeum* fired a "contemptible" opening shot at the *Origin*. The book was a snub to the clergy and an insult to humanity...Darwin was furious at the way the reviewer "sets the Priests at me & leaves me to their mercies"....
>
> "Since I read Von Bar nine years ago no work on Natural History I have met with has made so great an impression upon me", Huxley rallied Darwin...The new Reformation [evolution replacing Divine Revelation] seemed closer than he had thought. He reminded Darwin that "some of your friends...are endowed with an amount of combativeness which (though you have often & justly rebuked it) may stand you in good stead." Now Darwin was glad of it. Never one to enter the public fray, he needed a champion as Huxley needed a cause.

---

[199]Cyril Bibby, Scientist Extraordinary, the Life and Scientific Work of Thomas Henry Huxley, 1825-1895, 1972, p. 6

[200]Randall Hedtke, Secrets of the Sixth Edition, Darwin Discredits His Own Theory, 2010, p. 14

The two, so utterly unlike, seemed made for the occasion. Darwin's jubilation took a more traditional turn, "Like a good Catholic, who has received extreme unction, I can now sing 'nunc dimittis'". [201]

Hedtke puts it all into perspective:

It is ironic that the mark that Huxley achieved should be most popularly recognized as that of "Darwin's bulldog," a subordinate position to a man of lesser talents. Huxley is said to have enjoyed the luxuries of genius while Darwin possessed the bare essentials.[202]

Huxley's Early Years

Tom Huxley was born on May 4, 1825 in Ealing, just west of London, the youngest of six children. His mother was forty years old when he was born. His father was a teacher in the Ealing School,

Young Thomas Huxley

which Tom started attending when he was eight years old. The school, like many others in the area, was suffering because of the recession, and enrollment was down. It closed in 1835 when Tom was ten. Those two years were all of the education he got until he was able to attend Sydenham College at the age of sixteen.

Tom's father, George Huxley, got a job managing the new Savings Bank in Coventry in the midlands of England, and the family moved there in 1835. George had grown up on a farm there just outside town, and his father, Tom's grandfather, had also owned a large inn there. Coventry was known for silk-weaving. Unfortunately, it turned out that people in the weaving

---

[201] Adrian Desmond, Huxley, From Devil's Disciple to Evolution's High Priest, 1997, pp. 259, 260

[201] Randall Hedtke, Secrets of the Sixth Edition, Darwin Discredits His Own Theory, 2010, p. 15

business were distrustful of the new concept of banks. As the bank struggled mightily, so George struggled to support his family.

Tom had a strong desire to obtain knowledge, possibly seeing it as the only way to make something of himself.

> Not satisfied with the ordinary length of the day, he used,
> when a boy of twelve, to light his candle before dawn, pin
> a blanket round his shoulders, and sit up in bed to read
> Hutton's "Geology." [203]

We are told that young Tom Huxley read Hutton's *Theory of the Earth* twice in his youth. It appears that it was the original book written by Hutton himself, not John Playfair's much more readable rewrite, a testament to his high level of interest in the subject. Judging by the apparent pleasure he got from that book, it must have had a profound effect on his psyche, and may be a prime reason why he so readily adopted Darwin's hypothesis when he first heard about it. So, this becomes the third leg extending forward in time from James Hutton, dramatically influencing the following century. The other two were his effect on Erasmus Darwin (who had an effect on the thinking of his grandson, Charles Darwin) and Charles Lyell, who also affected Charles Darwin's thinking as a young man, and then later as a friend and confidant.

Huxley wrote a note to his mother in April of 1841, as he was studying to enter college the following fall. He was staying with his sister, Lizzie, and her husband, John Salt, in London:

> I got the books alright but is there not a Latin Grammar at
> home, & an Euclid? I am glad my father sent Hutton for I
> like it much the best but the college requires Euclid. [204]

Tom had three brothers and two sisters. The only two that he was close to were his brother, Jim, who was four years older than he, and his sister Lizzie, who was nine years his senior. Lizzie doted on him, even after he had long since reached maturity. Both Lizzie and his other sister, Ellen, married medical men in 1839.

---

[203] Life and letters of Thomas Henry Huxley, by his son Leonard Huxley, Volume I, Chapter 1.1 1825-1842
[204] Adrian Desmond, Huxley, From Devil's Disciple to Evolution's High Priest, 1997, p. 14

Ellen's husband, John Cooke, started training Tom in medicine when he was thirteen. Cooke was a teacher of medicine, not a practicing doctor, but what he taught included the dissecting of cadavers and surgeries on live patients. These were traumatizing experiences for a thirteen-year-old, but it made Tom grow up in a hurry. Cooke apprenticed Tom at the age of fifteen to a general practitioner named Thomas Chandler, who had a practice in London's squalid east end, the stuff of Dickens' writings. The horror that Tom saw in the doctor's office then took a back seat to what he saw in the streets. Extreme poverty and the most miserable sanitation and disease were almost too much to bear. I'm sure it contributed to Tom's intense desire get a proper education, so that he would not personally ever end up in a place like that.

In the fall of 1841, Tom enrolled in Sydenham College, which was behind University College Hospital in London. It was no Oxford or Cambridge, but it had the potential to get him a degree in medicine and provide an opportunity to expand his world. Pervading every nook and cranny of Sydenham College was a deep antipathy for anything Oxbridge (the word used to describe anything having to do with Oxford or Cambridge Universities). The collusion of the Anglican Church with those two universities ensured special privileges to those who were Oxbridge-trained. In medicine, that meant the Oxbridge graduates got the top jobs while the people graduating from places like Sydenham would be general practitioners in the slums and lower class areas. I'm sure anyone who had been through what Tom Huxley had been through would have a pretty low view of Christianity as represented by the Anglican Church of that day. Compounding that would have been the indifference of the church to the grinding poverty of the poor. People were needlessly dying of starvation and disease. A little humanitarian help could have prevented a great deal of suffering. Eventually the government provided some help, but the church did not directly respond to the needs of the poor in a meaningful way. Tom would have been aware of that, and throughout his life he demonstrated that he was aware of the needs of those less fortunate than he. In later years after Dr. Cooke had passed on, his sister, Ellen became an alcoholic, and Tom put her on an allowance. Many times she blew that and came asking for more. I'm not aware that he ever turned her down. His extended family was a disaster, between drugs and alcohol and various kinds of graft, there was no end to the requests for funds from Tom. Even though he was not a wealthy man, it seems he helped every time he was asked.

In the fall of 1842, when Tom was seventeen, he and his brother, Jim, were admitted to Charing Cross Hospital's medical school. He had earned a scholarship allowing him to attend free. It was another step in Tom's knowledge that would be useful after those years in his work involving anatomy. He spent three years there and graduated with honors.

On HMS *Rattlesnake*

A friend from the college, whose father had been a ship's captain on many ships in the Atlantic and Caribbean, got him interested in going to sea. The friend, Joseph Fayrer, told Tom all about going to exotic ports when he had sailed as a midshipman on some of those ships. As a trained surgeon, Tom had an inside track toward getting on as a surgeon's mate, which paid pretty well by Tom's standards. At Fayrer's urging, he wrote directly to the Surgeon General of the Navy, Sir William Burnett, requesting consideration for a position on a ship in Her Majesty's Navy. With Fayrer's help he wrote the following:

> Having a great desire to enter the Medical Department of Her Majesty's Naval Service and being at the same time totally unprovided with any friendly influence by which the attainment of my object might be accelerated–I take the liberty of addressing myself directly to you as the head of the department... [205]

In addition to his excellent educational credentials, he had to provide five references as to his character. In March, 1846, he was informed that he had been accepted and would be going out that year. He was put on HMS *Rattlesnake*, whose job it was to survey the coast of New Guinea and the ship passages in that part of the world. It was also their responsibility to secure the northern part of Australia from encroachment by other nations who might like to claim that sparsely populated part of the island continent for themselves.

The *Rattlesnake* departed Portsmouth harbor on December 11, 1846 with Captain Owen Stanley of the famous Stanley family of England guiding her. They were to be gone four years. The first stop, as always on those long English voyages, was the Island of Madeira.

---

[205] Ibid, pp. 36, 37

Huxley, knowing that Darwin reported finding on the deck of the *Beagle* red grit from the Sahara winds, looked for the same on the *Rattlesnake* but found none. They were eight days removed from port, but already the climate felt tropical, even though they were a good bit above the tropic of cancer. They spent December 19th through the 25th on Madeira.

Being a surgeon's mate on one of these voyages meant also being the ship's naturalist. Huxley had spent a fortune (for him) on a microscope that he took with him. He also had a few books he had purchased, among them Buffon's natural history. Buffon was one of the first naturalists to openly espouse a much longer history for the earth than was allowed by the Bible. Buffon was more than likely a prime source of information for a young James Hutton a hundred years earlier. Huxley also had nets with which to catch creatures from the sea for dissection. Having such an active naturalist aboard caught the fancy of the midshipmen, and maybe prevented some boredom.

On the 26th of December, they set off for Rio de Janeiro. After an exciting week in Rio, it was off across the Atlantic to the Cape of Good Hope. They were secluded there for a month longer than they planned because of the weather in the Indian Ocean. Finally, after a 24-day tack across the Indian Ocean, they came to the tropical island of Mauritius on May 4, 1847, his twenty-second birthday. On the 13th of May, they were on their way to Tasmania, an unscheduled destination, but one Captain Stanley made anyway, since his brother and his new wife had recently moved there. They sailed into Storm Bay and the new city of Hobart on the 24th of June. Every port of call up to that point had been decidedly non-English in nature, with tropical foliage and bright sun, sparkling seas and everything else one sees in the tropics. But Tasmania, especially Hobart, had England written all over it. It brought about some homesickness.

On the 3rd of July, they made their way into Port Jackson Harbor and Sydney, Australia, the penal colony that was in the process of trying to reform itself into a respectable copy of the motherland. They were there three months. Huxley, though not exactly a socialite, was coerced into taking part in some of the social activities, which were numerous. At one of the dances he met Henrietta Heathorn. What had become a rather monotonous trip now had some excitement. She was later to become his wife.

On the 11th of October, they sailed north to begin their mapping of a passage through the Great Barrier Reef for the future use of steamers. They reached Moreton Bay near present day Brisbane on

October 17th, and were there until November 4th. As they headed north, they could find no fresh water to restock their supplies, so they had to go back to Sydney. That took five weeks. It didn't break Tom's heart though, as he would get to see "Nettie" again.

On April 29th 1848, they were on their way north from Sydney once again. They made their way slowly up the coast, surveying as they went, tacking back and forth across the bays and inlets. They let off a party of 13 at Rockingham, whose job it was to make their way north overland and meet up with the ship at Cape York 600 miles to the north, the most northerly point of mainland Australia. On September 5th, the *Rattlesnake* reached Cape York, but there was no sign of the overland group. The cloying heat and humidity were so oppressive Huxley stopped writing in his diary, and as hot as it was on ship, he had no energy to go on land when they docked. On November 2nd, Stanley gave up on the other party and headed west. They circumnavigated the Australian continent and were back to Sydney via Perth, Melbourne and Tasmania on January 24th, 1849. On March 5th, a schooner arrived at Sydney with the three survivors out of 13 from the overland expedition. The unspeakable horrors they had endured were the talk of Sydney for a long time. Between starvation, disease, predation by aborigines and the vexing of the mind that takes place under those conditions in that kind of heat, they had long odds against them. William Carron, the Australian botanist, was one of the three that was still alive but he was so emaciated his elbow and hip bone were protruding through his skin.[206]

Again, they left Sydney harbor on May 8th, 1849, bound for New Guinea this time. They went to the most easterly islands of New Guinea, and made their way westward as they took soundings for future steamer passages. Along the way, they had a few encounters with the Papuans, who had a reputation for being some of the fiercest people on earth. Huxley and a few of the other sailors were enjoying the encounters, and although they were cautious, they didn't think there was much to fear most of the time. The captain, Owen Stanley, however, was quite fearful, and refused to have anything to do with them. As they worked their way west, he shut down all contact with the natives, staying some distance off shore. Ironically, though, the highest mountain range in Papua New Guinea is named after him. It runs right down the center of the

---

[206] Ibid, pp. 109, 110

island, and he never set foot upon it! Stanley was feeling the stress of commanding this group of men with the constant threat of being sunk on a shoal or being eaten by some islanders. Of course I'm sure he felt responsible for the disaster that happened to the overland expedition. Huxley expressed the view that Stanley was becoming more unstable all the time.

Upon coming back to Cape York they were met by a provisions ship, and mail was delivered. That is when Stanley learned that his brother, Charlie, whom they had stopped to see in Tasmania on their first trip to Sydney, had died of a stomach infection. Upon reaching Sydney, he got another letter telling him that his father, the Bishop of Norwich, had died in September. Then, while they were in port at Sydney, the 38-year-old Stanley, working alone on the ship one evening, had a seizure and died. Such was life on the sea in those days. Any voyage could be expected to lose several of its passengers before the final port of call. However, it wasn't usually the captain.

May 2nd, 1850 they left Sydney for the last time with extra passengers aboard on their way to England. All told, they had 230 people on their 107-foot ship, with provisions as well. It was a sad time for Huxley, because even though he and Nettie had agreed that they would be married, they had decided that he needed to get established professionally first, and neither of them knew when or if that would happen. He had gotten word that the papers he had sent home had met with success in the scientific community, so he had high hopes that it would be sooner rather than later.

From Sydney, their next port of call was New Zealand. It was unscheduled, but the *Rattlesnake* was leaking badly, so they decided to re-caulk part of it there. It was only three days, but it gave Huxley a chance to do a little exploring, and he liked what he saw of New Zealand. From there they made their way toward Cape Horn, a dangerous place any time of year, but especially so in wintertime, and they would be there in mid-winter. But, other than being very cold and having rough seas, they had no complications. They landed at Chatham, England on November 2nd, 1850, glad to be home. Huxley was also anxious to start his career in science.

After the *Rattlesnake*

Like Darwin, Huxley's science had preceded him, and like Darwin, he met Charles Lyell in his first month back. Within the first year back, he met John Tyndall, who was to become a lifelong friend, and Joseph Hooker, who also became a good friend. He also met

Richard Owen, who supplied him with valuable references. Owen, who had become known by that time as one of Britain's great men of science, was not someone Huxley liked, but he knew he had to put up with him until he became established himself. It wasn't too many years, though, until Huxley began offending Owen on a regular basis. Huxley enjoyed every minute of it. Owen is most famous nowadays as the one who coined the term *dinosaur* (terrible lizard).

While he found that he had gained some notoriety, and there was potential to capitalize upon it, being an accomplished scientist in those days did not automatically convert to making lots of money, or even to job security. He cut a deal with the Navy to remain in the service, but be stationed near London and to do research. The pay was piddling and did nothing for the huge debt he'd piled up, but it put bread on the table until he could find something better. He then learned there was more money for him in writing about science than doing it, and he learned he had a knack for writing. He also had a flair for controversy that became apparent when he began his writing career. At the end of 1853, it had been three years since his voyage on the *Rattlesnake* and he still hadn't procured anything stable enough to allow him to bring Nettie over and get married.

1854 was the year his fortunes changed. Robert Jameson, who had been the professor of natural history at Edinburgh for over fifty years, died, leaving an opening. Huxley's friend, Edward Forbes, who until that time had been the professor of natural history at the Royal School of Mines, was chosen to succeed Jameson, while Huxley followed Forbes at the School of Mines. Forbes had actually occupied three chairs at the School of Mines, natural history, geology and the geologic survey. Huxley got the first two, but didn't feel qualified for the third. A year later, however, when that position opened up again, he expressed a desire for it, since he had some exposure to geology during that time. He was given that chair as well. Combined with the writing he was doing, he was then earning a pretty good living.

Huxley began branching out. He gave talks to varied audiences, to academics and to working people. Many of his talks were transcribed and became articles in magazines. He was a regular contributor to the *Westminster Review*. He gave lectures in institutions.

Allegedly, he was involved in the famous debate with Bishop Samuel Wilberforce at Oxford in 1860. Wilberforce asked him whether it was on his mother's side or his father's that the ape appeared in his ancestry. That, of course, brought a howl from the audience. Huxley's response was that he would rather have an ape in his ancestry than be a man of great talent but one who suppresses debate upon such subjects (implying that Wilberforce was doing just that). Since there was no written record of those events at the moment they happened it is not known how accurate the above story is, but it seems likely that there was some kind of interaction of the sort between the two men.

In 1863, he released his book, *Man's Place in Nature*, which at that time was the most aggressive defense of man originating from an ape that had been seen in the public sphere. Lyell published his *Antiquity of Man* in the same year, but even though its title makes it sound like a strong evolutionary statement, Lyell's book only discussed the possibilities. It did not make a definitive declaration in support of the evolution of man. Darwin was quite disappointed with Lyell on that account.

After helping to start two short-lived periodicals, Huxley was a major player in the startup of the magazine *Nature,* which is still published and has a large readership today.

Huxley served in various capacities on numerous scientific boards and commissions. He was secretary of the Royal Society from 1871 to 1880 and president of that august body from 1883 to 1885, when he resigned. He was president of the Geological Society from 1868 to 1870. He was president of the British Association for the Advancement of Science from 1869 to 1870.

Huxley, the mesmerizing artist

By the 1870s, he was beginning to receive honors of all kinds, both within Britain and elsewhere. He was knighted in Sweden. By the mid 1880s he was beginning to have health problems, which caused him to retire from official duties in 1885, when he was 60. The British Parliament voted him a handsome pension of 1,500 pounds per month. He still wrote profusely and was still much in the news, but he spent more time at the sea shore than he had previously. Despite all the good science he had done, he was most known by the public as the man who brought evolution into the mainstream of society. He was also, more than any other man, responsible for changing science from an avocation for wealthy men to a profession for which training was required. By the time he retired, a person could go to school to learn science instead of having to train in medicine and hope to get the science on the side.

New York newspaper depicts Huxley smashing the statue of Moses with the bust of Milton

Thomas Huxley died in 1895 at the age of seventy. Despite there being no announcement of his funeral 200 people showed up. There was no mention of a higher power, which was just the way he wanted it, but undoubtedly a big disappointment to Nettie. Huxley was a caring father and husband, and helped his extended family on numerous occasions. He supported social causes that helped the poor and under-privileged. He advanced the cause of education in Britain more than any other man. He served on the newly-created London school board from 1870 to 1885. His friends knew him as a kind and understanding man. His enemies knew him as ruthless. He had nowhere near the tact of Charles Lyell, but unlike Lyell, with Huxley you knew where you stood. He lamented the moral depravity he saw around him in the England of the 1880s and 1890s, but ironically, did not realize that he was partly responsible for it by his continued attacks on Christianity and promotion of evolution, which was diametrically opposed to the Bible.

Huxley and Natural Selection

After the publication of Charles Darwin's book in 1860, evolution was embraced by a large segment of society, because, unlike the previous discussions of evolution, such as those by Buffon, Hutton, Erasmus Darwin, Lamarck, Lyell, Chambers, and others, Charles Darwin provided a mechanism to make it work, or so it was thought. He provided details, even if the details were just the out-workings of his overactive imagination. Charles Lyell believed in the production of new species, but he offered no suggestion as to how it might have happened.

The big idea that separated Darwin's system from all the others was natural selection. Darwin adapted Thomas Malthus' ideas on population control to suit his purposes for evolution. But, as we showed in the last chapter, after eleven years of defending his theory against attack, Darwin himself seemed to lose enthusiasm for natural selection, as he admitted in his sixth edition of *Origin* in 1872. His closest friends, Joseph Hooker and Charles Lyell, also remained unconvinced that it was a valid mechanism to accomplish all that Darwin had given it credit for. The upshot is that Huxley, "Darwin's Bulldog," never believed in natural selection either, at least not in the type that Darwin described in his book. Huxley obviously spoke in public at great lengths about evolution, and it was no accident he got credit for making it popular. But he never used natural selection in his talks. He used morphology (the similarity of various body parts in different animals) to argue for descent from a common ancestor. He was a very good artist, and could hold audiences spellbound for long periods of time drawing those parts and showing their similarities. A creationist would simply say, "It shows they were created by the same designer," but it is easy to see those predisposed to believe in evolution accepting Huxley's arguments unreservedly. Huxley, like Lyell and Hooker, never publicly said anything that would raise the issue of whether he believed in natural selection, but there is plenty of information showing that he did not.[207]

---

[207] Ibid, pp. 268, 269

Darwin's frustration with Huxley over the matter was evident after one of Huxley's lectures that Darwin had the rare opportunity to attend. Darwin states:

> I succeeded in persuading myself for 24 hours that Huxley's lecture was a success. Parts were eloquent & good & all *very* bold, & I heard strangers say "what a good lecture." I told Huxley so… [but] after conversation with others & more reflection I must confess that as an Exposition of the doctrine the Lecture seems to me an entire failure…. He gave no just idea of *natural selection*. [208]

Knowing Darwin's great respect for Huxley, Huxley's continued rejection of natural selection may be a major factor in why Darwin finally lost confidence in it.

In *Darwiniana*, published posthumously in 1896, the year after Huxley's death, Huxley makes the following comments:

> The Darwinian hypothesis…may be stated in a very few words; all species have been produced by the development of variety from common stock…by the process of natural selection, which process is essentially identical with that artificial selection by which man has originated the races of domestic animals…[but] without the breeder there would be no selection, and without the selection no race…it must be proved that there is in Nature some power which takes the place of man, and performs a selection *sua sponte*. [209]

Huxley is reiterating the point that if we can use all the resources available to man to produce a new species, does that mean it can happen by accident in nature? Additionally, he had previously made the point that man, with all his technology at his disposal, had *not* been able to produce new species. So we have two major stumbling blocks disclosed by Huxley that prevent a rational person from having confidence in natural selection.

We saw previously that Darwin eventually grew tired of defending natural selection, and Huxley, evolution's greatest salesman, never did believe in it, so why did evolution not fail the test and end up as just another crazy idea that we all laugh about?

---

[208] Ibid, p. 270
[209] Thomas Huxley, Darwiniana, 1896, pp. 71, 17

The answer lies in how evolution could be used to further societal causes of the secularists, and there was no one individual that this concept applied to more than to Thomas Henry Huxley. If the public could be talked into believing it, who cared if it was true? I believe that Huxley may have believed that evolution did happen, but believing that just how it happened is unknown.

What Did Huxley Think About the Church and Christianity?

Huxley states his position as follows:

> My screed was meant as a protest against Theology & Parsondom...both of which are in my mind the natural & irreconcilable enemies of Science. Few see it but I believe we are on the Eve of a new Reformation and if I have a wish to live thirty years, it is that I may see the foot of Science on the necks of her enemies. But the new religion will not be a worship of the intellect alone.[210]

Huxley lays out his intent with respect to Genesis in a letter to Frederick Dyster:

> I do not believe that any meaning which would be put by a *disinterested* Hebrew scholar upon the words of Genesis is in any way reconcilable with the most elementary and best established facts of geology. If it be permissible to turn and twist the Scripture phraseology as the rationalistic orthodox do on Genesis, I for my part will undertake to prove that rape, murder and arson are positively enjoined in Exodus.[211]

Huxley laments the situation that modern Christianity is still practiced while other practices of the ancients have been forsaken:

> The myths of Paganism are as dead as Osiris or Zeus, and the man who should revive them...would be justly laughed to scorn; but the coeval imaginations current among the rude inhabitants of Palestine...have unfortunately not yet shared their fate, but, even at this

---

[210] T. H. Huxley, Letters and Diary, January 30, 1859, To Frederick Dyster
[211] Ibid

day, are regarded by nine-tenths of the civilised world as
the authoritative standard of fact…[212]

Desmond describes the scene:

> With this Heavenly sanction the Sultan of biology
> [Huxley] slaughtered the orthodox. And after the carnage
> he gave thanks, as "Extinguished theologians lie about the
> cradle of every science as the strangled snakes beside that
> of Hercules." The orthodox army of occupation was left
> "bleeding and crushed if not annihilated." [213]

The X Club purchased a weekly periodical called the *Reader*, in
order to have their own voice in the public debate about science and
church/state issues. To refresh your memory, the X Club consisted
of nine men. Those nine men were a part of the club until their
death, and they were not replaced. The names familiar to our readers
would be Huxley, Hooker, Tyndall, and the atheist writer, Herbert
Spencer. Huxley wrote a scathing article in the *Reader* in which he
said,

> Science exhibits no immediate intention of signing a treaty
> of peace with her old opponent [religion], nor of being
> content with anything short of absolute victory and
> uncontrolled domination over the whole realm of the
> intellect. [214]

In writing to his old protégé at Oxford, George Rolleston, who
was critical of Huxley's harshness in the article, Huxley stated:

> The fact is that you have read into the article what you
> know or think you know of my opinions…there is not a
> word in that article opposed to any forms of belief in a
> revelation of the Unknowable…. All that I affirm is that all
> these beliefs & traditions will have to find a scientific basis
> & that those which cannot…will have to go. [215]

---

[212] Adrian Desmond, Huxley, From Devil's Disciple to Evolution's High
Priest, 1997, p. 262
[213] Ibid, p. 262
[214] T. H. Huxley, The Reader, Science and Church Policy, December, 1864
[215] Adrian Desmond, Huxley, From Devil's Disciple to Evolution's High
Priest, 1997, p. 332

To any modern Christian who wants to find a way to include evolution into their theology, let them consider this warning from the founder of modern evolution himself. He wanted no truck with Christianity in any way, shape, or form! It was his way or the highway and he wasn't about to discuss compromises, so why are people now saying the two worldviews can coexist? They weren't designed to coexist; they were designed for war, and today, the occupying generals of evolution feel the same way.

Huxley's best friend and coadjutant, John Tyndall, had the following advice for all who opposed them:

> We claim, and we shall wrest from theology, the entire domain of cosmological theory. [216]

Of course, the logical course for Huxley's opposition to Christianity was to proceed from Genesis to eventually reach the New Testament and Christ Himself. Huxley was a member of the Metaphysical Club, as was Prime Minister Gladstone. Gladstone was a defender of Biblical history, but was not the most informed, and because of that, took a beating whenever Huxley took a notion to expose him in public (which was often). On January 11, 1876, Huxley addressed the Metaphysical Club on his views about the resurrection of Christ. He went into a long discussion about how Jesus only appeared to be dead when he was taken off the cross and put into the tomb. He takes the usual course of those who make such arguments, leaving out many facts that support the standard Biblical interpretation and then claiming that there isn't enough evidence to say that he came back to life from the dead. Of course, like Hutton, Lyell and Darwin before him, he asserts that the writers of the gospels (he doesn't include John's gospel) were too primitive and crude to have known any better and couldn't possibly have been able to communicate the truth in the situation in a way that a modern reader could understand. He states in his discourse:

> ...the question whether Jesus died or not, in our modern scientific sense of the word, not only never can be answered, but never could be answered. And if it is not possible for us to say whether the body of Jesus underwent molecular death or not, it would be a mere

---

[216] Ibid, p. 445

futility to discuss the further question, whether he was miraculously resuscitated or not.... When such a story as the miraculous version of the Resurrection is presented to them [modern scientists] for acceptance, they not only decline to believe it, but they assert that, from their point of view, it would be a moral dereliction to pretend to believe it. Looking at fidelity to truth as the highest of all human duties, they regard with feelings approaching to abhorrence, that cynical infidelity which, when Reason reports "No evidence," and Conscience warns that intellectual honesty means absolute submission to evidence, attempts to drown the voice of both by loud assertion, backed by appeals to the weakness and to the cowardice of human nature.[217]

Later in 1876, Huxley made his first trip to America, a trip that was made especially exciting because it would give him his first chance in over thirty years to see his favorite sibling, his sister, Lizzie, who by then lived in Tennessee with her husband, the physician, John Salt. Salt had done something, and it is not known to this day and probably never will be, what it was, but it required them to make a hasty retreat out of Britain to the continent. They still didn't feel safe there, so they went to back country Tennessee in order to obtain the anonymity they felt was necessary. By that time they had taken the name of "Scott" instead of "Salt." Desmond comments about Huxley's arrival in New York Harbor:

Catching his first sight of the Manhattan skyline on 5 August he asked about the two conspicuous towers. Told they were the *Tribune* and Western Union Telegraph buildings, "Ah," he replied, "that is American. In the Old World the first things you see as you approach a great city are steeples; here you see...centres of intelligence." [218]

As happened so often, something out of France was causing consternation among Christian Brits. This time it was Albert Reville's *Prolegomenes de l'Histoire des Religions,* which was furthering the cause of the X Clubbers by devaluing the Bible, but using a

---

[217] T. H. Huxley, Address to the Metaphysical Society, January 11, 1876, The Evidence of the Miracle of the Resurrection
[218] Adrian Desmond, Huxley, From Devil's Disciple to Evolution's High Priest, 1997, p. 470

philosophical point of view, rather than a scientific one. William Gladstone, the former prime minister, out of office at that time, was writing about how modern discoveries in paleontology were actually validating the Genesis account of creation. In an 1886 essay, Huxley gives his view of the import of Genesis and how it differs from Gladstone's:

> My belief, on the contrary, is, and long has been, that the pentateuchal story of the creation is simply a myth. I suppose it to be an hypothesis respecting the origin of the universe which some ancient thinker found himself able to reconcile with his knowledge, or what he thought was knowledge, of the nature of things, and therefore assumed to be true. As such, I hold it to be not merely an interesting, but a venerable, monument of a stage in the mental progress of mankind; and I find it difficult to suppose that any one who is acquainted with the cosmogonies of other nations–and especially with those of the Egyptians and the Babylonians, with whom the Israelites were in such frequent and intimate communication–should consider it to possess either more, or less, scientific importance than may be allotted to these.[219]

Huxley was furious that a man of Gladstone's stature had been so outspoken in defending Genesis. In private he was fit to be tied. As with the uniformitarians of today, there was no reasoning about the matter, only name-calling and belittling of his opponent. Nettie, in private, exposed the fact that Huxley had come unglued about this. He was so polished and reasonable in public. But, those who have no real points in their favor usually do get angry. It is the only response they have left.

Preparatory to Huxley's book, *The Natural History of Christianity*, he wrote a forty-page article for the *Nineteenth Century* called *The Evolution of Theology*. In it he attempted to show that theology was a construct of man in ancient history, designed for the purpose of making intelligible that which the finite mind cannot fathom. He goes on to propose that it evolved just like everything else, being built upon by the ancient Jews, who conjured up the ghost known as Jahweh. In reading Huxley's article there is an overriding awareness

---

[219] T. H. Huxley, The Nineteenth Century, Mr. Gladstone and Genesis, 1886, pp. 191-205

that he regards ancient people as being very primitive, not capable of attaining to the accomplishments of 19th century man.

He proposed that Moses got the Ten Commandments and the moral teaching of the law, along with much ritual, from the Egyptians. Huxley had become aware that the new discoveries in Egypt, such as *The Book of the Dead*, revealed a moral code that was more advanced than what he had previously given the Egyptians credit for. He tries to draw a parallel between ancient Israel and primitive societies all over the world. He has some points, but the biggest point that this author took from it, and one overlooked by Huxley, is that it is one more evidence of the connectedness of all those societies at a recent period in time. An alternative to his view would be one world religion that manifested itself in a general revelation immediately after the Flood, and various cultures assimilated different parts of it. He marvels that animal sacrifice was known to be practiced all over the world, but why should that surprise us, when the Bible tells us that the first created family sacrificed animals, and our mutual ancestors, the family of Noah, made it their first priority to sacrifice animals upon landing in the Ark?

We saw previously that Huxley got quite upset when the prime minister delved into the field of science, which Huxley considered his own private domain, but he had no problem at all with putting on his theologian's cap when it seemed possible to grab a little of the theologian's territory. As he began to reach the last years of his life, he no longer disguised his religious interest behind science. The majority of his writing was about religion, not science. That should tell us much about what his motive was for his advocacy of evolution.

The following quote should dispel all doubt that Tom Huxley understood well the battle he was waging. This is from an 1890 article he wrote in *The Nineteenth Century* called *The Lights of the Church and the Light of Science.*

> My utmost ingenuity does not enable me to discover a flaw in the argument thus briefly summarised. I am fairly at a loss to comprehend how any one, for a moment, can doubt that Christian theology must stand or fall with the historical trustworthiness of the Jewish Scriptures. The very conception of the Messiah, or Christ, is inextricably interwoven with Jewish history; the identification of Jesus of Nazareth with that Messiah rests upon the

interpretation of passages of the Hebrew Scriptures which have no evidential value unless they possess the historical character assigned to them. If the covenant with Abraham was not made; if circumcision and sacrifices were not ordained by Jahveh; if the "ten words" were not written by God's hand on the stone tables; if Abraham is more or less a mythical hero, such as Theseus; the story of the Deluge a fiction; that of the Fall a legend; and that of the creation the dream of a seer; if all these definite and detailed narratives of apparently real events have no more value as history than have the stories of the regal period of Rome–what is to be said about the Messianic doctrine, which is so much less clearly enunciated? And what about the authority of the writers of the books of the New Testament, who, on this theory, have not merely accepted flimsy fictions for solid truths, but have built the very foundations of Christian dogma upon legendary quicksands? [220]

If only modern theologians would take the same stand! He knew that if he could prove part of the scriptures were not true he could throw considerable doubt upon the authenticity of the rest of them. After using Darwinism to undermine the older doctrines of Christianity, such as the special creation and the Genesis Flood, he spent the latter years of his life attacking the rest of the historical narrative from Abraham to Christ and the Apostles. Nothing was sacred to Huxley, and no heretical argument was spared in attacking Christianity and the Church of England. Huxley mainly waged his war against Christianity through the periodicals. Desmond wrote about

the way Huxley made Christianity just another regional religion, with a largely borrowed mythological base. What was atheist fanaticism in the 1840s had become mainstream pulp by the 1890s. [George] Holyoake had been jailed 50 years earlier (to deny God then was treasonous in an Anglican State). Now working-class political weaponry had become middle-class professional ideology, and he [George Holyoake] gave up editing the *Reasoner* "because his views were abundantly advocated

---

[220] T. H. Huxley, The Nineteenth Century, The Lights of the Church and the Lights of Science, 1890

in the most respectable Quarterlies." There was no incarceration for Huxley. [221]

The Huxleys visited Downe, Darwin's home, years after Darwin had passed on. Darwin's wife, Emma, was still living there. The most telling part, as it relates to Huxley's influence on the world, is the reaction of the cook.

> The Huxleys visited Downe for the first time in years, but it was "rather sad" – even if Parslow the butler, looking in on old Emma, reminded them of the glory days. "What times those days were!" Huxley reminisced. He conjured up Homeric images, as if "warfare has been my business", something forced on him by the times… He was the man who had symbolized the hopes of the Unitarian and secularist manufacturers, the man whose coming had been dreaded by the old Iron Duke of Wellington [William Gladstone]. But in the naughty nineties no one cared – except, it seems, the new cook. She walked out on learning of the godless household she was expected to cater to. [222]

This woman was obviously a Bible-believing Christian, but to risk her job that way, she must have had very strong convictions about the evil caused by Tom Huxley.

In 1892, Huxley came out with his 625-page book, *Controverted Questions*, which was his agnostic take on seemingly every theological question. Desmond observes, "Ironically, after a life in science, his biggest book was of Biblical criticism. But it left an overall impression of ridiculing, not clerical naivety so much as Gladstone's obscurantism." [223]

Amazingly, despite his excellent study of the life of Huxley, Desmond still doesn't get it; it was never really about science at all. And if he's disappointed that Huxley only used ridicule, he should know that was one of the main weapons he ordinarily used when it came to his observations on Christianity, and that is still the modus operandi today when Christians point out the shortcomings of the secularist props, such as evolution. Instead of defending their worldview through rational discussion, the evolutionists ridicule the

---

[221] Adrian Desmond, Huxley, From Devil's Disciple to Evolution's High Priest, 1997, p. 587
[222] Ibid, p. 589
[223] Ibid, pp. 592, 593

Christian in ad hominem attacks and use bait-and-switch tactics designed to mislead and distract. Huxley was also great at misleading and distracting.

Huxley's impact in advancing the hypothesis of evolution and the humanism that would grow out of it cannot be overstated. Darwin was a timid man who had no stomach for controversy. Charles Lyell, while being very desirous for the overthrow of the Church, could not gather the faculties to be as direct and charismatic as Huxley was, and those traits were necessary in order to carry the day with the public and with the media, who had such a big part in the advancement of the X Clubbers' cause. Tyndall and Hooker were absorbed in other matters, and needed the encouragement of Huxley to continue the fight. If you opposed Christianity in those days, you would say that Mr. Huxley was the right man for the job at the right time. One that would agree with you and a man who always had a smile on his face at the mention of Huxley was Charles Darwin.

> Huxley's about-face warmed Darwin. He devoured [Huxley's] lectures. So did Hooker, who found them "overwhelming", "like the old Scotch wife who said, "Ae, it was a grand discourse, I couldna understand the ane half of it." But it was not their "revolutionary" nature that struck Darwin. It was Huxley's gall. He mauled Owen in the lectures. Mere mention of his name had "the old adam in T.H.H." rising to fight, such "is the nature of the beast." Owen's "Archetypal Ideas" were consigned to oblivion; his parthenogenesis was denounced and his classification derided….
>
> Huxley was honing his skills as a controversialist. All knew it. The tyro was mugging the old men. It was a job he relished, trashing reputations and received wisdom – and perhaps essential work if Darwin's big book was to sweep the world before it.
>
> Darwin himself ground on, terrified at going public, wishing *"most heartily"* that he had never started. [224]

Huxley's purposes are summarized as follows:

> Though Darwin was careful not to say it, the *Origin* ultimately meant that man, "with all his lofty endowments and future hopes, was…never 'created' at all, but was merely…a development from an ape." But without the

---

[224] Ibid, pp. 225 - 227

> promise of Heaven or the fear of Hell, why should we live
> a good life? Huxley knew that this was the crux, even as
> he trashed Wollaston's "stupid review" [Thomas
> Wollaston had written a scathing review of *Origin*]. [225]

This was exactly why Huxley's grandson, Aldous Huxley, many years later, said he liked evolution. It allowed him, and anyone who believes in it, to live their lives in any manner they see fit, because there are no eternal rewards or punishments for behavior.

Thomas Huxley, to a large extent, accomplished his goal in his lifetime: to make science the arbiter of all things. Since, by the end of his life, science had been raised to a level of prominence that it was beyond questioning, it was necessary to make sure that evolution, the basis for his godless worldview, would be looked at as science, and not philosophy. He was successful there as well. Evolution could huddle under the umbrella of science and insulate itself from all attacks. It did not need to be a proven hypothesis, as long as the critics were not allowed to attack it. It obtained that status during Huxley's life, and it has remained immune to attacks ever since.

Professor Huxley

To get a true perspective on Huxley's influence on the world one has to look no further than this statement by the famous Harvard University professor of biology, Ernst Mayr, who was no friend of the biblical world view: "It can hardly be doubted that [evolutionary biology] has helped to undermine traditional beliefs and value systems" [226] Huxley had more to do with that trend than any one else.

Huxley was different from Hutton, Lyell and Darwin in the respect that he had to struggle hard to obtain material success in life.

---

[225] Ibid, p. 266
[226] Internet, http://en.wikipedia.org/wiki/Thomas_Henry_Huxley, accessed 02/25/2011

Nothing was handed to him. One of the oppressive institutions that helped make it harder for him was the Church. He could not get into Oxford or Cambridge because he didn't have the money or connections that were required. Later, when he was fighting for science to be included in the curriculum in schools, one of the forces opposing him were men from the clergy and government officials, who marched lockstep with the bishops. You could say the fight against the church, and hence Christianity, was a personal issue with him.

We will next review where this state of affairs has gotten us.

CHAPTER 7
CONCLUSION

ONE of the problems of negotiating settlement terms with a despotic ruler is that the ruler is often not aware of the gravity of the situation in which he is involved. He thinks his situation is better than it is because none of his advisors will tell him the truth, for fear of suffering punishment lest he not wish to hear it. The more despotic the ruler, the harder it is for him to get accurate information from his sources.

The old adage of "punishing the messenger" has application to our world as well. Most of us have heard the tale of *The Emperor's New Clothes* by Hans Christian Andersen. The emperor was convinced by some con artists that they could make a cloth that was so light it would look invisible to people who were simpletons, but would be beautiful to those who were sophisticated. Of course, that cut the costs of materials for the tailors considerably! He took them up on their offer and had a suit made of their "cloth." When he wore it, no one had the nerve to tell him he was naked for fear of incurring the emperor's wrath, or appearing to be a fool. Only when a small boy exclaimed that the emperor was naked did some of the others second his observation. The emperor, however, was not convinced and still deluded himself that he was wearing a beautiful suit, although in his mind, he thought he looked naked too, but didn't want to embarrass himself by admitting it.

Emperors rule over geographical territories and a powerful emperor can drastically affect how the citizens of the country live their daily lives. The citizens of Cuba can vouch for that. Cubans don't risk their lives crossing 90 miles of ocean because they are happy where they are. Americans can be thankful that no one person has that much influence over their lives.

But our lives are not ruled only by political considerations. Ideology is ultimately the guiding force for most of us. Another term for that is *worldview*. The number one component of worldview is religion; what do we do with the concept of God. After all, most cultures claim there is a god or gods who supersede the affairs of men. Some cultures may have more truth in their concept of God than others. Individuals must come to an understanding of how they are personally going to relate to that deity. Will they follow the religion of their culture or will they deny that the cultural religion is valid? Maybe they will make the choice to follow a religion that originated with another culture. More and more, modern westerners have chosen to deny that there is a god at all. The path people choose to follow on this question will guide their decisions on lesser worldview issues.

There are forces brought to bear that will put pressure on people to follow one path or another. It is a battle for the mind. Those who win that battle and convince the most people that their worldview is correct control many people, maybe to a greater degree than political emperors. We could call these people *emperors of the mind.* The thought that immediately comes to mind is the case of "Reverend" Jim Jones and the Jonestown massacre in Guyana in 1978. His faction was so deluded by his teaching they followed him to their death.

There are those who could say their science guided them to their beliefs about God. I've heard this most often from people who work in the fields of astronomy and microbiology. In those two fields one views things on a daily basis that tax the mind to comprehend: the enormity of space on the one hand, and on the other, the complexity of systems absolutely essential to the process of life, but so small they must be viewed through high-powered microscopes, and even then, may be too small to be seen.

The opposite extreme, however, includes a large number of people. These are the ones who use their beliefs about God to guide them to their science. The four emperors, Hutton, Lyell, Darwin and Huxley, are the ultimate in that regard, and their "science" has had a sweeping and destructive influence upon the world.

Many modern westerners not guided by a religious ideology are guided by popular culture. Their worldview is determined primarily through the educational system and the media. So, you could say that whoever controls the education and the media controls the minds of a large share of the population. Those people in control are essentially emperors over the minds of the others. As we've shown previously, John Dewey and the secular humanists resolved in the early part of the last century to take control of the educational system. They have been successful in setting the wheels in motion that are moving our society closer and closer every day to complete atheism. According to figures I have seen, a century and a half ago somewhere around 1% of the population admitted to being atheist or agnostic. The latest figures I have seen for the present day are between 15% and 25%, depending upon which country you are polling. Knowing how these things explode exponentially, our time is growing short to reverse that trend. Many polls show there is still a large number of people who believe in a god or "higher power", but the problem is people are not as sure of who the higher power is as they used to be. Also, I think those who believe in a god of some sort are not as sure in their convictions as those of 50 or 100 years ago.

The media follows as well as leads. They follow the current thinking of the public in order to determine what sells. Then, their publicizing of that agenda influences people even further in the direction they are already headed. The media is also a product of the educational system, since most people in the media are well educated and therefore have a high regard for education. The media seems to assign authority to any research that comes from an academic setting. So, in the end, the educational system has more to do with the public worldview than any other single factor.

It wasn't always that way. At one time, the churches ran the schools and could control what was taught, but public education put an end to that. Thomas Mann pushed for an end to church-sponsored schools, and John Dewey continued pressuring to change to public funding for schools everywhere. Even many of our leading universities were once connected to Christian denominations. They have now cast aside those connections, and some of them are leading the charge away from God. Additionally, upwards of 75% of the institutions of higher learning that call themselves Christian do not teach a literal Genesis.

We know that changes in the worldview of a culture do not happen overnight, or even in a single century. When Dewey and the secular humanists of the early twentieth century set out to change the world, they were only acting out the dreams of those who went before them. Those dreams started in the seventeenth century with Rene Descartes, John Locke and other philosophers, who sought to free the world of religion, which at that time was represented to them as Christianity, as seen through the lens of the Catholic Church and the Church of England. But it was James Hutton in the eighteenth century that gave "scientific" support to the idea of there being no God. His system would have died a natural death if not for the works of Charles Lyell. As we have seen, both Lyell and Hutton had a disdain for the church and Christianity. Then, Darwin took Lyell's long ages and used them to make his hypothesis of evolution appear credible. Huxley took Darwin's hypothesis and force-fed it to the world. Even though there are many reasons to believe he had some doubts about its authenticity, he was willing to push it onto everyone else because of its utility in destroying Christian faith.

The social Darwinists took it from there, pushing evolution into every nook and cranny of the social fabric. The social Darwinists were not concerned about verifying its scientific validity. They saw the uses for it in creating a world without God, looking right past any possible problems with its scientific credibility. In the 1860s through the 1890s, science had captivated the world. The telegraph and later telephone, steam engine, electricity and many time-saving inventions such as the cotton gin and the grain reaper were impressive departures from the methods known for hundreds, if not thousands of years. People were beginning to believe that all of the world's problems would eventually be solved by science, and men of science were admired and respected. Since evolution had been classified as science, the social Darwinists relied on its icons, Huxley, Darwin, Lyell, Hooker, Asa Gray, Tyndall et al, to give them a true accounting of origins. In other words, they believed because they wanted to believe it and they trusted the authority figures who told them it was true. After all, they were scientists, weren't they? Even the theologians were convinced. Rather than fight it, they devised ways, no matter how counterintuitive, to try to incorporate evolution into the Bible. In order to do that, they had to render the words of the beginning chapters of Genesis, which are very straightforward prose, meaningless.

While many people have been involved in the establishment of modern humanism, the five men that were by far the most prominent were James Hutton, Charles Lyell, Charles Darwin,

Thomas Huxley and John Dewey. They were, and still are, emperors of the minds of modern people. They rule with an iron hand, and do not tolerate competition. Karl Marx, Friedrich Nietzsche, Joseph Stalin and Adolf Hitler were all fans of Darwinism, as exhibited by their efforts to cull the "less desirable" elements of society. All make mention of that fact in their own memoirs. Marx was a friend of Darwin's.

James Hutton could not even convince his contemporaries of the truth of his system. He was able, apparently, to convince his best friend, Joseph Black that his system was valid, although Black never lifted a finger to try to convince anyone else to take it up, so we have to wonder how deep Black's belief was. I'm sure he valued his friendship with Hutton enough that he wouldn't have wanted to offend him. The young guys, John Playfair and Sir James Hall, believed in Hutton's system primarily because of Hutton's persona and standing in the scientific community in Edinburgh, and kept it alive for the next generation. Hutton may have also had a hand in converting Erasmus Darwin into a committed uniformitarian and evolutionist. Darwin's writing took a decided turn toward naturalism after he met Hutton, and Huttonisms such as "millions of ages" abound in his writing.

Charles Lyell repackaged Hutton's ideas in his book, *Principles of Geology*, which gave no convincing arguments for the antiquity of the earth. Both Hutton and Lyell expressed their disdain for the church and Christianity, and their total unwillingness to even recognize the reigning paradigm of that day, the creationist position, gives them away as totally subjective. They took the position they did because it was a way to combat the truth of the Bible.

Charles Darwin proposed evolution by means of natural selection. He wedded his grandfather's ideas with Lyell's long ages, and published his book espousing natural selection, but gave examples of artificial selection only. Darwin's publicist, Thomas Huxley, never believed in natural selection as a mechanism for species-changing adaptation, but drew support for evolution by referring to homology, the similarities of different body parts in different creatures being evidence for their origination from a common ancestor. He was such a good speaker, artist and writer that he was able to convince many people, especially those who had the power to control the educational system and the media. Huxley could be said to be the first social Darwinist, because he was less concerned about the scientific aspect of it than he was about its affect

192 | M I L T   M A R C Y

on society. He was keen to see the church and Christianity in general lose their grip on the minds of men.

In Huxley's old age, a cadre of young social Darwinists arose, spreading the evolutionist gospel throughout society, from science to history to current events and beyond. Evolution was assumed to be true, and when that point was reached, the masterminds of the new society decided the time was ripe to use it as a foundation to build the edifice of formal humanism, which would seep into the court system, legislatures, education, the entertainment industry, the media and even the church. Once it got started, there was no stopping it.

Formal humanists are still a small minority, but they have the ability to carry others along with them, people who do not have their morals firmly anchored in Judeo-Christian values. Many other people are humanists, for all intents and purposes, but do not call themselves humanists. For example, the concept of situational ethics has been formally adopted as one of the tenets of humanism, and much has been done to spread this concept among the society, but many people who don't even know what humanism is have adopted situational ethics as a part of their lifestyle; it seems to them that their life will be easier if they can change their ethical stance to fit their needs for every particular situation. It is important for Christians to know why they believe what they do or they can be deceived into accepting some of those humanist concepts in their own lives. Humanist values appeal to the licentious side in each of us.

In 1973, the American Humanist Association wrote a new manifesto called *Humanist Manifesto II*. It was still strongly tied to evolution, as it was in *Humanist Manifesto I*, but some of the particulars are especially interesting. The third section deals with ethics. It states:

> We affirm that moral values derive their source from human experience. Ethics is autonomous and situational, needing no theological or ideological sanction. Ethics stems from human need and interest.... Happiness and the creative realization of human needs and desires, individually and in shared enjoyment, are continuous themes of humanism. We strive for the good life, here and now. [227]

---

[227] Weep for Your Children, Dr. Murray Norris, p. 25

This quote sounds as if it could have come right out of James Hutton's *Principles of Knowledge.* An eighteenth-century geologist and a twentieth-century social document have exactly the same worldview! Could it be that the geologist actually had social objectives as his first priority, and that the framers of the twentieth century document endorse evolution only in order to obtain their social objectives?

We find more Huttonian thinking when they address the issue of morality:

> The myths, the dogmas, the rituals of traditional religion – with their authoritarian tone – are irrelevant to the resolution of our problems...humans must be the sole judge of right and wrong because ethics and morality do not need theological sanctification...morality is a product of human experience...higher authorities must not be allowed to dictate morality. [228]

James Hutton said the same thing almost 200 years earlier, albeit in a more discreet manner. Let's see what they have to say about religion:

> We believe, however, that traditional dogmatic or authoritarian religions that place revelation, God, ritual, or creed above human needs and experience do a disservice to the human species. Any account of nature should pass the test of scientific evidence; in our judgment, the dogmas and myths of traditional religions do not do so. [229]

Didn't Tom Huxley say that religion should be required to be scientifically verified? Nothing new here. The modern humanists are only repeating what the founders of evolution previously expressed in their philosophical digressions.

One common denominator of the emperors was that they took great pride in the accomplishments of their generation, and viewed the ancients as savages with small brains that had no power to understand, much less change, their environment. Ironically, Lyell grew up just a stone's throw from one of the wonders of the ancient world, Stonehenge (no pun intended). In Lyell's day they would not

---

[228] Ibid, p. 21
[229] Ibid, p. 24

have been able to budge one of the limestone blocks that make up that megalith, let alone place it in position with the preciseness exhibited in that ancient edifice. The architects of that structure had accurately predetermined the amount of sinking that would take place in the ground when a column was put in place, so that when the horizontal members were placed on top they would be level and rest evenly on each column. If Lyell had any objectivity whatsoever, he would have been deeply impressed by that, but as we have pointed out numerous times, he had a great ability to completely ignore any evidence that did not support his view. He did not offer counter arguments. He just pretended there was no other view but his own. In that respect, he was no different than the other emperors or modern evolutionists.

It must have been necessary for them to take the view they did toward the ancients in order to support their worldview, since the religion they so hated (Christianity) grew out of that ancient past. You could say they believed the way they did because it was the only choice they had that would allow them to maintain their worldview.

Modern secular humanists are mostly unaware of the shaky foundation that supports their beliefs. If they've studied their movement at all, they know that the first two tenets of the *Humanist Manifesto* mention the belief in evolution, but they don't investigate any further to see if that trust is warranted. Of all the present day population that says they believe in evolution, probably not one in a hundred knows anything about Siccar Point, which was supposed to be Hutton's prime proof for his system. And if they do know about it, would they know about all of the difficulties involved in defending Hutton's analysis of it? For that matter, not many more of them would even know who James Hutton was! Do they know that Charles Darwin's long ages needed for evolution come from Hutton? Do any of them know that Thomas Huxley did not believe in natural selection? Would they know who Huxley was?

It seems our emperors are just as naked when it comes to real science as the fairy tale emperor was with his clothes and people are just as intimidated about voicing any objection to evolution as the emperor's subjects were about his clothes. Many reasons exist for that fact, threat of job loss or demotion, ridicule by others, or just the herd mentality that discourages thinking outside the box.

In writing a contract, it is not so important what the document actually says as it is what the parties to the contract *think* it says.

Many times people have had their rights abused because they did not know what their contract actually said. The illusion is often just as good as the real thing, if the perpetrator has done a good job. The perpetrators of evolution have done an excellent job. And the humanism that has grown out of it has produced a public that has no moral compass, because there is no generally accepted standard by which we may determine right and wrong. If evolution is true the Bible is wrong and if the Bible is wrong we must look elsewhere for ultimate answers. The authority that was previously assigned to God's Word, which guided our society, has now been eroded and that has left us with no authority, save the opinions of men. We are back to where the Hebrews were at the end of the book of Judges.

Before his death, Tom Huxley lamented that society seemed to have lost its morality, but he was the most prominent person responsible for kicking the foundation of morality, Christianity, to the curb!

The emperors have gotten what they wanted, a society that no longer regards the Bible as a guiding influence. Many modern people, including quite a few churchgoers, view it only as a book of fables, or at best a series of moral lessons. The emperors saw this situation as freedom, but I don't think any of them had any idea what happens to a culture when it becomes pagan. Each man does what is right in his own eyes, and if there is a conflict, a judge decides who is right using a standard that varies from judge to judge and from case to case. Often violence has taken place between the warring parties by the time the judge gets involved. Led by God two thousand years ago the apostle Peter prophesied of these days.

> ...knowing this first: that scoffers will come in the last days, walking according to their own lusts, and saying, "Where is the promise of His coming? For since the fathers fell asleep, all things continue as they were from the beginning of creation." [the present is the key to the past?] For this they willfully forget: that by the word of God the heavens were of old, and the earth standing out of water and in the water, by which the world that then existed perished, being flooded with water. But the heavens and the earth which are now preserved by the same word are reserved for fire until the day of judgment and perdition of ungodly men. (II Peter 3:3 KJV)

Note that these people are *willingly* deceived. We could even go a step farther and say they *wanted* to be deceived. The phrase, "all things continue as they were from the beginning of creation", is an apt description of evolution. The term *scoffers* is about as good as any to describe those who scorn God's Word and choose instead to believe the lie of evolution in today's world. They don't use reason. They only ridicule and cast aspersions on those who believe the Word of God. But, no matter how much men turn away from God, He always provides a way back to His good graces.

> ....if My people who are called by My name will humble themselves, and pray and seek My face, and turn from their wicked ways, then I will hear from heaven, and will forgive their sin and heal their land. (II Chronicles 7:14 KJV)

The emperors were not just tyrants, who are still imposing their will on the nations of the twenty-first century; they are thieves of the highest order. They have stolen the awe and wonder of God and hidden it away, out of sight of the people of the world. A person reading the Psalms, if he has swallowed the lie of evolution, can no longer follow along with the psalmist when he rhapsodizes about God's creation, because he has been convinced that everything he sees was not created, it came about by chance and accidents. The child turning on the television to a nature show will not learn about the wonders of God's creation. He will be told that millions and millions of years ago a particle exploded for some unknown reason and matter organized itself through gazillions of accidents into everything we see today. He will be told the plant and animal world is in a battle with mortal consequences for those who do not have the facilities to win the fight. There is no higher purpose for life or for anything in the universe, for that matter. We are all consigned to live out our days just plodding along looking for excitement wherever we can find it.

The idea of an original perfect creation that God made for His created beings, that He repeatedly expresses His love for in His Word, is a foreign concept to those who have bought the lie of evolution and the humanism that comes with it. And because they have not been able to accept God's majesty and benevolence in His past works they are hard pressed to envision Him providing a future restoration of that original paradise.

Even those who have become believers in creation often have trouble putting aside their old assumptions about the world around them because these concepts are deeply ingrained in the subconscious mind. It is difficult to "unlearn" all the various concepts that have been accepted as truth throughout one's life.

The number one thing I would like to see accomplished by this book is that all will see that evolution and Christianity cannot be wed. It would be like a marriage of God and Satan. Evolution was designed by the emperors to destroy Christianity, and despite the appearance of a scientific objective its only real objective was the destruction of Christianity. There are many in the evangelical church today, including many leaders, who would like to see the church unite in accepting evolution as true and try to fit it into the Bible somehow. They see creationists as divisive and disruptive to the evangelical cause. In answer to those people I would like them to think about the fact that all the leaders, in both evolution science and atheistic thought, often one and the same people, agree that if evolution is true that means Christianity is not true. It's that clear cut. Richard Dawkins, Sam Harris, Christopher Hitchens and P.Z. Myers are just some of the many who have expressed their views on this matter.

In the area where I live, a popular bumper sticker shows the Christian fish with a diagonal line through it and off to the side the word, "Darwin." The thousands of people who drive around with that sticker on their car have no doubt that if Darwinism is true it means that Christianity is not true. Furthermore, they believe that everyone who sees their sticker will understand the message they are trying to get across. Everyone understands except the clergyman who wants to make Darwin right at home in his congregation!

The Soviet Communists called Western sympathizers "useful idiots' because they naively supported the communists, thinking it was the right thing to do, not realizing that the communists, if they got their way, would eventually exterminate them as well as all others. The Christians who would include evolution in their world view could be and are very aptly called useful idiots by the evolutionists/atheists that have foisted this deadly world view upon us. It is akin to going to buy a house. You are told by the seller that the house has termites. But you, the buyer, won't accept his statement of fact, but insist the house does not have termites. It would seem to any objective person that the seller ought to know if the house has termites and why would he tell you it does if it does not? It would be utter foolishness to ignore the seller's statement. The people who "sold" us evolution in the first place and the ones who are still selling it to us now claim it disproves Christianity, not that the two can be combined in some happy Shangri-la.

Lest one think that things have changed since the days of the emperors let us see what two of the more prominent modern evolutionists have to say about it. First, Jerry Coyne of the University of Chicago:

> [Evolutionists may be] religious scientists and Darwinian churchgoers. But this does not mean that faith and science are compatible, except in the trivial sense that both attitudes can be simultaneously embraced by a single human mind. (It is like saying that marriage and adultery are compatible because some married people are adulterers). [230]

Thank you, Mr. Coyne. I am convinced a more appropriate statement could not be made. Of course, faith and science *are* perfectly compatible, but he and I would differ about what true science is. The point is that Coyne's science [evolution] has no intention of allowing faith to co-exist.

William Provine, of Cornell University also has his say:

> ....implications of modern science produce much squirming among scientists, who claim a high degree of rationality. Some, along with many liberal theologians, suggest that God set up the universe in the beginning and/or works through the laws of nature. This silly way of trying to have one's cake and eat it too amounts to deism. It is equivalent to the claim that science and religion are compatible if the religion is effectively indistinguishable from atheism. Show me a person who says that science and religion are compatible, and I will show you a person who (1) is an effective atheist, or (2) believes things demonstrably unscientific, or (3) asserts the existence of entities or processes for which no shred of evidence exists (Provine 1988, p. 10).[231]

Provine's belief in an unproven evolution is a religion (or anti-religion) as well. Based on his statement, option two above would indicate that he doesn't think creation science is scientific, and I would be happy to debate him about that, but the thing to take from

---

[230] Answers in Genesis website, Why Orthodox Darwinism Demands Atheism, accessed 07/28/2010, p. 4
[231] Ibid

his statement is how ridiculous it is to try to wed a compromise of the two.

I will leave you with three thoughts:

If there really was a six day-creation 6,000 years ago, what would we expect to see in the strata of the earth? We would expect to see all species fully formed, with no antecedents, no transitional species and creation legends in cultures all over the earth. What do we find? We see all species fully formed, with no antecedents, no transitional species and creation legends in cultures all over the earth.

If there really was a worldwide flood as Genesis tells us there was, what would we expect to see? Building on a phrase used by Ken Ham of *Answers in Genesis*, we would expect to see billions of dead things buried in rock layers, laid down by water all over the earth, with sea shells on all the highest mountain tops and flood legends in cultures all over the earth. What do we find? We see billions of dead things buried in rock layers, laid down by water all over the earth, with sea shells on all the highest mountain tops and flood legends in cultures all over the earth.

If all the languages came from one language in one place as the Bible says, what would we expect to find? We would expect to find evidence that all languages are derived from one source in one location in the Middle East. What do we find? Linguists tell us that all languages are derived from one source in one location in the Middle East.

If the Bible really is God's Word, we would not find it remarkable that prophecies in it were made that were fulfilled in detail hundreds and sometimes thousands of years later. In all their writings about theology, Hutton and Huxley never wrote about prophecy. Lyell, Darwin and Dewey tried not to think about theology or prophecy at all. I guess it was too disturbing.

I must say that after delving deeply into the lives of these five men, they all had some good qualities. They also exhibited their poor qualities from time to time and revealed their humanness. Unfortunately, they were all driven to deny the religion of their culture and they were determined to draw others away as well. Another thing they all had in common was their disgust when others tried to retain their Christian worldview and mix theology with evolution.

We should have that same disgust.

APPENDIX A

What Is Happening to the World We Live In?

I started writing this book in 2009. A couple of times during the year I received one of those bulk e-mails, which many of you probably received as well. It was a look back 100 years to the year 1909. The facts it rattled off were not too surprising, I suppose, but when they were all presented at once it was kind of mind-boggling, and I marveled at the change that has taken place in that small window of human history. To wit:

- The average life span was only 47 years of age in 1909.
- Only 14% of the homes had a bathtub.
- Only 8% of the homes had a telephone.
- There were only 8,000 cars in the whole country and only 144 miles of paved roads.
- Fuel for the few cars there were, was purchased at drug stores.
- The maximum speed limit in most cities was 10 miles per hour. .
- The average wage was 22 cents per hour.
- The average worker made between $200 and $400 per year. Dentists made about $2,500 per year and mechanical engineers made about $5,000 per year.
- More than 95% of all births took place at home.
- 90% of all doctors had *no* college education!
- Sugar cost four cents a pound. Eggs were fourteen cents a dozen.
- Most women washed their hair only once a month, and used borax or egg yolks for shampoo.
- Canada passed a law that prohibited poor people from entering their country for any reason.
- The five leading causes of death were:
    1. Pneumonia and influenza
    2. Tuberculosis
    3. Diarrhea

4. Heart disease
5. Stroke

- The American flag had 45 stars. And so, there were only 45 states at that time.
- The population of Las Vegas, Nevada, was 30!
- Crossword puzzles, canned beverages, and iced tea hadn't been invented yet.
- Two out of every 10 adults couldn't read or write.
- Only 6% of all Americans had graduated from high School.
- Marijuana, heroin, and morphine were all available over the counter at local drugstores. Back then, pharmacists said, "Heroin clears the complexion, gives buoyancy to the mind, regulates the stomach and bowels, and is, in fact, a perfect guardian of health."
- There were about 230 reported murders that year in the entire USA!
- 95% of the taxes we have now did not exist in 1909.

All of the above information is quantifiable and verifiable without a great deal of effort because we have records of those things. I've even stopped sometimes, during the process of moving, for example, and pulled an old newspaper open that was being used to wrap something, and upon seeing the age of the paper, taken a few minutes to catch up on what things were like back then. It can be fascinating.

But I think there has been just as great a change in social conditions as we see in the above e-mail relating to living conditions. It is much harder to measure, however, because in many cases we are dealing with information that is hard to quantify. But, let me try.

One of the more graphic examples pertains to my experiences as an insurance agent. I like to contrast the process of filling out an application for auto insurance back in the mid 1980's (when I started in the business) to what it is like now. At that time, if two young people of different sexes, between the ages of say, 18 to 24, applied for auto insurance, most of the time they were married. Today they almost never are. They are just cohabitating, but since they live together, they must be on the same policy. Or how about this: if you were rating on a married couple but accidentally checked the same sex for each of them, the computer would give you an error message at the bottom of the page and not let you proceed to the next page. Now it lets you go right on with the insurance quote and will let you issue the policy that way.

What is happening to the world we live in?

According to the people who keep track of such things, the divorce rate has leveled off in the last 20 years. But many people today aren't even bothering to get married, so how can they get divorced? Obviously, the statistics are skewed. The National Institute of Child Health and Human Development states:

> Cohabitation, once rare, is now the norm: The researchers found that more than half (54 percent of women of marriageable age today) of all first marriages between 1990 and 1994 began with unmarried cohabitation. They estimate that a majority of young men will spend some time in a cohabiting relationship. ... Cohabiting relationships are less stable than marriages and that instability is increasing, the study found. Just over 50% of first cohabiting couples ever get married.

The percentage of adults between the ages of 20 and 54 that are married has gone from 78.6% in 1970 to 57.2% in 2008. That's a drop of 21.4% in only 38 years! The percentage of first marriages intact went from 77.4% to 61.2% in that same period. Perhaps the most troubling statistic is in the percentage of births to married parents. It went from 89.3% in 1970 to only 60.3% in 2008 and by 2008 only 61% of all children in this country live with their own married parents.

What is happening to the world we live in? [232]

An article in the September 2009 issue of the Philadelphia Trumpet states,

> In July, the level of sexual depravity reached a new low in Britain when the National Health Service produced a sex education pamphlet for school children. According to the Daily Mail, the publication complained that when it comes to sex, sociologists pay too much attention to 'safe sex' and 'loving relationships' and not enough to the subject of

---

[232] www.americanvalues.org, accessed 07/28/2009, The Marriage Index, A Proposal to Establish Leading Marriage Indicators

sensual pleasure. Teenagers, says the pamphlet's author, have as much right to a good sex life as do adults.

Britain, it should be noted, has the highest teen pregnancy rate in Europe and second highest in the developed world, trailing only the United States. Of the 40,000 British girls who will be impregnated this year, half will opt for abortion. [233]

Artwork by Matt Marcy

Speaking of abortion in this country, over 50 million babies have been aborted since seven unelected judges unconstitutionally mandated legal abortion on the federal level in 1973. This is almost a thousand times as many people as were lost in the Viet Nam war and far over-shadows the other evils of the modern age. The soldiers that were lost had families that cared about them, whereas the little ones hadn't developed those attachments yet when their lives were snuffed out. Rest assured though, God loved them every bit as much as He loved the soldiers.

Fifty years ago if an unmarried girl got pregnant, it was a major event. Usually, she would seek refuge with a distant relative until the child was delivered, and then the baby would be given up for adoption. Yes, there were some illegal abortions done, but the number was miniscule compared to today. Nowadays, the unwed

---

[233] www.thetrumpet.com, accessed 10/01/2009, The War Against Family

mother may prefer to have the child and keep it, since it increases her ability to get government assistance, but if she decides not to she can have an abortion.

What is happening to the world we live in?

In 1973 we didn't have the internet, but today there are 1.3 million pornographic websites; 260 million pages. The U.S. adult DVD/video rentals in 2005: almost 1 billion. The number of hardcore pornography titles released in 2005 in the U.S.: 13,588. The number of adults admitting to internet sexual addiction is 10% and interestingly 28% of those are women.

According to ComScore Media Matrix more than 70% of men from 18 to 34 visit a pornographic site in a typical month. 20% of internet pornography involves children. In what would seemingly be a pretty objective bunch, the American Academy of Matrimonial Lawyers came out with a very revealing statement at a 2003 meeting of their association. Two thirds of the 350 attendees said "the internet played a significant role in the divorces in the past year, with excessive interest in online porn contributing to more than half such cases. Pornography had an almost non-existent role in divorce just seven or eight years ago."

It really gets interesting when we look at a 1996 Promise Keepers survey at one of their stadium events, revealing that over 50% of the men in attendance were involved with pornography within one week prior to attending the event. A 2001 survey by Christianity Today disclosed that 37% of the pastors surveyed said that pornography is a current struggle for them. Over half of evangelical pastors admit to viewing pornography in the last year. 57% of pastors say that addiction to pornography is the most sexually damaging issue to their congregation (Christians and Sex Leadership Journal Survey, Fall 2005).

34% of female readers of Today's Christian Woman's online newsletter admitted to intentionally accessing internet porn in a 2003 poll, and 1 out of every 6 women, including Christians, struggles with an addiction to pornography (Today's Christian Woman, Fall 2003).

Average age of first exposure to pornography: 11 years old (Internet Filter Review).

Largest consumer of internet pornography: 12 – 17 year-old age group (various sources, as of 2007).

1 in 5 children (10 to 17 years old) receives unwanted sexual solicitation online (Youth Internet Safety Survey, U.S. Department of Justice, 2001).

To sum it all up, the U.S. Department of Justice made the following statement in 1996:

> Never before in the history of telecommunications media in the United States has so much indecent (and obscene) material been so easily accessible by so many minors in so many American homes with so few restrictions.[234]

What is happening to the world we live in?

Pornography is very addictive, but there are many other addictions which seem to have taken over our country as well. The elephant in the closet on this one is gambling. Fifty years ago if you wanted to gamble you could, but your options were pretty limited. There was always the horse or dog track if you lived in or near a metropolitan area. There were illegal gambling operations in most major cities if you wanted to take that chance. Or, you could take a trip to Las Vegas or Monte Carlo, which of course, limits the options for those who aren't wealthy enough to do that.

Now, we have all of the above, plus state-sponsored video games, state and interstate lotteries, Indian casinos and on-line gambling. I have personally witnessed the destruction of several families because of gambling, so I guess I have an antipathy for it that is stronger than it would be for most. Some will say that it is the gambler's fault, not the institution offering the gaming opportunity that should be blamed. But, if that is the case and we have no responsibility as Christians to remove temptation from in front of our brother's nose, why have we not given this same nod to the tobacco companies, who for many years have had their little warning on the side of the pack of cigarettes? They have had to pay billions for the health risks their product has caused, but we use gambling to create revenue for the state. Am I the only one who sees the inconsistency here?

From a November 14, 2009 article in The Oregonian newspaper about the complicity of the state in the gambling addictions of its citizens, we read the following:

> The Oregon Lottery is addicted to addicted gamblers. More than half the money the lottery collects from video gambling, about $375 million last year, comes from a small

---

[234] U.S. Department of Justice, Post Hearing Memorandum of Points and Authorities at l, ACLU v Reno, 929 F. Supp. 824 (1996).

number of Oregonians, many with big gambling problems.

These gamblers tell the lottery they lose more than $500 a month, every month. They represent only 10% of Oregon's video gamblers but account for 53% of the money lost, according to an analysis of three years' worth of the lottery's data obtained by the Oregonian under the state's public records law.

Losses from these heavy gamblers prop up the lottery's profits, which in turn prop up the state budget.

Lawmakers covet lottery cash to pay for schools, parks and other state services, but most have no idea what the real costs are.

"Unless you're in it, you can't understand the depths of a gambling compulsion," says Nate Peterson of Portland, who lost $5,000 on video gambling in eight months before he sought treatment last year [2008]. "You're scared to tell anyone, there's such a stigma. But I was killing myself, I was really dying inside."

These problem gamblers are your neighbors, coworkers and family members who sit at video screens and slip dollar after dollar into high tech slot machines that are programmed to eventually take their money. Many sink into debt, lie to friends and steal from their employers and loved ones.

"People in the legislature have no idea about these numbers and the damage that is done to people's lives," says Rep. Carolyn Tomei, D-Milwaukie, "It's a message that frankly wouldn't be welcomed in the legislature right now, because we've become so dependent on the lottery's money."

Many people who have no problem with compulsive gambling do not feel sorry for these people, just as they don't feel sorry for the alcoholic or the drug addict, but I'd like to ask those people a question: What about the innocent children whose lives are degraded by this addiction? Do we have any sympathy for them?

The gambling industry has grown tenfold in the U.S. since 1975.

37 states now have their own lottery and most of the ones who don't have one take part in an interstate lottery.

15 million people (that's about 5% of the American population) display some signs of gambling addiction.

Two-thirds of the adult population placed some kind of a bet last year. In 1973 state lotteries had $2 billion in sales. By 1997, the revenues had grown to $34 billion.

Gambling among young people is on the increase: 42% of 14-year-olds, 49% of 15-year-olds, 63% of 16-year-olds, 76% of 18-year-olds.

There are now approximately 260 casinos on Indian reservations (in 31 states and with $6.7 billion in revenue).

After casinos opened in Atlantic City, the total number of crimes within a 30 mile radius increased 100%.

The average debt incurred by a male pathological gambler in the U.S. is between $55,000 and $90,000 (it is $15,000 for female gamblers).

The average rate of divorce for problem gamblers is nearly double that of non-gamblers.

The suicide rate for pathological gamblers is 20 times higher than for non-gamblers (one in five attempts suicide).

65% of pathological gamblers commit crimes to support their gambling habit.

Most people recognize that this situation has gotten exponentially worse in the last 25 years (the gambling industry has grown tenfold in that time period). In *Turning the Tables on Gambling*, Gregory L. Jantz, 2001 states:

> The biggest obstacle to changing this situation is that governments have become hooked on gambling themselves, namely the revenues derived from the mostly poor people who make up the bulk of the problem gamblers.

What is happening to the world we live in?

When we are speaking of addictions, most people think of drugs and alcohol. The U.S. has certainly not been spared in this world-wide phenomenon. It wasn't that long ago that illegal drugs were something middle-class Americans knew little about. They were used only by the more seedy elements of society, or perhaps a few of the very rich. All of that changed with the hippie movement of the late 60s. Since then, we have seen many additional drugs added to the mix; the drugs of preference have changed from time to time, but the usage of drugs has not diminished. The old standbys of marijuana, LSD, cocaine, and heroin were not enough to satisfy the hunger of the consumer for more and better drugs, so we had the development of ecstasy, crack cocaine, meth amphetamines and others. In addition to that, the improper use of prescription pain killers has exploded. And this doesn't even address the often unwarranted, but prescribed use of mood-altering drugs for every minor ailment that comes along, by a medical profession that has a drug to prescribe for every condition imaginable.

According to an article in an issue of the 2001 Philadelphia Trumpet, "America leads the world in demand for mind-damaging, escapist-type drugs. Over 77 million Americans have sniffed, smoked, swallowed, or injected themselves with illegal drugs; 22 million (about 7% of our population) identify themselves as regular users. Among children age 12 to 17, a staggering 10.9 % are regular drug users!" The routine availability of illegal substances is now a fact of life for young people. Keith Hellawell, the former "drug tsar" for Great Britain said that

> drug-taking among well educated teenagers from stable families is the fastest growing part of the drug racket. Forget cannabis, these kids are going straight for cocaine.

From the National Institute of Drug Abuse: Drug abuse and addiction are a major burden to society. Estimates of the total overall costs of substance abuse in the United States, including health and crime-related costs, as well as losses in productivity, exceed half a trillion dollars annually. This includes approximately $181 billion for illicit drugs, $168 billion for tobacco, and $185 billion for alcohol. Staggering as these numbers are, however, they do not fully describe the breadth of deleterious public health and safety implications, which include family disintegration, loss of employment, failure in school, domestic violence, child abuse, and other crimes.

Of course, the number one drug is still alcohol. If you look on the internet for Alcoholics Anonymous meeting places in any American city you will find a wide array of choices and literally hundreds in each major city. If you get in your car and drive by those places, as I have, you will see the parking lots full during prime meeting times and in the off hours you will still find quite a few cars parked there.

The number of therapists and treatment centers has exploded, and you now see advertisements for them on prime time in major media.

An estimated 43% of U.S. adults have had someone related to them who is currently, or was, an alcoholic.

Three million U.S. citizens older than 60, abuse alcohol or require it to function properly.

6.6 million minors in the U.S. live with an alcoholic mother or father.

About 14 million U.S. residents (around 5% of the total population) battle an alcohol addiction.

As the baby boomer generation settles into retirement, alcoholism is becoming more prevalent among the elderly.

Alcohol comes with a staggering price tag, socially and economically. Alcoholics have higher rates in divorce and marriage separation, crime, automobile accidents, property damage and injuries to persons, depression and suicide. They, their families, and their friends all end up being the losers.

Alcoholism, more than any other addiction, has often led to the innocent loss of life because of accidents caused by someone under the influence of alcohol. It is also more subtle than other addictions, since drinking is legal and it is often unnoticed by friends and family members that the drinker is no longer in control of his drinking until something serious happens to alert everyone that the situation is out of control.

With such a large percentage of our population addicted to drugs, alcohol, gambling, and pornography, it seems obvious that people are looking for a means of escape from their everyday lives.

What is happening to the world we live in?

We now turn our attention to homosexuality. Back in 1980 I got to know a fellow who had come to Portland with his friend from San Francisco. Their purpose for making the move was to remove themselves from their friends and to change the general living environment they had in San Francisco. They both had become Christians and wanted to get out of the homosexual lifestyle. Of the two men, the one I got to know the best was a man of about 35 who had previously moved to San Francisco from New Hampshire when he was quite a few years younger. Over time, he became aware that homosexuality was not something condoned by God and was earnest in his quest to rid himself of anything to do with it. He had been a quite active leader among homosexuals in San Francisco before he came to Christ. His time in Portland was quite different, however, as he spent time preaching the gospel from street corners.

Because of the 180 degree change in his life, I found him to be a most interesting fellow. We also enjoyed sharing our experiences as committed Christians. More than once he told me, "Milt, I can tell you from having been on the inside looking out that there are some big changes coming from the homosexual activists. They are going to try to convince the public that they are that way because they were born that way, and there is nothing they can do about it. They feel that by doing that, they will be able to capture the sympathy of more people than they would if they were belligerent, and it is numbers from the general public that they need on their side to allow them to enforce their agenda.

"Then, after they have won enough people over to their side, they will try to force many changes upon society, like creating a special minority status for themselves just the same as you see for ethnic minorities, religious minorities, etc. Eventually, they will even try to legalize marriage amongst homosexuals."

Since I could see that he was right about the direction things were heading, my reaction was to ask him how long he thought these things might take. His answer was, "about 30 years for the whole agenda." He could not have been more right, and it looks as though the masterminds of the homosexual movement had everything figured out pretty well, since the American public has acquiesced to much of the whole package. It must be noted however, that until recently, no state has approved homosexual marriage by a vote of the people, but even that was something the masterminds had seen ahead of time. I think they knew there were judges that would be more likely to rule in their favor than the people would.

Let me be clear: I don't view homosexuality as being any worse than any other sin, but I definitely do view it as a sin. Any objective person cannot read the Bible without seeing that every reference made to homosexuality condemns it. If it weren't obvious to begin with, Leviticus 18:22 and Romans 1:24, 26 and 27 make it clear that it is not in line with God's design for his creation. Nowadays we are getting more and more laws pertaining to it. The ones I have a real problem with, besides the marriage laws, are those pertaining to employment. The number one and two places where people meet other people are at school and at work.

In 2009, a gay newspaper reported, "Gay and bisexual men account for half of new HIV infections in the U.S. and have AIDS at a rate more than 50 times greater than other groups, according to Centers for Disease Control & Prevention data . . . ." [235]

I have a friend whose brother and brother-in-law both died in their 30s in the same year from AIDS. They were both enticed into the homosexual lifestyle when they were in their teens by older men they worked with. So far as I know, there are no laws that tell me I

---

[235] Dyana Bagby, "Gay, bi men 50 times more likely to have HIV: CDC reports hard data at National HIV Prevention Conference," *Washington Blade*, August 28, 2009.

can't refuse to hire someone because they have cheated on their wife, but with all of the negative consequences of homosexuality, I can't protect my other employees from this perversion? Does this make any sense?

If you had mentioned the idea of homosexuals marrying each other 40 or 50 years ago you probably would have gotten a laugh or a sarcastic response. Some would say that is because those people were so unenlightened they didn't know any better, but the people making that accusation must remember that the unenlightened people in 1909 mentioned at the beginning of this chapter had 230 murders per year in the whole USA, and marijuana, morphine and heroin could be sold over the counter without it creating a drug addiction problem. I might add that divorce was rare in that society. In fact, if we go back to the early 1800s, the Frenchman, Alexis De Tocqueville, upon visiting America for the first time, published his book, *Democracy in America*, in which he said, "There is certainly no country in the world where the tie of marriage is more respected than in America or where conjugal happiness is more highly or worthily appreciated." I don't think, were he around today, he would make that same judgment.

What is happening to the world we live in?

Adding up the percentages, it seems that about 25% of the U.S. population has some kind of addiction, and since children are not usually addicted to anything yet, the percentage of adults with an addiction must be in the 35% to 45% range. Those addictive behaviors also affect many more people than just the addict, so when you look at the big picture the majority of our population is severely handicapped by these addictions.

Of course there are other addictions that have less serious or less immediate consequences, such as video games, overeating, and compulsive shopping.

But, the change in our society is not just limited to the obvious conditions mentioned above. In fact, the underlying causes of these overt behaviors, is, I believe, more insidious than anything we've discussed so far. There is an old saying that there is a God-shaped vacuum in every heart, and if it is not filled with God, people will fill it with something else. Not nearly as many people are filling that vacuum with God nowadays.

In the last few years there has been a lot of talk about dishonesty in high places. We have had major cover-ups by people in government, and many have been forced to resign for their moral failures. The Watergate scandal that came to a head in 1973 seems to have been the public start of this phenomenon. It seems as though since that time the number of scandals in government has increased steadily until now, so that today when we look at the news there are a number of government scandals that are being investigated at any given time all over the country. They range from personal immorality issues like sexual indiscretions to improper use of public funds or campaign funds to major rip-offs of the public for personal enrichment or the enrichment of friends.

Another source of corruption that has really come to the forefront in the last decade or two has been the corruption in big business. We have seen several Ponzi schemes exposed where investors have been extorted for millions (or even billions, in some cases). In other cases it is the stockholders who have been ripped off. Workers have had their pensions stolen. They've routinely been lied to about company intentions so that the company could keep people working when they might have left had they known the truth of the company's intentions. In other cases, it is the consumer who has suffered the abuse of an unethical company when they purchased a product improperly sold, or promises of performance were made that could not be fulfilled. In many cases the company never had any intention of fulfilling those promises.

One of my big pet peeves is dishonesty in advertising. This is a good example of how instructive it is to go back and read a newspaper from 50, 75 or 100 years ago (or even longer) and see the way things have changed. Long ago, an advertisement simply contained verbiage highlighting the good qualities of a product. Yes, they left out the bad, but still, the deception seemed to be less. Nowadays, actors are hired to give testimonials that clearly indicate they are supposed to be consumers who have used the product, and the statements they make are in many cases just bald-faced lies. Attempts are made to associate products with famous people in order to appeal to the vanity of some. Some products contain little or none of the product that the label says it contains.

Many people rail against big government, and others rail against big business, but a more fundamental question is where do the people come from who work in those positions in big government and big business? The vast majority of them come from rather humble backgrounds. That is the nature of the American way of life. The opportunity to achieve big things is there if one is willing to prepare, and many people do just that. So, those people that we love to hate usually started out just like us. How is it that they became corrupt along the way? Or, is it possible they were corrupt all the time but we just didn't notice it because they were not in a position to do anything offensive enough to get noticed until they got into a position of power? I will opt for the latter choice.

The general public is morally bankrupt, and that is why we are seeing the breakdown in the integrity of large institutions. The people that run those institutions usually come from the general public. According to a CNN Money Poll from March 10, 2010, 19% of the responders admitted to cheating on their taxes. I wonder how many more cheat but won't admit it?

How many times have you heard someone say they have a real problem with their car, and then get the advice from a friend or family member to sell the car to someone else before it finally breaks, while of course, failing to mention the problem with the car to the prospective buyer?

Real estate transactions require that the seller leave anything attached to the house when a sale is made, but in many cases the reality is there are usually a few things missing. In my case, when I bought the house I live in now, the seller took all of the drapes, the bathroom wall fixtures, the fireplace accessories, including the screen and carriage, and some of the plants out of the yard.

Being an insurance agent, I get a quarterly publication from the state insurance division intended to update agents on the latest news in the industry. The back page or page-and-a-half is devoted to listing all of the agents who have been reprimanded by the state for improper and illegal transactions with the public. I'm sure every professional group has the same problem.

I have a friend who is an auto mechanic. He expressed his frustration to me that every place he has worked there has been extreme pressure to "create" a problem where there previously was no problem instead of being honest with the customer. Being a Christian, he felt as though he simply could not work for most of the shop owners he had considered working for.

We mentioned the problem of divorce earlier, but what is the essential underlying problem in most bad relationships? I believe that whether we are talking about marriage, business partnerships or any other relationship, things start to deteriorate when one or the other side is not honest in the relationship. Sometimes both sides are dishonest.

I was first shocked into acknowledging how much life had changed in terms of personal honesty a few years ago when I was reading about the annual budget projection of a large retail chain. One of the items mentioned was something they called *shrinkage*, a rather kind term for theft. But the shrinkage in the report was more particularly called employee shrinkage and the amount allotted was 5% of the total budget. In other words, for every twenty dollars they earned one would be stolen by an employee! It would seem the figure would be at least as high for the amount stolen by customers or people posing as customers.

In 1990 two researchers, James Patterson and Peter Kim, did a massive national survey to determine just how honest the average American is. The results were published in *The Day America Told the Truth*. The distinctive feature of the survey was that absolute anonymity was promised to the people involved, so it was felt that the results were a true representation of the feelings of all Americans. There were over 2,000 people from all over America polled and they each answered over 1,800 questions.

The survey revealed that only 13% of us believe in all the Ten Commandments. 40% of us believe in five of the Ten Commandments.

The following results were found based on various questions, in the proportion shown:

- I will cheat on my spouse – after all, given the chance, he or she will do the same (53%).
- I will procrastinate at work and do absolutely nothing about one full day in every five. It's standard operating procedure (50%).
- I will use recreational drugs (41%).
- I will cheat on my taxes – to a point (30%).
- Other results found:
- Only 31% believe honesty is the best policy.
- Over 50% now believe living together is acceptable.
- 31% of all married Americans have had, or are now having, an affair.

The problem seems to be getting even worse, because the young fared much worse than older people. The following questions were asked:

- "Would you consider lying to achieve an important business objective of the firm?"
- "Yes" said 66% of the high school seniors, vs. 29% of the adult executives.

- "If a building is damaged by a storm, would you include all damages covered by insurance, even though not caused by that storm?" "Yes" said 50% of the high school seniors, vs. 26% of the grown-ups.
- "Would you cheat on a highly important business certification test?" "Yes" said 36% of the high school seniors, vs. 14% of the adults.

Some more of the findings:

- 58% of us went to church services regularly while growing up, but only 27% do so today.
- Only 52% of us say the Bible has some right to tell us what's right or wrong. At the same time, 81% want schools to teach moral values to our children. That's a head scratcher! I guess they figure that values are a good thing for their children, but not for them, and quite a few of them don't want their children to get their values out of the Bible. I wonder how many of them are aware America got most of her values out of the Bible?

The authors, who show no obvious bias toward any particular ideology, conclude: There is absolutely no moral consensus in this country – as there was in the 1950s and 1960s. There is very little respect for the law or for any law.

- "90% of all Americans believe in God. It is who that god is that contains the surprises."

No big surprise here:

- "Religious people are much more moral than nonreligious people."

Some of the other conclusions:

- "One of the most devastating findings: One in every seven Americans has been sexually abused as a child. This number far exceeds the statistics published to date. Child abuse is actually creating sociopaths in this country – at an alarming rate."
- "American marriage is in crisis. More than half of all Americans genuinely believe there is no good reason for anyone to get married."
- "Moral ambivalence: Most Americans see the great moral issues of our time in shades of gray rather than as clear-cut moral choices."
- "The United States has become a greedier, meaner, colder, more selfish, and more uncaring place. This is no

wild inferential speculation but, rather, the informed consensus of the American people."

The above survey is now over 20 years old but I don't think things have gotten any better. In fact, I'm sure if the same survey was done again today we would be shocked at the exponential deterioration of our culture.

We have a problem with dishonesty in America, and the only reason more average Americans don't have the reputation of Ken Lay, Bernie Madoff or Rod Blagojevich is that they just haven't had a big enough stage on which to display their dishonesty.

During the writing of this appendix, I received a second e-mail similar to the one at the beginning of the chapter, but this one didn't cover quite as long a period of time.

> One evening a grandson was talking to his grandfather about current events. The grandson asked his grandfather what he thought about the shootings at schools, the computer age, and just things in general.
>
> The grandfather replied, "Well, let me think a minute. I was born before television, penicillin, polio shots, frozen foods, Xerox, contact lenses, Frisbees, and The Pill. There were no credit cards, laser beams, or, ball-point pens. Man had not invented pantyhose, air conditioners, dishwashers, or clothes dryers. The clothes were hung out to dry in the fresh air, and man hadn't yet walked on the moon. Your grandmother and I got married first, and then lived together. Every family had a father and a mother. Until I was 25, I called every man older than me, 'Sir.' And after I turned 25, I still called policemen and every man with a title, 'Sir.' We were before gay rights, computer dating, dual careers, daycare centers, and group therapy. Our lives were governed by the Ten Commandments, good judgment and common sense. We were taught to know the difference between right and wrong, and to stand up and take responsibility for our actions. Serving your country was a privilege; living in this country was a bigger privilege. We thought fast food was what people ate during Lent. Having a meaningful relationship meant getting along with your cousins. Draft dodgers were those who closed front doors as the evening breeze started. Time-sharing meant time the family spent together in the evenings and weekends—not purchasing condominiums. We never heard of FM radios, tape decks, CDs, electric typewriters, yogurt, or guys wearing earrings. We listened to Big Bands, Jack Benny, and the President's speeches on

our radios. And I don't ever remember any kid blowing his brains out listening to Tommy Dorsey. If you saw anything with Made in Japan on it, it was junk. The term making out referred to how you did on your school exam. Pizza Hut, McDonald's, and instant coffee were unheard of. We had 5-&-10-cent stores where you could actually buy things for 5 and 10 cents. Ice-cream cones, phone calls, rides on a streetcar, and a Pepsi were all a nickel. And if you didn't want to splurge, you could spend your nickel on enough stamps to mail 1 letter and 2 postcards. You could buy a new Chevy Coupe for $600, but who could afford one? Too bad, because gas was 11 cents a gallon.

"In my day, 'grass' was mowed, 'coke' was a cold drink, 'pot' was something your mother cooked in, and 'rock music' was your grandmother's lullaby. 'Aids' were helpers in the Principal's office, 'chip' meant a piece of wood, 'hardware' was found in a hardware store and 'software' wasn't even a word. And we were the last generation to actually believe that a lady needed a husband to have a baby. No wonder people call us 'old and confused' and say there is a generation gap. And how old do you think I am?"

This man would only have to be 59 years old!

This little story was received in 2009, so this fellow would have been born in 1950. His age sounds about right for this story.

If I seem as though I am being unduly negative, I should say that there are many honest, hard working, God-fearing Americans. The point I am trying to make is that there is a growing problem in our country, and all over the world really, that is dragging us down in a moral and spiritual way. Even many older folks are in denial that there really is a problem. It is like the frog in the water that doesn't notice the water gradually getting hotter until it is too late, and the frog has been boiled alive. If it had happened all at once they would have recognized the problem and taken measures to nip it in the bud.

APPENDIX B

I'm sure there are some who, in reading this book, have thought to themselves that even though the foundations that evolution was built on were faulty and the original reasons for the long ages were wanting, surely modern science has been able to verify the soundness of these doctrines, after all. In writing this book my intent was not to deal with these issues. They have been dealt with deftly and exhaustively in other literature. But, I will give a brief synopsis of some of those subjects here and then refer the reader to more thorough works in appendix C.

Age of the earth:

Geologists are primarily responsible for setting the age of the earth. They do it the same way today they did in the time of Lyell, by using the fossils as indicators of age. They *assume* there was no world-wide flood. So, in effect, they assume the Bible is wrong in order to prove the Bible is wrong. Of course, the paleontologists set the age of the fossils based on the age of the layers they are buried in. Yes, that circular argument is essentially how it works, although they will tell you it is not that simple.

The media sometimes mentions radiometric dating when they want to make a point that the age of something has been precisely calculated. That reveals their ignorance, because geologists seldom mention radiometric dating, knowing all of the pitfalls that go with it. For instance, when the historical age of a sample is known, such as rocks created from the eruption of Mt. St. Helens, Hawaii Volcanoes, Krakatoa, Vesuvius, etc., the age as dated radiometrically is almost always about 100,000 times what the actual age is and the radiometric age has an estimated range that varies from a low age that is $1/100^{th}$ of the estimated maximum age. In other words, if you just guess the age you will probably be just as accurate. Rocks created in the Mt. St. Helens eruption of 1986 were sent to two independent radiometric dating laboratories to be dated in 1996. They came back with results ranging from 27,000 years to 3 million years. There are now many other methods to measure age, but they all start with assumptions that end up yielding just as wildly variant ages as radiometric "dating" does.

There over 400 ways to date the earth. All of them have their assumptions, but it is an instructive study none-the-less. 95% of those methods don't allow an age anywhere near old enough to satisfy evolutionists and in most cases they only allow a few thousand years. The 5% that do allow an age old enough to satisfy the evolutionists also allow an age young enough to satisfy the facts of the Bible.

What are some of those methods? I'll mention a few. Let's look at the salinity of the ocean. We can determine the rate at which the ocean is getting saltier. Extrapolating backward we see that only a few thousand years ago there would have been no salt in ocean water at all, and that is allowing that there was no salt in the ocean to begin with, so even those few thousand years should probably be shortened. The river deltas in the ocean are expanding all the time. At the rate they are expanding just a few thousand years ago there would have been no deltas at all. We can see that silt is accumulating on the mid-ocean floor at a known rate. Again, extrapolating backward a few thousand years there would have been no silt.

We know that the moon is moving away from the earth at the rate of about 2 inches per year. You do the math. Helium escapes from all substances in which it is enclosed. There is helium in the basement rocks of the earth. It would only take a few thousand years for it all to escape. And the amount of helium in the atmosphere should be much greater than it is if the earth were more than a few thousand years old.

We know the earth's magnetic field is being cut in half every 1400 years. Going back 5600 years the magnetic field would have been 8 times greater than it is now, very conducive to life, but if you go back another 1400 years it would have been 16 times greater than at present and that would have been too strong for life to exist.

Why is it that our oldest living things, the redwood trees and bristlecone pines are about 4,000 years old? Those old trees, for the most part, give no indication that they are about to die. The Bible tells us there was a world-wide flood about 4,400 years ago. If those trees can so easily make it to 4,000 years, why is it none of them have made it to 5,000 years?

Well, you say, "what about starlight that we see from stars that are billions of light years away? Doesn't that mean that it has taken billions of years to get here, and if so, that means the universe must be at least that old? This is a question that I feel creationists have allowed to be a bigger problem than it should be. There are a number of creationists that have devised ways of answering this question. They all seem to answer some of the questions but leave others unanswered.

It should be pointed out that this question is problematic for evolutionists as well. They attribute the beginning of the universe to a "big bang." That should have produced light that is variable throughout the universe, but measurements have shown that the distribution is amazingly even. All sorts of contrivances have been devised to deal with this problem but none of them have ever been observed to happen in the real world.

The Bible, which should be our first source for information on everything, tells us that in the creation everything had "apparent age", that is, things looked mature, but were actually exceedingly young. We may presume that Adam probably looked about 25 years old on the day he was created. The trees that were providing fruit for him must have looked at least a few years old. Trees don't produce fruit until they have had a few seasons of growth. Should we not think that light also had apparent age? Many creationists have a problem with this because they say it makes God look to be a liar. If we observe something happening, such as a supernova, in the present that is coming from a distant star and if we don't believe the earth is over six thousand years old, we are actually saying the supernova never happened. God just made it look that way.

I think that sometimes we creationists can be just as narrow minded as our evolutionist friends. Doesn't God have more ways of solving this problem than the few options we seem to be giving him? I think we should remember that God is way beyond our understanding. Some possible solutions, but by no means all, are that God has changed the speed of light over time. There is some experimental evidence for that idea. He also may have changed the speed of light in other parts of the universe, while leaving it constant here.

He created the stars on day 4. Did Adam only see the ones whose light could have gotten there in two days at the present rate of the speed of light? If so, he would only have seen a few planets! Even the light of the sun would have taken nine minutes to arrive. He told Adam to mark the seasons by these bodies. Surely, if Adam could not see any stars until several years went by that would have been mentioned in the Bible. Many of the stars that are now visible would not have been seen in Adam's lifetime if we make the assumption that God did not use apparent age with regard to light.

There are many problems that are produced by men thinking that God cannot act in any ways that are incomprehensible to man. This applies both to evolutionists and creationists. The speed of light question seems to bring out this attitude more than most arguments.

It still remains that the most authoritative and influential single fact that demonstrates the great age of the earth for the evolutionist was James Hutton's wave of the hand and his saying, "these rocks must be very old."

Appendix C

Resources

The search engines of these sites are equipped to answer the questions that readers may have. These sites do not always agree about everything, but they adhere to the same high regard for scripture and most of them have a treasure trove of information that the average inquirer would not otherwise have easy access to, a definite plus for the modern age.

www.answersingenesis.org
www.icr.org
www.creation.com
www.creationtoday.org
www.creationevidence.org
www.genesisveracityfoundation.com
www.creationscience.com
www.mtblanco.com
www.trueorigin.org
www.creationism.org

Books regarding the speed of light question:
Dr. John Hartnet: Starlight, Time and the New Physics
Dr. Russell Humphreys: Starlight and Time

Books regarding evolution:
Dr. Jonathan Sarfati: Refuting Evolution
Dr. Duane Gish: The Fossils Still Say No
Dr. Lee Spetner: Not by Chance!: Shattering the Modern Theory of Evolution

Book Providing an Overview of the Creationist Model:
Dr. Henry Morris and Dr. John Whitcomb: The Genesis Flood

For In-depth Creationist Geology:
Book by Michael Oard: Ancient Ice Ages or Gigantic Submarine Landslides
Dr, John Baumgardner: Planetary Cataclysm DVD
Articles by Dr. Tas Walker on www.creation.com website, by Dr. Andrew Snelling on the www.answersingenesis.org website or by Dr. Henry Morris or Dr. John Morris on the www.icr.org website.

These resources are by no means an exhaustive list. There are literally hundreds more that I don't have the space to list here and some will provide information beyond that found in the resources listed.

INDEX

The author, Milt Marcy, is a 66 year old businessman in Portland, Oregon, who has been involved in the Creation-Evolution debate for many years. Many probably know him for his work in the search for living specimens of creatures thought to be extinct by mainstream science. However, his interests were upon the whole spectrum of issues in the controversy. It became increasingly obvious to him over the years that there was more to the source of the conflict than what was being presented to the public, which was that the evolutionists were just honest scientists presenting their theories, which just happened to be diametrically opposed to what the Bible teaches, and that creationists were just religious fanatics that were trying desperately to hold on to the Bible as truth, even though they had no science to back up that claim. The further he got into the research for this book the more his suspicions were confirmed. There was a very powerful philosophical current pushing anyone not firmly anchored in the Bible and in apologetics toward a godless worldview that evolution, and later humanism, which is based upon evolution, was designed to support.

In writing the book, Marcy sought out the opinions of many of his peers. Even though many of them did not have access to the mountain of information he had, they were not surprised by the conclusions to which he came.

Made in the USA
Charleston, SC
24 March 2013